The Handbook of Professional Communication Effectiveness

West Chester University of Pennsylvania

Fall 2011 – Spring 2012

D1358714

FOUNTAINHEAD
PRESS

Our green initiatives include:

Electronic Products
We deliver products in non-paper form whenever possible. This includes pdf downloadables, flash drives, & CDs.

Electronic Samples
We use Xample, a new electronic sampling system. Instructor samples are sent via a personalized web page that links to pdf downloads.

FSC Certified Printers
All of our printers are certified by the Forest Service Council which promotes environmentally and socially responsible management of the world's forests. This program allows consumer groups, individual consumers, and businesses to work together hand-in-hand to promote responsible use of the world's forests as a renewable and sustainable resource.

Recycled Paper
Most of our products are printed on a minimum of 30% post-consumer waste recycled paper.

Support of Green Causes
When we do print, we donate a portion of our revenue to green causes. Listed below are a few of the organizations that have received donations from Fountainhead Press. We welcome your feedback and suggestions for contributions, as we are always searching for worthy initiatives.
Rainforest 2 Reef
Environmental Working Group

Book Design: J. Kanan Sawyer
Design Revisions and Page Composition: Doris Bruey

Books may be purchased for educational purposes. For information, please call or write:
1-800-586-0330
Fountainhead Press
Southlake, TX 76092
Web site: www.fountainheadpress.com
E-mail: customerservice@fountainheadpress.com

First Edition
ISBN: 978-1-59871-514-9
Printed in the United States of America

Table of Contents

An Introduction xi

Chapter One: Models of Communication in a Business Context 1

Evolving Communication Models 2

    Advantages of Models 3

    Limitations of Models 3

    Early Communication Models 3

        Shannon-Weaver (1949) 4

        Schramm (1954) 6

        Berlo (1960) 7

Basic Elements Elaboration 8

Models of Communication Recap 15

**Chapter Two: Organizational Structures – How Communication
Moves through Businesses** 17

Who Talks to Whom 17

    Business Structures' Impact on Communication 17

    Building on Schramm 19

Organizational Hierarchies 21

    Tall vs. Flat 21

The Evolution of Business Structures 23

    The Development of Business Structures 24

        Classic Business Structures 24

        Modern Business Structures 28

Who Talks to Whom Through What Structure? 30

Chapter Three: Listening to Others' Communication 33

Being Present 33

    Audience: Ethos, Pathos, Logos 34

Listening in the Workplace - A Functional Choice 35

    Defining Listening 35

    Attention to Listening 36

        A Classroom Setting 37

        Why Haven't We Studied Listening? 37

    Listening in the Business Setting 38

        Getting along with others at Work 38

The LQ (Listening Quotient) 39

Barriers to Effective Listening 41

    Barriers According to Us 42

        Common Listening "Selections" 43

External And Environmental Barriers 45
Improving Listening Effectiveness **46**
   Practical Steps to Listening 46
Finally... Listen Up **49**

Chapter Four: Leading and Meeting in Business Groups **51**
Group Work? **51**
An "Emergent" Nature **52**
   The Patterns of Group Work Experience 52
Leadership As Role Emergence **56**
   Initial Views on Leadership 56
      Emotional Intelligence 57
   Shared Leadership and Group Roles 58
      Tasks and Relationships 58
      Coping with Dysfunction 59
   Leadership "Styles" of Influence 61
      Four Styles of Influence 61
Addressing Conflict in a Group **62**
   Groupthink... a Bad Thing 63
   A Problem-Solving Approach to Conflict Resolution 64
      The Reflective Thinking Approach 64
   Creating Conflict On Purpose 66
When Groups Meet **68**
   Writing a Formal Agenda 68
      Agenda Common Elements 70
      Sending an Agenda 71
   Adjusting A Meeting Environment 71
   Keeping a Meeting Moving 72
Leading & Meeting – You Can! **73**

Chapter Five: Research: Having Ethos with Business Audiences **75**
How Can I "Know"? **75**
Why Start with Research? **76**
Quantitative vs. Qualitative Evidence **77**
   Quantitative 77
   Qualitative 78
   A Good Place to Start 80
How Much Research Do I "Need"? **83**
   Cite it... Don't Steal it 86
   Contemplating Your Rhetorical Situation 87

Gathering Evidence...**90**

Audience Analysis... 90

Informal Audience Analysis...................................... 91

Formal Audience Analysis 92

Formal Audience Analysis Question Formats............94

Survey Questions Formats... 94

Evaluating Evidence **98**

Published Material Credibility.................................. 99

The Website Credibility Checklist 101

What to "Know" Final Ideas..**102**

Chapter Six: Organizing Your Thoughts for the <u>Ideal</u> Business Speech **103**

Framing What You Know..**103**

Speech Preparation...**104**

Selecting Your Topic... If You Can 104

Why Talk About Topic Selection Now?...................... 104

Creating a Path 106

Determine Your Purpose 107

General Purpose 107

1.   To Inform.. 108

2.   To Persuade.. 108

3.   To Entertain.. 109

Specific Purpose.. 110

Your Primary Argument: Crafting The Thesis **112**

Why Argue?.. 112

Elements of the Thesis/ Primary Argument............. 113

Organizational Patterns..**118**

Organizing Ideas 118

Patterns of Organization... 118

Informative Patterns of Organization 119

Persuasive Organization Considerations 121

Persuasive Patterns of Organization........................ 122

Laying Out Your Main Points **124**

Matching Main Ideas with Organizational Patterns.............. 125

Main Point Creation.. 125

Incorporating and Organizing Your Evidence.............. 129

Linking Ideas..**130**

Organization Between Main Points – External Transitions 130

Organization Within Main Points – Internal Transitions 133

Getting In and Getting Out 135
  Opening Your Talk.. 135
  Closing Your Talk 138
A Final Frame on Organization 140

Chapter Seven: Words, Voice, Movement: Business Presentation Delivery.. 141
  Talking the Talk.. 141
  Addressing the "Nerves" Issue 142
    The Right Mindset 143
    Practical Steps 143
  Modes of Delivery 146
    Linking Delivery Style to Rhetorical Situation.................... 146
  Verbal and Nonverbal Considerations 151
    Verbal Effectiveness... 152
      Language Strategies 152
      Common Elements of Oral Style 153
      Individual Elements of Oral Style 154
      Verbal Speaking Strategies.. 156
    Nonverbal Effectiveness 159
      Considering Your Space.. 165
    Presenting With a Group 166
  Practicing for Effectiveness 170
    Become One with the Ideas.. 170
    Go Beyond Visualization 170
  You are Ready!... 171

Chapter Eight: Aiding Business Presentations with Visuals................. 173
  Connection as the Foundation 173
    A Communication Model: Aristotle? 174
  Visual Strategies 176
    Usage Overview.. 177
      All Visuals Can Distract.. 178
      Avoiding the "Boomerang Effect" 178
      Content vs. Medium.. 179
  Visual Content 179
    Content: The Stuff that Goes on Aids 180
      Text and Font 180
      Numbers 183
      Charts, Diagrams, and Tables... 184

Graphics and Illustrations 185
Images (Pictures).. 186
Color... 187
Sound 187

Visual Mediums **188**
Low vs. High Tech Mediums 188
Do and Do Not (Use Strategies)............................. 190
Handouts (low-tech) 190
Overheads/ Transparencies (low-tech) 191
Overhead Transparency Hints 192
Models and Objects (low-tech) 192
Model and Object Hints 193
White and Chalkboards (low-tech) 194
Flip Charts/ Posters (low-tech) 194
Picture Slides (low-tech) 196
PowerPoint® and Keynote® (high-tech) 197
Internet Use (high-tech).................................... 199
Videos/ Movies/ Audio Visuals (high-tech)...... 200
Smartboards/ IWBs (high-tech) 201

Delivering Messages with Visuals **202**
Practice... 203
Presenting on Others' Machines 203
Staying In Sync... 204

A Final Word on Visual Stuff..................................... **205**

Chapter Nine: Résumé and Cover Letter Communication **207**
The Résumé & Letter Experience............................... **207**
What is a Résumé? **208**
Résumé Creation 209
Résumé Formats for YOU 210
Templates and Trends 210
Organizational Formats 211
General Formatting 211
Chronological Format 211
Functional Format 213
Content: What to Include and Not Include................ 215
Length: How Long Should Your Résumé Be? 215
Crucial Contact 216
Potential Categories 217
Visual Language and Style 230
Language.. 231

Style 232
Résumé Don'ts / Stuff Not to Include 233
The Killer Typo 233
Avoid "References Upon Request" 234

Cover Letter Creation **235**
What is the Purpose of Your Cover Letter? 235
Length of Your Cover Letter? 235
Cover Letter Content 236
Purpose of the Paragraphs 236
Cover Letter Language 240
The Look of Your Materials 240
Signature 240
Example of Full Page Letter with Formatting 241
PDFs 242
Online Résumés and Portfolios 242

A Final Word **243**

Chapter Ten: Interview Me? Interview You! **245**
Two-Way Communication **245**
Interviewing Others **246**
What Employers Want 246
How Do Employers Prepare 247
Organizing the Interview of Others 247
The Opening 247
The Middle 248
The Closing 249
Developing Probing Questions 249
The Question Types 249
Question Purposes 250
Interview Sequence 252
External Evaluations of the Candidate 254
What They Look At 254
What They Can See 255
What To Manage 255

Being Interviewed **256**
Interview Types 257
Just Me? Or With Others? 258
Interview Modes 259
The Telephone Screening Interview 259
The Face-To-Face Interview 259

Preparation Elements of Your Interview 262
   General Interview Preparation 262
   Finding Practice Interview Questions 264
   Practice Answering Common Questions 265
   Organizing Your Answers 268
   Tactics for When You Can't Answer a Question 270
   Managing Illegal Questions and Interactions 271
   Prepare Intelligent Questions to Ask 273
   Developing Confidence 274
"Day-Of" Interview Behavior 274
   Dress for Success 275
   Timeliness 276
   Interaction Do's and Don'ts 276
Post-Interview Follow-Up 277
   "Write" a Thank You Letter 278
   How to Inquire About Your Status 278
   What to Do With an Offer 279

Looking Back on Interviewing **281**

Chapter Eleven: Ethical Business Choices – How are they Made? **283**
Communication Ethics at Play **283**
  An Ordered World 284
Foundational Ethics Perspectives **285**
  Kant: Universalism and Deontology 286
  Mill: Utilitarianism 289
  Aristotle: Virtue Ethics 291
  An Over-Simplified Model 293
A Final Recap and Reflection **295**

References **297**
  Chapter One References **297**
  Chapter Two References **298**
  Chapter Three References **299**
  Chapter Four References **302**
  Chapter Five References **303**
  Chapter Six References **304**
  Chapter Seven References **304**
  Chapter Eight References **306**
  Chapter Nine References **308**
  Chapter Ten References **309**
  Chapter Eleven References **313**

An Introduction

Welcome to *The Handbook of Professional Communication Effectiveness.*

Most professors don't assign the introduction to a book but I hope that yours has. If not, and you are reading this, well, thanks! I just wanted to take a minute to tell you what you are getting in to. This text was written to aid students and new professionals in the art of communication in the workplace. While some of the material will cover written forms (e.g., résumés and cover letters – or how not to sign off on an email to your boss), the primary substance of this text is verbal and nonverbal communication.

Verbal and nonverbal communication strategies are woefully overlooked in college level materials. Sure, you can get books on how to write reports and briefings and even résumés but when it comes time to actually say something to another person, many texts ask you to just wing it.. or let your PowerPoint slides do most of the work. Eek.

You will learn skills in this text that help you to feel prepared to send messages in a business context. The book was written, by me, to have 100% of the focus on business examples. Therefore, you won't need to worry about wading through chapters on Rhetorical Strategies that were adapted from unrelated materials. To be fair, this text will cover rhetoric. My training is, in fact, in the rhetorical arts. However, full chapters on rhetorical cannons or ethos and how to write bad news have been edited down and incorporated into relevant, real-world examples and explanations. You'll get prepared without wading through the excess.

This text has also adopted an unconventional writing style. It is far more conversational than other texts and may be a completely novel approach to textbook writing. Why is it so different (you may ask)? Well, most text-books are boring. They don't actually "talk" to us. The author of this one felt that since this was a book about how to talk – it should be written just as we talk. It is chatty but tries to keep things professional with a keen eye to being *real*. (A student editor of mine actually said, "wow… I would actually read the assignments in this book." High praise!)

Now… if you are putting together a paper for your class, do NOT adopt the style that you see here. Most classroom papers ask for a professional style that is far more formal than what you are about to read. For every-thing there is a time and a place. We keep the chattiness between us – and you can send the formal stuff to them. Fair?

I hope that you enjoy this text. It would never have materialized without the help of a group of kind and motivated fellow scholars who contributed to the construction of the text. More specifically, it would not have been possible without the hundreds of students who read this text and provided pages of feedback to earlier editions. I listened, changed, and (hopefully) rose to every challenge.

I hope that the readers will now use this text to master the challenges of business communication! (Enough said).

Chapter One

Models of Communication in a Business Context

COMMUNICATION CONSTRUCTS AT PLAY

In survey after survey of major employers, communication skills are stated as the number one quality that companies desire in applicants (Morreale, 2001; Morreale & Pearson, 2008; North & Worth, 1996). OK. But what does that actually mean? If you know how to talk (or just have the ability to speak), does that mean that you have strong communication skills? Unfortunately, it does not. *Communication is what connects you to other people – it's actually what gets work the done.* Whether a person is in business, medicine, government service, or any other field; that person will rise to the top of their field if he or she has mastered effective communication. You want "that person" to be YOU!

The core concept in effective communication comes from achieving shared meaning between two or more people. An employee might talk all day, but if the audience (e.g., other employees, a boss or manager, a potential client) doesn't share the employees understanding about the subject, then the communication has not been effective. Before you begin to think that effective communication means changing every listener's perspective to you own… it does not. **Communication is the art of expression whereby others can grasp your intended meaning**.

With so much expectation on the giving and sending of messages in professional settings, it would be ideal for companies to train you in this all-important skill. Ah but remember, they expect you to *come in* with strong communication skills. Even when employers offer small seminars in developing sales presentations or giving talks to clients, your post-graduate communication training will be limited. Companies are in the business of making money – not offering speech training. If you come through the door having communication skills in your repertoire of experience – woohoo! You are well ahead of your colleagues and likely to be far more successful.

Scholars have spent years discussing and debating what constitutes effective communication, how to define it, and how to track it. These discussions – and, of course, their conclusions – are instrumental in being prepared to enter the workforce with a strong background in what all employers want communication skills. This initial chapter will provide you with a vital understanding of models of communication as they apply to business settings including their evolution and primary elements.

EVOLVING COMMUNICATION MODELS

You've been using language to communicate since you were, well, about two years old. That's a whole lot of time to master this intricate interaction and it might leave you asking, *why do I need a model on how to communicate?* Well, models are simply visual representations of all the components that make up a construct. Communication, while a seemingly simple notion, is actually a combination of many crucial elements, which continue to evolve over time.

As you look through each of the models that are about to be described… don't get fooled. Models help you understand the key elements of communication but they are not the full picture. University of Wisconsin-Madison Communication professor, C. David Mortenson (1972) breaks this down for us; he argues that models have clear *advantages* and *disadvantages*.

Advantages of Models

- Models are a tool to help us ask better questions
- Models help to clarify or organize complex ideas
- Models are metaphors that allow us to look at one thing *in terms* of another

Limitations of Models

- Models can lead to oversimplification
- Models can result in confusion between the <u>model</u> and the <u>behavior</u> that it actually portrays
- Models can limit our thinking and leave areas outside the model unexplored

So, as you read on, be sure to take advantage but don't be limited! Use these models to see how notions of communication, especially in business contexts, have evolved over time – and can be used to help make us successful in a corporate context.

Early Communication Models

Communication models involve two parties in the sending of messages: senders and receivers.

Sender ⟶ Receiver
(Message)

If this were all that there were to communication then you would hardly need training in it. You would open your mouth, messages would come out, and receivers would be affected. Alas, it just isn't that simple (and if you have ever sent a message that did not have the result that you intended then you know this!). Understanding what functions are needed to have their intended communication effects is the goal of all communication research.

Shannon-Weaver (1949)

In the late 1940s, Shannon and Weaver (1949) published a novel notion of how communication works. Their ideas were originally spawned from a mathematical model applied in an engineering context. Math – in communication?! Relax, here's what happened.

Claude Shannon was an engineer for the Bell Telephone Company. He was looking to guide the efforts of engineers in finding the most efficient way of transmitting (**send**) electrical signals from one location to another (**receive**). His logarithmic measures (*that was the math part!*) accounted for any potential interference in the electronic messages (**noise**). In other words, he wanted to get all of that static off the line that you can hear when picking up an old 'land line' phone.

While this model was created for a technical environment, it quickly became adopted by communication scholars who saw that it added key components to the sender-message-receiver idea—notions of *encoding*, *decoding*, and *noise*!

The Shannon-Weaver Mathematical Model, 1949

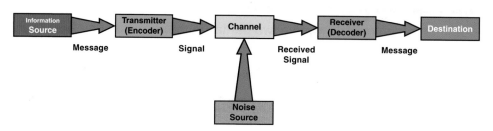

These new elements gave us a fuller picture of how to have effective communication and even how social factors could impact this effectiveness. In short, the model (with new elements highlighted) says:

1. A Sender will **encode** (i.e., put into a system of letters, numbers, or symbols) a Message and then send it through a **channel** .
2. Once messages are taken in by the Receiver then they are **decoded** (i.e., translated to a system of letters, numbers, or symbols understood by the receiver).

3. Message clarity can be helped or hindered by the worldview of each person, the environmental context, and/or any real or semantic **noise** (grammatical problems or word usage that the receiver can't decode).

From a business perspective, we can see how this more developed model gives us insight into becoming more effective speakers. If you are informing your colleagues on crucial changes to information systems as they are all grabbing lunch from the sandwich guy then you have obvious noise that will hinder your success. You may also consider a need to change your use of language when training new employees to eliminate jargon—or trade specific language and abbreviations—until they have a full concept of what those terms mean!

Given how useful this model has been to language scholars, it is ironic that Claude Shannon (1948) wrote, "(language) aspects of communication are irrelevant to the engineering problem," (p. 1) and then his work guided communication/ language models for decades! (Ironic, huh?). Our understanding of communication, however, did not end with this basic model. We have learned from it and developed it further.

Schramm (1954)

Wilbur Schramm (1954) came along a few years later to modify Shannon-Weaver's (1949) model because Schramm saw that, while more thorough, this original model still was missing a pivotal element necessary for effective communication—*feedback*. **Feedback** is the information/ message sent from the receiver back to the sender to show the extent of understanding. Schramm also further conceptualized how sender and receiver fields of experience (what background the sender has for encoding or the receiver for decoding) and labeled these **Interpretation**.

Schramm's Model of Communication, 1954

**Schramm actually developed several models; this is a compilation of those ideas from his 1954-1977 publications.

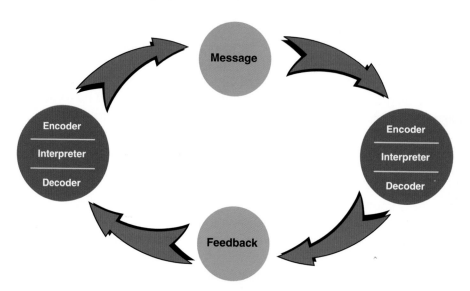

Have you ever sat in a meeting and someone looks right at you and asks, "Which part didn't you get?" How did they know that you were confused? They probably knew because it was written all over your face. Had that person ignored your facial feedback, he or she would have been "speaking" but, according to Schramm, not *communicating*. After all, the message was not having its intended impact. Feedback permeates every aspect of corporate communication. We need it to gain information about client and customer needs. We need it to be sure that our sales pitches and training seminars are effective. We need it to alter any communicative practices that did not work the first time but can work the second time. To get the feedback that we want, we must fully appreciate what shapes our communication.

Berlo (1960)

When David K. Berlo (1960), former head of the Communication Department at Michigan State University, fleshed out his idea of communication… it was not about identifying the elements (folks had already done that). But, he gave his attention to what 'made up' each of the individual communication elements. He called his model **SMCR** (from the elements of sender-message-channel-receiver).

Berlo's SMCR Model

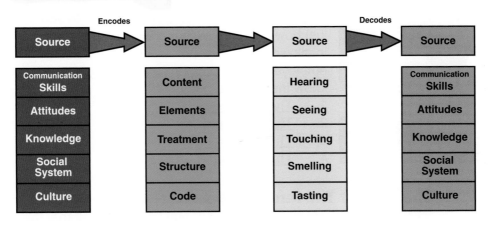

If you are sending a message, you are a source. But you are more than that, right? You are perhaps an entry level employee from a Catholic background who was raised in Texas in a middle income family who has an extensive background with blogs and online social media. You are more than a lable and Berlo understood this. He understood that who we are determines what message we will send through which channel—and how the person to whom we send our message will be able to receive it. By offering what now may seem like obvious information, Berlo helped to initiate audience analysis (see Chapter Five) and refine message clarity!

Every communication model contains the basic elements that we first discussed: sender, message, and receiver. To follow Berlo's lead, we must fully understand each of these for truly effective communication.

BASIC ELEMENTS ELABORATION

It's very easy to say that communication comes from senders through messages to receivers. Each of the above models uses these terms but until now we have done little to explain to you just how complex each is. Given their importance in allowing you to show current and future employers your communication skill, you must know the intricate nature of:

1.   **The Sender**
2.   **The Message**
3.   **The Channel**
4.   **The Feedback**

1. The Role Of The Sender: Senders are the originators of any message—this is where it all starts! At first you may think that this is you. If you are where a message originates then this is true. You already have a fairly good idea of your own worldview that will help to frame your message (although doing more self-analysis can help you to understand why you send the messages that you do). If, however, you are receiving a message then you need to know more about the sender to see what has *motivated* the communication.

A sender shares his or her idea with someone else because that sender was first <u>stimulated</u> and then <u>motivated</u> to do so. Motivation is the driving force or inspiration that results in a behavior. Have you been motivated to speak up at a meeting? What inspired you to do it? Have you ever tried to persuade a customer at work to buy something that they had not originally intended to purchase? Consider why you did that.

Examples such as these should not imply that *all* messages are all sent intentionally.Watzlawick, Beavin, and Jackson (1967) argued that it is impossible *not* to send messages. We may be sitting in silence, but our nonverbal communication screams loud and clear. We may be hoping to restrain our impressions, but they shine through. The important idea here is that you should be aware, especially at work or as a new employee, that you are sending messages all of the time and should be careful what you send!

Encoding

Do you speak Mandarin? Sign language? Pig Latin? If you are sending a message, will you compose your message using any of these means? The manner in which a person crafts a message in his or her head using words and phrases is called **encoding**.

Notions of message encoding are part of numerous long-standing communication theories (e.g., Jakobson's, 1960, interpersonal verbal communication theory to Hall's, 1980, media context theory or McQuail's, 1983, mass communication theory). While the details of each theory differs due to its context, each theory explains how codes are developed through:

    a) **sender experience**: personal knowledge, background, understanding, and familiarity

    b) **culture**: socialized traditions, customs, and ways of life

If two communicators are not from the same culture, they will encounter obstacles in producing effective communication. For example, word choice, language choice, inflection or accent. People say things because they expect a certain response—and that expectation comes from culture.

2. **Selecting a Channel:** Usually, we use the word channel to talk about changing something on television or selecting radio frequencies. In communication models, **channel** refers to the different *mechanisms* for conveying a message from one person to another. Message channels take the forms of either:

    a) **face-to-face**: messages sent using direct contact between senders and receivers (e.g., two people standing in a room having a conversation)

b) **mediated**: messages sent using direct contact between senders and receivers. (e.g., messages sent using phones, written text, Skype™, fax machine, etc.)

How does someone select a channel? Unfortunately, it isn't as easy as hitting a remote control—but is often done with just as little thought. Selecting the correct channel for your message is key to both making sure that the message is received and understood. Channel selection must <u>consider</u>:

a) **channel richness**
b) **task ambiguity**
c) **relationship maintenance**
d) **noise**

Channel Richness

Have you ever given notes to a friend who missed class? Then the test comes and you know the information but your friend (with the same notes) doesn't. Why do you think this is? Those who study communication models will guess that the *richness* of your channel was the differentiating factor! Channel richness, so says Richard L. Daft (2007), is <u>the amount of information that can be transmitted during a communication episode</u>. For instance, the richest channel is face-to-face communication (where you get information from all 5 senses), while the least rich channel might be a telegram. When selecting a channel, consider that greater nonverbal capacity is better because it creates redundancy (or recurrence of the message in a different way). *Redundancy is good*!

Managerial and business settings offer unique opportunities to benefit from channel richness. For instance, Alice Johnson and Albert Lederer (2005) write, in the Journal of Management Information Systems, that the more frequent the communication and the richer the communication channel between CEOs (chief executive officer) and CIOs (chief information officer), the more that they will agree on future goals and long-term financial decisions.

Task Ambiguity

The nature of the task (the thing that you want to other person to do) will also help you to determine in which channel to send your message! Consider the following: you are having trouble with your computer (shock… don't we all?!). You find out that you must take the computer apart to fix it and you have not done anything like this before. Would you like a bulleted list of directions—or would it be better to have a video to watch someone who goes through the process? Hhhhmmmm – tough call, right?!

Some tasks are by nature ambiguous. Russ, Daft, and Lengel's (1990) *Management Communication Quarterly* article explains that managers who choose more *rich channels* for more *ambiguous tasks* and more *lean channels* for *unambiguous tasks* are more effective. Be strategic about choosing your channels.

Relationship Maintenance

Messages play a role in building relationships—the wrong channel… and the message will be unclear or lack a shared meaning with the audience. How can message channels impact relationships? They do this by the **tone**—or manner or character in which a message is sent.

If you have recently been hired as the big boss at a new company, you can imagine that people will be somewhat skeptical of you. Newness, after all, creates levels of tension (see Chapter Four). This is a time when you will need to be careful about the channels that you select. If you are about to change the décor in the company lunch room, you are probably good selecting to send a mass email. If you have decided to completely revise employee vacation allotments, well, you might wish to have a company meeting that allows you to go through your decision face-to-face.

You can see that message channel have the power to maintain, strengthen or even weaken relationships—and that you should choose them depending on your goal.

Noise

Some channels lend themselves to… noise. Do you have a cell phone that automatically spells words for you as you are texting? Have you ever sent a word that you did not mean to send? Or even a *message* that you did not mean to send? Have you ever hit "reply all" on a work email only to realize that your boss just got your sarcastic reply intended for a friend down the hall?

Shannon and Weaver's (1949) concept of **noise in a channel** was originally coined to talk about static in the telephone line ("Can you hear me now?") but is just as easily applicable to other contexts. Noise can take on a variety of forms:

a) **psychological noise:** distractions from your head (e.g., thinking about hunger, dismay, distress, discomfort, or even hatred)

b) **semantic noise:** the problem associated with differences in the meaning that people assign to words (e.g., the many interpretations of the word business: an industry, "getting down to business," an affair, an amount of work, etc.)

c) **mechanical noise:** an actual interruption of a message signal (e.g., a wireless printer creates static on your television)

d) **cultural noise:** differences in worldview expectations (e.g., wishing a group of people a *Merry Christmas* when some of them are Muslim)

e) **physical noise:** disturbances that surround and overrun the message (e.g., sitting in an uncomfortable chair, thunder or a marching band)

Controlling for noise is the best way to have your receiver get the message that you had intended for them to be given.

3. **Role of the Receiver:** Communication always <u>starts</u> with a sender—one or more people who want to get their idea across to someone else. We have a tendency to focus on the speaker, particularly in U.S. culture where speakers have more status than listeners, but scholars have known since Aristotle (that's

2,300 years ago!) that the *receiver* is the key to successful communication.

Appealing to Receivers

Communication is about audiences. Speakers send messages that are *for* audience and *about* audiences *to* audiences. This does not mean that you have to pander to the preferences of your audience and say only what you think they want to hear – absolutely not! What it does mean is that you need to understand where your audience is coming from if you want get them where you want them to go. You have to meet them where they are, first. Aristotle argued that we must do this by appealing to our audience in all three of the following ways:

- **Ethos:** Our information should be of the highest quality and credibility in the eyes of our audience. It should not be what we think is the best source but what the audience will think is the best source. If we are speaking to a group of college students then our examples might be about EA Sports® games but if we are speaking to a group of Wall Street brokers then the *Financial Times* will provide our best ideas. Credibility comes when our audiences believe that we have ethically done our best to provide them with what they need.

- **Logos:** Our ideas should also be organized in a *manner* that supports our argument but in a *structured* form that makes sense to our audience. Whether this structure be an entire presentation or just a single argument, audiences should never think, "Huh?" If you have not understood an audience's needs then it is likely that you cannot layout a sensible argument to them.

- **Pathos:** What we present should have emotional resonance, or connection, with our audience. This never means that those sending messages should say things that make *them* feel but instead should figure out what will make the *audience* feel the way that the speaker wants him or her to!

It is crucial to connect with your audience so that they are not only capable of changing (becoming more informed or persuaded to change an idea or path), but also will indeed choose to change.

Decoding the Message

Decoding involves knowing what message was intended and working to understand that message. This means that the receiver must both understand **denotative** (actual dictionary definitions) and **connotative** (ideas and images associated with the word) meanings. Decoding a message is much like a military game.

In World War II, the U.S. Marines used Navajo Indians to send messages using their native language. The language was the only code that the Japanese <u>never</u> broke (*Naval History & Heritage Command*, 2009). Why? Well, the Navajo "code talkers" did not want to be decoded.

> *(An expert) believed Navajo answered the military requirement for an undecipherable code because Navajo is an unwritten language of extreme complexity. Its syntax and tonal qualities, not to mention dialects, make it unintelligible to anyone without extensive exposure and training. It has no alphabet or symbols, and is spoken only on the Navajo lands of the American Southwest. One estimate indicates that less than 30 non-Navajos, none of them Japanese, could understand the language at the outbreak of World War II (para. 3).*

Try to apply this decoding scenario to your first day on the job. When all of your co-workers are using jargon and abbreviations to refer to necessary tasks and you do not yet speak their language. How effective can you be? This is the reason to use feedback to search for message clarification!

4. **Creating a Feedback Loop:** How can anyone be sure that a message is interpreted correctly—where both parties have a shared meaning? Feedback! A **feedback loop** cycles back and forth between sender and receiver until both are satisfied that they are on the same page. Tra la! (Well, not that easy).

Basic Rules Of Feedback

Feedback is more than simply reacting. It follows rules:

- The most effective messages *suggest* a way to respond.
- Without a response, the sender does not know if shared meaning was achieved.
- It typically takes <u>several cycles</u> of sending-receiving-feedback to achieve shared meaning.
- Feedback is a message in itself that must be encoded, sent, and decoded.
- Once feedback is decoded, it starts the next message in the model.
- It turns out that when the sender and receiver have overlapping experiences it is easier to reach a mutual understanding.

Who could have imagined that asking someone to "pass the salt" could be so complex? Given the infinite number of ways that messages can go wrong, it's amazing we accomplish anything at all—and yet the world is becoming more globally coordinated every day!

MODELS OF COMMUNICATION RECAP

Professional people often communicate successfully without *actively* thinking about every element of their communication. As someone who is new to business, you will not have had years of practice to test and receive feedback on your message. You can have a good idea of how the elements of communication work (and work together) before you begin your job by attending to these models and details.

Communication models are an excellent place to start our journey looking at business and professional communication. By understanding how communication flows, you will be able to see how it moves through corporate structures, how to listen so that you receive your desired feedback, lead business meetings, create presentations, conduct and perform in interviews and be ethical in your approach to life as a business communicator.

Chapter Two:
Organizational Structures – How Communication Moves through Businesses

WHO TALKS TO WHOM

If you rise to be the top dog at your company—fantastic! The top, however, is not where most new employees will start. Many companies start even their executive hires at lower level positions in order to teach the person all levels of the company structure (for example, UPS or Sparkletts water). Organizations have 'pecking orders.' A **pecking order** is a hierarchy of status seen among members of a group of people or animals (originally as observed among <u>hens</u>!). This pecking order will determine to whom you will report and who will send information to you. How are these orders determined? They are the result of how the business is organized—or structured.

To be fair, this is not a text to introduce you to the myriad of *business* concepts available to you. It is a text to help you understand how <u>communication</u> moves within and impacts business. In order to do this, you need to understand business structures so that you can effectively send your messages through the right channels and to the correct receiver.

Business Structures' Impact on Communication

Have you ever had a complaint about a co-worker? Perhaps that person was not doing his or her fair share of work. Maybe that person was stealing or even harassing you. In these situations, it's important to know who is in charge because you will want to know to whom you should report these infractions!

In small organizations, such as the local water ice store you worked at last summer or your dad's accounting firm, you would go straight to the top. You go to the boss—because there are likely few, if any, levels in the company through which you would go to get to the boss (e.g., a vice-president, a manager, a senior supervisor). In larger organizations, your access to the boss will be limited and determined by the structure of the particular company.

Organizations are structured so that communication follows a clear path. Let's be clear. Things that *should* happen are not always the things that *do* happen. This is especially true of communication. Take for example the following scenario:

> Perhaps your direct supervisor <u>should</u> have let you
> know about a change in some system but he or she
> told a co-worker of yours instead—and that person in-
> effectively relayed the details to you. You then acted on
> the information only to have your boss become angry
> that you took such counter-productive measures. Do you
> tell your boss that it's your co-worker's fault? Nah—that
> will just look like you're passing the buck and can't take
> responsibility. You should have gone to your boss or
> checked the information before acting on it. ?#@*&%!

Information that you hear, which does not come through formal communication channels, comes through the **grapevine**—or informal communication channels. Why would you receive information through a grapevine? Grapevine communication tends to exist where business structures have not adequately specified the path for communication—or when a business has adopted a poor communication structure. After all, models for communication are not as simple as they might seem.

Building on Schramm

By now, you are familiar with the most basic components of sending communication messages. There is a sender, a message, a receiver, and feedback. We can see this in Schramm's (1954) model that shows how messages are sent.

Schramm's Model of Communication, 1954
* see Chapter One for details

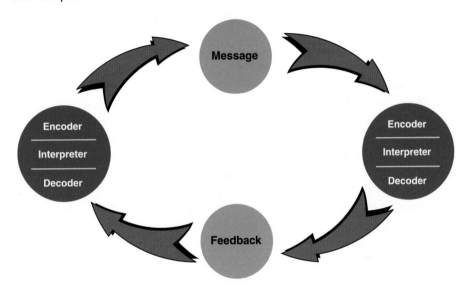

Schramm's model, along with each of the others previously discussed, only depicts a single sender and a single receiver. This is hardly the case in most business settings. As you send a message to Person X, another person is also sending a message to Person X. At the same time that you are both sending a message to Person X, both of you (the senders) are bombarded with messages about any variety of topics. You know that becoming effective with your communication is not about sending messages into a vacuum, but receiving and reacting to as many messages and as much feedback as you get.

The whole thing can get a bit sloppy…

Example:

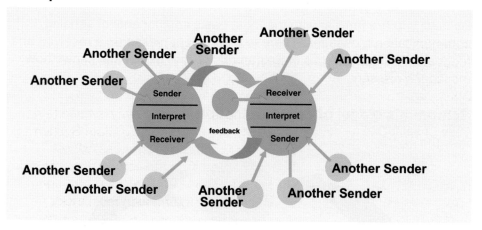

The nice thing about this type of *multiple-incoming-messages* communication is that we're used to it. Think about your life: your mom calls just as your roommate is in the middle of telling a story and you are on the computer trying to finish a report that goes out tomorrow when suddenly a gripping story is told on the news. That's a whole ton of information! But, somehow, we process the information. We are able to filter through details and grasp overall concepts. This becomes easy because we place ourselves at the center of our own communication hub. Everything coming in is about us, for us, or from us. This will not be the same in a corporate world.

Business structures determine who is the hub of *corporate* communication. Rather than rely on informal communication channels to send messages, receive them, or offer feedback, knowledge of appropriate formal channels of communication can alleviate concerns over message sources and merit.

This chapter will review the differences between tall and flat organizational hierarchies as well as the development of classic business structures to show how both dictate the flow of communication in corporate settings.

ORGANIZATIONAL HIERARCHIES

Where do messages come from? Everywhere. Where should messages come from? Well, if you are talking about a business then it depends on the size and structure of that business. If the company is huge (e.g., Microsoft, the Pennsylvania State System of Higher Education, Starbucks, Whole Foods, FedEx) then the company most likely will have a whole series of levels through which company information must trickle. Smaller organizations (e.g., Georgetown Cupcakes, Social Strata in Seattle, Boardman Silversmiths, the New Jersey Brownstone) typically have fewer and need fewer levels. The number of levels in an organization through which communication flows is referred to as the **organizational hierarchy.**

Tall vs. Flat

Organizational hierarchies may be relatively simple or quite complex. In either case, these *preset* structures that will control communication from and for any individual or business. J. C. Worthy (1950) did a famous study of the *Sears and Roebuck* company (before it was just *Sears*). He used his study to determine that not all companies have the same number of 'levels' of supervision. He was likely the first to coin the terms of <u>tall</u> and <u>flat</u> structures.

- **Flat Business Hierarchies:** According to Worthy (1950), small organizations could get away with fewer levels of administration – a **flat structure** with a wide span of supervision. This is also called a horizontal structure.

  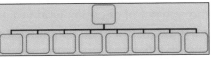

  In this type of business you will not see reporting levels *between* the employees and managers (i.e., if your boss is the only person above you then your organization is flat!), the long-term or trained employees are often part of the decision-making process and the company or division is relatively small. Many global companies first started as flat businesses and then moved into larger and more tall hierarchical structures.

- o <u>Examples</u>: Mom and Pop grocery stores, Georgetown Cupcakes, Social Strata in Seattle, Boardman Silversmiths, the New Jersey Brownstone
- o <u>Benefits of Flat Hierarchies</u>: Better manager satisfaction; Quicker decision making; faster communication (Donaldson & Hilmer, 1998; Ghiselli & Wyatt, 1972).

Tall Business Hierarchies: Conversely, **tall structures** were multi-levels of organization with a very narrow span of supervision. If you have a supervisor who reports to a department head who reports to a division head who reports to a vice-president who reports to a president who is responsible to a board… (and on and on), then, you have a tall structure.

- o <u>Example</u>: Microsoft, the Pennsylvania State System of Higher Education, WaWa, Whole Foods, FedEx
- o <u>Benefits of Tall Hierarchies</u>: Quicker conflict resolution; Larger profit margins; Clear promotion progression; Allows managers more time for direct subordinates (Carzo & Yanouzas, 1969; Pugh, 2003)

Some might think that because there are fewer people involved, flat structures are somehow better. Or, that with more levels of supervision, a tall structure is the mark of higher success. In fact, as you can see, each type of structure has its own benefits (and weaknesses) that have been the subject of decades worth of academic and professional investigation. As these hierarchies become more fully developed to determine who should talk to whom (when sending organizational information) and how each level is considered in the scope of the business, they become specific business structures.

THE EVOLUTION OF BUSINESS STRUCTURES

In American history, we have stories of industries rising out the drive of early settlers' work ethics. We can imagine the lone shoe repairman realizing that, instead of making a single shoe at a time for purchase (yes, this is originally how shoes were made and folks could come in to buy <u>one</u> to replace a single worn out shoe), he could create a mold to repetitively make hundreds of shoes that could be purchased off the shelves. Suddenly, mass production is born and business is forever changed.

When one man (typically, it was usually a man back then rather than a woman) worked in a shop with an apprentice, the hierarchy likely looked much like Wilbur Schramm's (1954) model of communication. The artisan spoke to the apprentice and then feedback would follow. This was pretty easy communication and the transfer of complicated and difficult information was less likely to break down due to such close and direct contact.

A business communication structure models a single person talking to another single person could not continue to work as our country came into an industrial age. Factories took over the jobs of small shops and the norm became a big boss hovering over masses of workers. One person gave information to all. Today, there are fewer and fewer instances of one person leading the masses (in industry). Instead, our work patterns have had to adjust to access to technology, global work groups, working on the road, multi-division companies, and more! How we communicate at work has changed with the times and understanding how communication was managed in those early days, gives us an understanding of both how it is managed today and how it might even be managed as industries continue to change.

The Development of Business Structures

Business structures fit with their times. As we have evolved in our means of communication, we have developed new understandings of the employee/employer relationship—as well as how they communicate – and businesses have had to adapt to facilitate these new understandings.

Classic Business Structures

1. **Scientific Management:** In 1911, Philadelphia native Frederick Taylor (1911) published *The Principles ofScientific Management*. He described how <u>the application of scientific principles could benefit the management of people and allow companies to achieve their highest levels of production</u>. In his day, craftsmen and artisans completed most productions individually (we talked about that above). In Taylor's eyes, companies could design one optimal means of production (e.g., *how* a dress was made) and then that process could be replicated again and again. Sounds fantastic, right? Isn't this what quality control is all about in a modern age? Not quite. Taylor applied his system to the idea of production but failed to adjust for *basic human needs*.

   Taylor (1911) was known for his time trials. He would stand behind an employee with a stopwatch and ask that the employee to work as diligently, accurately, and quickly as possible. He would note how long it took under these circumstances to complete a product and then insist that all other work be done just like this—for hours. Can you do that? Can you work at your optimal level for your entire shift? Some folks need to have water, visit the bathroom, stretch, etc. This was long before ergonomic workstations. The result was that employees could not meet employer set standards and were often let go. Employees were not permitted to give feedback on the process because scientific management only sends information from the top down.

   o **Bureaucratic Theory**: Max Weber (1947) furthered the functionality of scientific management theory by developing **BureaucraticTheory**. Weber saw that <u>tasks could be</u>

<u>routinized but that they must then be specialized</u>—not everyone could do just anything. To make this happen, formal rules were necessarily built into the overall organizational structure to insure stability and uniformity but only employees who were good at one task (e.g., making dress patterns) were given that task while others were given tasks for which they were best suited (e.g., sewing on dress buttons and zippers). So, employees would be assigned to special areas but within that area, no variation was permitted or less than maximum output.

How does this relate to communication? **Scientific Management** is not interested in the voice of the employee but only in the application of precise rules of governing by a single voice of management. Information is sent only from the manager/sender to the worker/receiver (as you can see, Taylor's 1911 studies were long before Schramm came around in 1954 to articulate the notion of feedback!). Scientific Management is the ultimate flat structures where there is a boss—and then *everybody* else.

2. **Human Relations:** As you might imagine, a widespread scientific management method of management could not last. Workers had goals that differed from that of management (like needing to pee) and managers could not reliably count on this structure for long term production. Elton Mayo (1933) recognized that workers would be far more effective if they were not simply told what to do but had *some stake in the process*—this is the crux of **Human Relations Management.** Mayo asserted that improved productivity would come from <u>*workplace satisfaction* and depended to a large degree on patterns established by social work groups</u>.

You have likely seen this in your own work experience. If you were ever a waitress, where the rules were technically the same for all employees but everyone knew that employees who worked weekday shifts had a different way of doing things than employees who go to work weekend evening shifts, then you have used the rules of a Human Relations structure. The means by which you and your team *informally organized* actually helped productivity! By sharing communication within informal work groups (weekday workers vs. weekend workers), you followed a pattern that fits with the Human Relations business structure – individual groups have individual needs. Meeting these needs helps the employees to become more productive!

The link between meeting group needs and subsequent productivity first became popularized in Elton Mayo's (1949) experiments (known as **the Hawthorne Studies**), which were conducted at the Western Electric Hawthorne Works in Cicero, Illinois (a suburb of Chicago). Mayo's experiments changed workplace environments to find out which met all employees needs (i.e., rest breaks, work hours, temperature and humidity). Ultimately, he found that those workers being studied improved performance *because* they were being studied rather than as a reaction to whatever manipulation the research did. Yes, it was the *attention* that made the difference. The groups studied felt that they were more important than groups that were not and the positive attention increased their productivity. (Ah… that makes sense, right?! Pay positive attention to me, I will feel better and, thus, work better!) This was Mayo's ultimate means of showing that workplace satisfaction was an important part of business.

Communication in a structure that values workplace satisfaction will necessarily differ from companies that do not value workplace satisfaction. In this environment, elements such as feedback and coding through proper channels are vital – whereas, in previous models, messages were sent through convenience channels with no attention to feedback. To facilitate such structures, companies moved from generally flat organizational models to taller business hierarchies with mid-level managers, thus, giving *teams* higher levels of attention.

3. **Human Resources:** Human Resources is a derivative of the Human Relations structure. Unlike the move from Scientific Management to Human Relations, which was an almost revolutionary change from a focus on productivity to a focus on

people, the **Human Resources** structure <u>considers employees to be as much of a resource to the company as necessary supplies, funding, final products, etc</u>. OK – so this makes people sound like sewing machines and typewriters – not the case. In fact, the Human Resources model, which is still in use today, considers people to be *invaluable* while acknowledging that *individual mindsets* about work (specifically, **how one is rewarded for work product**) will dramatically affect outcomes. These mindsets were the focus of Douglas McGregor's (1960) book, *The Human Side of Enterprise*, which offered up the Theory X and Y to differentiate the kind of mindsets that employees have about work.

> **Theory X**: Theory X hinges on the fact that <u>employees generally dislike work and must be controlled (or even threatened) in order to be productive and that they prefer not to take on additional responsibilities</u>. This is a difficult management position when you know that you really need those employees – and that they need you. McGregor (1960) saw that managers communicated one of two **"rewards"** messages to their employees. The first was a financial reward – do your work and I will pay you. The second was the reward of a pleasant working environment – do your work and I *won't* make life at this company rotten for you.

> o **Theory Y**: This theory does not argue that the reward system is the only way to get the best out of employees, but believes that <u>we can get the most out of these valuable resources if managers make the job itself satisfying with good working conditions</u>. McGregor (1960) saw in companies applying Theory Y forms of Human Resources management that managers viewed work is a natural human behavior. They believed that employee job satisfaction would lead to employees seeking responsibilities – and that creativity and imagination could solve problems. So, they communicated their value of employees by rewarding them with the best environment possible and listening to needs for creating that environment.

** From notions of treating employees well and providing **rewards** emerged management coordination of a range of worker related benefits (later known as 'personnel functions'). If your company offers you a retirement plan, a company picnic, paternity leave, puts up a picture of the Employee of the Month, or in anyway asks for your needs and responds to your *feedback* with rewards… then you are benefiting from ideas derived through Human Resources management.

Human Relations and Human Resources models of business have helped to shape our idea of modern business communication, but with a new age also comes a range of new and needed organizational models.

Modern Business Structures

4. **Systems Contingency:** Who hasn't been shopping during the U.S. holiday season? Well, probably smart people. If you have ever been shopping during this hectic time then you know that you will push through crowds and wines a frenzy unlike any other time of year (well, except for maybe the '*after* holiday' sales). If companies made no changes in their corporate structures (and general business practices) during the holiday season then you would likely interact with a whole bunch of ill-prepared and ill-equipped retailers. Alas, we do see changes! We see things like extra hours and employees, new set-ups for checkout and customer service, and perhaps even temporary standards for managing the retail floor. Such changes are '**contingent**' or dependent on changes in the environment.

   Systems contingency is the organizational model that works to be flexible for ever-changing needs in management and communication. Jay Galbraith (1973) argues that, *there is no one best way to organize and all ways of organizing cannot be not equally effective.* Such an idea flies in the face of what Frederick Taylor (1911) would argue. Taylor might contend: *if it ain't broke, don't fix it.* But, does that always work?

Contingency theory presents a new model for management and, subsequently communication, in which, "the best way to organize depends on the nature of the environment to which the organization relates" (Scott, 2003, p. 89). If the environment changes, then the company changes. Perhaps this could mean that communication messages that are normally sent from top to bottom begin traveling from the bottom to the top. It could mean that there is a time where employees change and desire more responsibility (moving from a Theory X to a Theory Y model). What is important to realize is that these changes can be made for short-term environmental changes (e.g., the holiday season) or longer-term global changes (moving all manufacturing plants from Asia to Texas). In general, contingency theory is guided by the general orienting hypothesis that organizations whose inside structures best match outside demands will achieve the best results (Scott).

5. **Transformational:** Systems contingency structures actually *plan* to make changes from time to time as they are needed. In that vein, the technologies and abilities that we experience in the 21st century have changed what it means to work for the one company – alas, the Transformational Model emerged.

The **Transformational Model** (first conceptualized as a leadership model by James MacGregor Burns in 1978) business structure is about organizing employee supervision and communication around a *vision* rather than around products, seasons, or a bureaucratic model. Timothy Johnpress (2003) examines the difference between **Transformational** businesses and **Transactional** businesses in his *Austin Business Journal* article. He quotes founder of the Stagen Leadership Institute, Rand Stagen's excellent distinction:

> *A transformational company provides a clear sense of purpose grounded in an unchanging set of core values and guiding principles. These companies maximize human capital by capturing the positive emotional energy of their workforce towards a common vision.*

A transactional company is clearly defined by its name – *transaction*. Employees will show up, do work and get paid. Or, in terms of employees, the idea is "pay us a fair price, and we'll provide you with appropriate products and services." Examples of *transformational* companies, according to Johnpress (2003) are Starbucks, Southwest Airlines Co., and Home Depot, Inc.—along with employee-focused Google, IKEA, and Richard Branson's Virgin Mobile. Examples of *transactional* businesses are trade unions, construction companies and 'old school' manufacturers.

This new theory of management, leadership, and organizational culture is directed and most closely tied to the relationship between <u>communication and organization</u> (Bisel, Messersmith, & Keyton, 2009). Transformation in any company relies on the implementation of effective marketing strategies and an eye toward keeping up with the times – but the payoffs are worth it! "When transformational leaders create organizational cultures of innovation and inspiration, their employees are more satisfied with their jobs and provide better customer service" (Bisel, Messersmith, & Keyton, p. 10). Transformational models can create happy (Google-like) places to work.

WHO TALKS TO WHOM THROUGH WHAT STRUCTURE?

In our nation's history, we have moved from individual craftsmen (sending direct messages and listening to single apprentices) to mass production (with Frederick Taylor standing over us with a stopwatch directing our progress and not listening to input). We have come from recognizing that attention to employees improves their job satisfaction (in the Hawthorne Experiments) to allowing workers to move to distant lands and telecommute, while focused on a single vision (as in transformational business). Each type of organizational models is built on how communication works its way through a business. As noted at the very beginning of this chapter, this is not a text to introduce you to *business*. It is a text to help you understand how *communication* moves within the constraints and confines of the corporate world.

Those of us who enter into any of the fast-paced careers available in various aspects of business cannot be successful by simply by doing our jobs in isolation. We all are part of a bigger picture. We all must participate in communication. To do this, we must know where to send our messages and from whom we should receive them!

Chapter Three

Listening to Others' Communication

BEING PRESENT

"I know that you believe you understand what you think I said, but I'm not sure you realize that what you heard is not what I meant."

Huh? Have you ever said something to someone and just known that the person to whom you were speaking didn't get it? Have you ever told someone something incredibly tragic and they said, "Hey, that's great!" Too often we send messages that are received – but clearly not *heard*. (Thank goodness for the feedback that lets us know when our messages are inaccurately absorbed.)

In the business context, missed messages can have disastrous, even fatal, results. Edward Tufte (2005) makes the argument that the use of PowerPoint as a message channel meant that NASA engineers were not heard when they announced that the Columbia Space Shuttle had a potentially (as it turns out, absolutely) fatal design flaw. While the validity of Tufte's argument is highly debatable, the notion that being heard in business it vital <u>cannot be over stressed</u> (DiSalvo, 1980; Sypher, Bostrom, and Seibert, 1989).

Just because we speak does not mean that our audience will listen – and the difference is crucial. Vincent Ferraro and Kathryn C. Palmer (1999), in *Speaking and Arguing* state:

We give speeches and make presentations with the assumption that people will listen to us. It is therefore essential that a speaker understand what listening involves. The speaker can legitimately expect that an audience will hear the words spoken, but hearing does not necessarily constitute effective listening.An audience is not actually listening unless it is attentive enough to comprehend fully the meaning of the speaker's words (para. 1).

Speeches are not just the practiced 5 minutes talks that you give with the aid of PowerPoint slides but the response to a colleague in a meeting, the request email that you send to your boss for attending an out of town sales call, or even the interaction with a co-worker while grabbing a cup of coffee in the cafeteria. When we speak, in any circumstance, it is not enough to be loud and make sure that your microphone is on. Creating an atmosphere that encourages listening is about so much more.

Audience: Ethos, Pathos, Logos

The first chapter of this text introduces the concept of "appeals". In the context of sending and receiving messages (Chapter One), appeals are crucial elements to be sure that you are crafting the best message. Now, let's flip that around.

Appeals to the audience are necessary for those in the audience to listen to your message. Recall that speakers send messages that are *for* audience and *about* audiences *to* audiences. We must meet our audience where they are culturally, emotionally, logically, and ethically. Aristotle presented us with the notions of ethos, logos, and pathos so that we could be heard – and the concepts are still crucial to business communication today.

- **Ethos:** Our information should be of the highest quality and credibility in the eyes of our audience. It should not be what we think is the best source but what the audience will think is the best source.

- **Logos:** Our ideas should also be organized in a *manner* that supports our argument but in a *structured* form that makes sense to our audience.

- **Pathos:** What we present should have emotional resonance, or connection, with our audience.

Imagine receiving information from a disreputable source (e.g., Bernie Madoff telling us where to invest) or trying to follow a disjointed attempt at a message for even if we are presented with a speaker that is devoid of emotion or too emotional (e.g., Dean should have thought of this before that eager yell that lost him the presidential bid). These are all cases where the speaker ignored the importance of appealing to the audience and we would tune them out.

How do we know how to make our presentations, interviews, and all communication *for* our audiences, *about* audiences, and *to* our audiences? Rather than guess – we listen. We gather data. We go through the steps of processing expected and unexpected information.

As you can see, listening is a process. In this chapter, you will get a leg (or an ear) up on the function of listening, how to test your listening quotient, facing and overcoming barriers to listening.

LISTENING IN THE WORKPLACE - A FUNCTIONAL CHOICE

What does it mean to say that something is functional? To say that it 'functions' is a bit redundant. Instead, consider **functional** to be that which is practical and operational. Now let's put them together. As we consider listening in this chapter, your focus will not be on listening as an <u>academic</u> term. Instead, your work here will be practical and applicable in helping you operate in a workplace. It (listening) will be a *functional* choice.

Defining Listening

Considering what you know about business communication thus far, you likely have a good idea of how listening fits into business structures and communication models. That being said, let's break it down for the sake of clarity. Senders send messages through channels to receivers. If the receiver chooses not to take in the message, then that receiver is not listening. If the message is never received, then there is no feedback and no communication. But simply taking in the message does not mean that the person was listening. If that were the case then you would never be congratulated for bad news, and teenagers would rarely scream at their parents, "You never listen to me!"

So what is listening? At its most clinical level, **listening** is an intentional act that involves taking in and processing *all* of a message (Fredriksson, 1999). Contrast this to **hearing**, which is what most of us do, that can be either a conscious or unconscious behavior involving the physical awareness of sound (Fredriksson).

Barker and his colleagues (1980) developed the notion of listening and communication one step further to argue that in order to *truly* listen, a receiver must take a message and provide feedback on three levels:
1.   *self-feedback* – did I get that?
2.   *listener-to-listener feedback* – did you get that?
3.   *listener-to-speaker feedback* – did you say that?

Attention to Listening

While we may not be fully cognizant of it, we spend a great deal of our time listening. In the same Barker, et al (1980) study mentioned earlier, the results showed that college students spend over 18 ½ hours a day communicating. Of that 18+ hour communication day, over half of that time is spent listening. This means that we are spending a good amount of our lives attempting to gather and understand messages. While additional studies debate the actual number of hours, those analyzing how we divide our time during the day always attribute more time to listening than to writing, reading, or even speaking (for review, see: International Listening Association, n.d.).

Given the amount of time we spend doing it, you would think that we would spend a great deal of time studying it. You would think wrong. The time we spend learning about the critical communication skill of listening is woefully inadequate. One core reason for this is how we are accustomed to thinking about listening. Take a minute to reflect back over your years of education. If it was a traditional public school education, you spent most of your day listening. In fact, if you talked during class, you could be sent to the principal's office. We learned very quickly how to shush.

A Classroom Setting

During all of that time that we spent listening in class, we spent precious little time studying the *process* of being quiet and paying attention. Listening, as a learned communication skill, was either entirely or almost entirely neglected in formal education. The great irony here is that the more educated we become, the worse we listen! *The Encyclopedia of Business and Finance* (2010) observed:

> Research indicates that we hear only 25 percent of what is said and, after two months, remember only one-half of that. This has not always been the case. In first grade we heard 90 percent of what was said, in second grade 80 percent, in seventh grade 43 percent, and by ninth grade only 25 percent. It is imperative that we strive to improve our listening skills (p. 1).

Bearing in mind the time and dedication that you have spent (as well as possibly the money) on a formal education, it is frightening that you – or any of us – were not able to grasp much of the information that was sent to us. It is sad that with this being the case, listening gets the least amount of curricular development of any learned skill (Ifert Johnson and Long, 2008; Janusik, 2002).

Why Haven't We Studied Listening?

A couple of factors may help explain educations' inattention to the skills needed to listen. First, because we are so poorly educated about listening, we equate hearing and listening. If we can hear, we can listen, right? Wrong! Consider the differences: physical *awareness* of sound versus an intentional act (Fredriksson, 1999). There is a world of difference between the two. Second, our culture is action-oriented. In the communication process we see talking (which is visibly, assertive, and expressive) as more important than listening (which is passive and receptive). In the business world, we think "In order to sell, I have to talk." While this may ultimately be true, in order to know what to say, we have to first listen to understand our customers' needs.

The Pay Off for Studying

If we learn how to listen effectively, the payoff can be huge. Wolvin and Coakley (2000) note that listening is so important that it is actually a better predictor of educational success than either reading or academic aptitude. Effective listening translates into faster and deeper learning. The benefits of listening effectively, however, are not confined to the classroom. Professionals have recognized the importance of listening to organizational success for more than 50 years (Flynn, Vilikoski, and Grau, 2008).

Listening in the Business Setting

Consider all of the day-to-day workplace tasks that need your listening skills. Taking notes, conducting interviews, receiving instructions, and even handling complaints all demand alert and active listening. Effective listening is crucial to running a business efficiently. As the Encyclopedia of Business and Finance (2010) explains:

> Most people make numerous listening mistakes every day, but the costs—financial and otherwise—are seldom analyzed. Because of listening mistakes, appointments have to be rescheduled, letters retyped, and shipments rerouted. Any number of catastrophes can arise from a failed communication regardless of the type of industry. Productivity is affected and profits suffer (p. 1).

Getting along with others at Work

Effective listening also translates into improved working relationships. You only need to recall the fallout of your relationship with a disliked co-worker to understand the value of good working relationships. So how can listening help? Flynn, Vilikoski, and Grau (2008) found that creating an organizational culture that values listening will boost employee identification with the company and result in higher employee satisfaction! Additionally, **we know that customers trust salespeople more when they perceive that the salesperson is listening to them** (Ramsey and Sohl, 1997). In this vein, listening works as a marketing tool for the company to build a long-term clientele.

As you are building your clientele, you will be building your career through relationships. None of us ever enters the business world set on mediocrity – okay, maybe most of us don't. For the vast majority of us, excelling in our careers is very important. Well, guess what? Effective listening skills are essential to your personal career advancement (Flynn, Vilikoski, and Grau, 2008) – especially given that the higher you rise in the corporate structure the more time you will spend listening.

So… how well do you listen? Let's see how things look before your training has begun… and later you can check again. Take the quick test on the next page as a measure of your LQ (Listening Quotient).

As you take the test, be honest. Your LQ is not a number set in stone – it can be improved. If you don't truly know where you are beginning then you won't know how much attention to give to developing your skills. (Don't worry. No one will tell… and we all have room for improvement!)

THE LQ (LISTENING QUOTIENT)

INSTRUCTIONS: To check your listening effectiveness, take the following quiz. Compare your answers with the scale on the next page.

For each of these statements, select one of the following:
(Y)Yes, (S) Sometimes, (N) No

_____ I feel comfortable when listening to others on the phone.

_____ It is often difficult for me to concentrate on what others are saying.

_____ I feel tense when listening to new ideas.

_____ I have difficulty concentrating on instructions that others give to me.

_____ I dislike being a listener as a member of an audience.

_____ I seldom seek out opportunities to listen.

_____ I find myself daydreaming when others ramble on.

_____ I often argue mentally or aloud with what someone that is saying even before he or she finishes.

_____ I find that others often repeat things to me.

_____ I seem to find out about important events too late.

<u>**Count Them Up:**</u>

_____ Number of Times that you answered – Yes

_____ Number of Times that you answered – Sometimes

_____ Number of Times that you answered – No

Look for how to score your listening adeptness using the scale on the next page.

Scoring Your Listening Adeptness

CHECK FOR THESE RESPONSES:

If you answered *Yes* or *Sometimes* on less than (3) three questions, you perceive yourself to be a good listener.

If you answered *Yes* or *Sometimes* on (3) three to (6) six questions, you perceive yourself to be an average listener.

If you answered *Yes* or *Sometimes* on (7) or more questions, you must give immediate attention to your listening skills.

NOTE: The preceding scale on communication apprehension was taken from Wheeless, L. R. (1975). An investigation of receiver apprehension and social context dimensions of communication apprehension. *The Speech Teacher, 24,* 261-268.

Finished? How'd ya do? If you did well then you have an excellent foundation on which to develop your skills. If you struggled—do not fret! You are about to learn how to overcome barriers to listening and become a listening champ!

BARRIERS TO EFFECTIVE LISTENING

 With or without formal training, how you listen is subject to a whole host of factors that are difficult (and sometimes impossible) to control. Think of listening like seeing. With vision, we must overcome obstacles when someone steps in your way, it's raining, or you're looking at one of those stupid graphic pictures where if you relax your eyes just right you can see an image appear from inside the dots. Vision is a critical resource for information and we accept that we might have physical difficulties that impact how we see things. We are willing to get glasses and train our eyes—or ask people to step out of the way. Don't let listening be any different! Recognize the barriers to effective listening that are all around us and within us in order to take the steps toward improved listening ability.

Listening Barriers in the Brain

One impact on listening is that our brains are way too efficient at processing what we are listening *to*. The average person speaks at a rate of 100 words per minutes (on the slow side) up to 175 words per minute (on the fast side) with most of us falling around the 125 words per minute rate (Lee and Hatesohl, 1993; Zofi and Metzler, 2007).

The problem is that we have the mental ability to understand speech at an estimated speed of 400 words per minute on the conservative side (Lee and Hatesohl, 1993) and 600 to 800 words per minute on the high side (Zofi and Metzler, 2007)! So, when we are listening, we are using as little as 12.5 percent of our mental capacity and just under 44 percent at the most. While you may think that this would make us better listeners because we have so much ability, what in fact happens, is that our brains begin to wander and take care of other tasks.

Example:

> You are sitting in your company's annual employee meeting. Your CEO is hoping to get folks on board with the move from one location to the next. First, she details the problem with the current location. Second, she somehow lays out how the new location will fix the problems. Finally, she asks that you help in the process by giving details of...
>
> Oh gosh. You tuned out. Sure, you could tell what the main points were but after that—all of the details just ran together and, suddenly, you found yourself creating a grocery list in your head. (ps... you're out of bread.)

Barriers According to Us

Why don't you listen? That's not an accusation—like, "Hey, you never listen! How come?!" Quite the contrary. Since we know that the brain starts to pull our mind away from listening (and that we <u>all</u> do this), it's good to do a personal analysis of what factors cause your mind to pull away. Before you think that you are alone, take a peak at what some college students answered when they were asked: **What prevents you from listening?**

> Golen (1990), in the *Journal of Business Communication*, reported what college students saw as their own issues. While the students listed a whole host of reasons, their answers clustered around six main difficulties with listening.
> 1. Avoiding complex or time consuming subject matter
> 2. Cannot relate to the speaker
> 3. Don't agree with what is being said
> 4. Focused on the individual words rather than sentiment of the talk
> 5. Not interested in the speaker's subject
> 6. Distracted by external noise

Common Listening "Selections"

Selection means choice. Just like listening is a choice, so is the information to which we *select* to listen. You are aware of this all the time. Right now, go over to your stereo (hopefully you are at home because this example will backfire in a library, your parent's house, or in public). Turn it on and up as high as possible—on a station that you don't like. Now look in the mirror. Are you making that, "oh wow, that's awful face"? Can you feel yourself putting mental earmuffs on to block out some of the noise so that your eardrums do not explode? You are putting up **filters**—or screening devices to suppress unwanted information. You do it everyday in common situations. We all do. We choose:

1. **Selective Exposure**
2. **Selective Attention**
3. **Selective Perception**
4. **Selective Retention**

Understanding each of these areas will help you to know when you have your filter on, why, and what it does… even if what it does is sometimes a good thing.

1. **Selective Exposure:** Leon Festinger (1957) was the first to layout the notion of **selective exposure** as it connected to communication. When he first discussed this, it was in regards to political communication (but has since been picked up by communication and listening scholars). In brief, Festinger told us that we have all sorts of information to which we <u>can</u> expose ourselves… but we <u>choose</u> to only put ourselves in front of information that is consistent with our world-view. (His example was that if you are a Republican, you would not surround yourself with only Democrats but would choose to expose yourself— or primarily hang out with—those who are like you). In other words, it is rare and would be irrational for us to put ourselves in uncomfortable situations *all of the time*.

2. **Selective Attention:** What if we are exposed to something outside our worldview? Of course, this happens and some people even seek out contrary ideas when evaluating their own

positions. Even in the times where we do seek out alternative positions, we are still making listening choices about what gets our consideration. These choices are called **selective attention**.

For example, your (inept) co-worker walks in and begins to give a presentation on a business strategy with which you whole-heartedly disagree and know that your boss will squash in an instant. Do you spend your time keen on every word? Of course, not! You begin to go through your work-day list—or even your grocery list (you're out of bread, still)—in order to make better use of your time. You do what neurologists and psychologists (see Posner and Peterson, 1980), have long considered a natural reaction—you tune things out! This process of selective attention is actually considered to be our brain's way of best utilizing resources.

3. **Selective Perception:** Perception is our interpretation of messages. Because communication is ambiguous by nature, messages are open to interpretation. Through **selective perception**, we tend to assign meanings that are consistent with *our* expectations. ("But, mom... 1am *is* home early!") When a message doesn't fit with those expectations, we deny of the validity of the message, dismiss it as irrelevant, or compartmentalize the message to isolate it from our conflicting views (for original scientific analysis, see Hillyard, et al., 1973).

    a. <u>Perceptual Sets</u>: To do this, we develop **perceptual sets** or preconceived notions of *what goes with what* (Bugelski & Alampay,1961). For instance, good messages come from people we like whereas poor messages come from people we don't like (again, think how this can work in sales).

    b. <u>Perceptual Filters</u>: Along with matching one thing to another, we have pre-setup ideas of how experiences should play out—**perceptual filters** (Posner, 1980). For instance, if the manager down the hall has always been a jerk to you, when he calls you in for a meeting you are already set up to filter anything he says as 'jerk-like'— whether that's what happens or not.

Dearborn and Simon (1958) looked at how organizational culture, group interaction, and workplace politics have all *benefited* from understanding selective perception. How? These studies showed us that success in business is as much in *how people perceive us* (and, thus, listen to our ideas) as it is how valid our ideas are on their own. So… be sure that you are perceived well!

4. **Selective Retention:** The worst part about how our brains listen is that we may actually listen and then discard important details. **Selective retention** (McCroskey, Richmond & McCroskey, 2006) allows us to drop from memory both those nagging inconsistencies that do not fit with our worldview or are not evaluated as vital information.

   Has your boss ever said, "I have told you how to do this twice already!" Ugh—do you feel like you have Alzheimer's long before you should. Relax. You aren't losing your mind… your mind is letting go of information for strategic reasons (perhaps you have too much on your plate already and can't manage another work task). This doesn't make it a good or ok thing to 'forget' the details but it might allow you to understand why you do it and get better at not doing it later!

External And Environmental Barriers

Everything discussed, thus far, appears to be some level of psychological control over our ability to listen. It isn't always that complicated. Being hungry, or too hot, or too cold, or in pain, or tired, etc., will impact our ability to effectively listen. Did you or do you have a class in college that is just before lunch? Think about how hard it is to listen to the professor when your body is thinking ("mmm… turkey sandwich"). Additionally, what is happening in our physical environment can distract us from listening. Background noises, interruptions (like a cell phone ringing, the comfort level of your seat, and so forth, can be barriers to effective listening. These complications are commonly referred to as **noise** (think back to the Chapter One discussion of Schramm 1954 model of communication). The fact of the matter is that it's not all us that impacts our ability to listen – but that it is all on us to work on improved listening.

IMPROVING LISTENING EFFECTIVENESS

Does it seem like you simply cannot get into a good place to listen? Frustrated? It is that defeatist attitude that will lead to the selections that we have just discussed. Let it go. Let yourself see these barriers as challenges in the workplace and, while others are stuck behind them, you are improving the communication skills so that you to will truly have thenumber one quality that companies desire in applicants!

Practical Steps to Listening

Knowledge is power. You have more knowledge about what blocks listening than most others entering the workforce. With practice, you may become so skilled that 'listening skills' become something you even feel comfortable listing on your résumé (more on this in Chapter Nine). So, let's make this as practical as possible.

1. **75/ 25:** SSSShhhhhhh. Sometimes listening is that easy. We need to stop talking in order to start listening. In discussing fundraising, Schumacher (2008) highlights how *not* talking is the key to success. "When meeting with donors, you cannot listen to them if you are doing all the talking" (p. 41). This is good advice in all client relationships. You have to understand *their* needs before you can sell them your stuff!

   Conflict resolution and negotiating expert Robert Mayer has given a label to what most sales trainers recommend, the '**75/25 Partnering Secret**.' This is simple: spend 75% of your time listening and 25% talking. When we do this, we know what we are talking about and improve relationships along the way.

2. **Set the Scene:** There is a time and place for everything, right? Effective listening is no different. In order to maximize your listening ability, you need:

a. **Sufficient Time**: If you are pressed for time, you cannot give your undivided attention to understanding what is being communicated to you. For the record, multitasking is not the answer! Make an appointment for a time when you can focus on listening fully.

b. **A Lack of Physical Distractions**: Make sure that you have a setting that is amenable to giving the other party your undivided attention. Bierck (2001) advised avoiding having *serious* conversations in your office (e.g., performance reviews that won't go so well). Why? Because the unfinished projects, your phone, your e-mail, and other distractions can draw your attention away from the conversation, which is especially problematic when it is emotionally sensitive. Smart organizations actually create spaces that promote effective listening opportunities. Find a conference room or a private nook where you can converse without distractions and interruptions.

c. **A Lack of Mental Distractions**: You know from above that distractions come from outside and within. Give yourself time to remove these internal distractions. Arrive for your meeting early, which will give you some transition time to get out of the thinking mode you needed for whatever you were doing just before the meeting and to get into an appropriate mindset for this interaction. Review your purpose for being there and what outcomes you would like (Bierck, 2001). A little assessment time makes for better listening.

3. **Outline—on Paper or Mentally:** Listening is a behavior that you should *embody*. Lee and Hatesohl (1993) suggest three ways to productively hone your in the moment listening that revolve around the practice of tracking another person's ideas.

   a. **Anticipate**: Actively attempt to anticipate the speaker's next point. If you guess right, what you are learning is reinforced; if wrong, figuring out *why* helps to increase attention.

b. **Identify Support**: Identify the way the other person supports his or her position. Lee and Hatesohl (1993) observed that, "By and large, we use only three ways to build points: We explain the point, we get emotional and harangue the point, or we illustrate the point with a factual illustration." Figuring out how someone is supporting (or not supporting) his or her point can increase listening efficiency.

c. **Make Mental Summaries**: Periodically make mental summaries as you listen. A good listener takes advantage of natural pauses in the flow of ideas to think back and recap what has been said. These periodic summaries significantly reinforce overall understanding.

4. **Enact Listening Behaviors:** Even when you are listening, *demonstrating* listening to an audience will help reinforce your behavior. Demonstrating listening will also provide necessary feedback to those sending the message. The way to 'show' that you are listening comes from some basic phrases and nonverbal communication.

a. *Look!* **I am Listening**:Your nonverbal messages… speak volumes. These signals let people know if we are listening or not. So, when you are listening: a) give appropriate eye gaze (not staring but making contact), b) sit or stand in an engaging way (attentive, but not aggressively eager), c) avoid fidgeting or multi-tasking, and d) occasionally nod or signaling understanding.

b. **"So, What' You're Saying Is…"**: While jumping in to take over the conversation will hinder listening, providing small verbal indications of listening will help you to focus. Bordone (2007) suggests three key skills to use when actively listening: paraphrasing, inquiring, and acknowledging.

1. **Paraphrasing**: Restate what the other person has said (in a genuine manner). This serves to: a) give senders a chance to clarify, b) avoid misunderstandings, and c) show comprehension of the other point of view.

2. **Inquiring**: Get someone to elaborate on an idea by asking non-threatening questions.
3. **Acknowledging**: By showing that you understand not just the facts but the *feelings* underlying the other person's message then you can convey that you have listened to the 'big picture.'

5. **Practice:** Veering away from the conversation is inevitable. Let's not sugarcoat it. As Lee and Hatesohl (1993) confirm, listening intently is hard work. If done for a long period of time, it can leave us mentally (and physically!) exhausted. But, we can improve how well we listen with practice. Think of listening like exercise—the more you work out, the easier it gets.

Zofi and Metzler (2007) suggest, when faced with a challenging listening situation, to think of a trigger (something either physical or mental) on which you can concentrate to clear and refocus your mind. Perhaps this for you is a promotion ("if I get all the details, I can get ahead of everyone else!"), an ideal job… or even a good grade. If these are things that you want then a quick mental picture of any or all of them can help you reprioritize and get back to the task at hand.

FINALLY... LISTEN UP

Listening effectively does not happen naturally; it is a skill (like good communication) that has to be cultivated. Moreover, if the research is to be believed, the older and more educated we get, the worse listeners we become. Perhaps it is because we don't value listening, or it might be that we simply don't learn how to listen well. This does not mean that we can't get better! It is certainly worth the effort. If you do it well then you have the chance to fight the curve and become someone who improves your skills over time. Lee and Hatesohl (1993) perhaps said it best,"Listening is hard work… It's a challenge to be a good listener. But good listeners get big rewards."

Chapter Four
Leading and Meeting in Business Groups

GROUP WORK?

So, your boss assigned you to work in a group. Perhaps you're dreading it – in that case you've got a fair bit of company. Groups are like marriages, they take a great deal of work and patience, they are much harder than you might assume at first, and the dynamics (of groups—not marriages) cannot be easily predicted ahead of time. In fact, research shows that, like a marriage, there's only a fifty percent chance that your group will be successful (Bormann, 1990). If you are looking at the odds here—then there is also a fifty percent chance that you will realize all of the benefits of working in a group (or marriage). How so? By taking some very strategic steps.

Rather than throwing up your hands and surrendering to the "Bad Group" notion, a better strategy is to learn how to *guide* your group into having a successful experience and positive outcome. The best way to do this is to know what groups need in order to be successful, and work hard to make sure your group has what it takes!

The information in this chapter will guide you through relevant theories regarding group conditions, explain how leadership and groups roles can manifest, and finally how you can lead your group during an effective meeting.

AN "EMERGENT" NATURE

What does it mean to **emerge**? Most basically, it means that some element (in this case, elements of group work) will become apparent, important, and prominent. It also means that something has recovered or survived a difficult or demanding situation. Both notions of emergence apply to scenarios where you come together with your colleagues and are pursuing a common goal.

It would be easy to say that all groups follow certain steps and that if you follow them—you will be successful. Unfortunately, group work is not that simple. What is good to know is that scholars have been studying groups for years and can provide us with telling information about the conditions of group work. What you see below pools resources from the prominent scholars in group communication and function!

The Patterns of Group Work Experience

"Who are you?"
"What do you do?"
"Wow—you can do that?"
"Look what we can do together!"

Does this sound familiar? We experience group work in similar patterns. We come together, we experience tension and breakthroughs, we figure each other out, and then (hopefully) we come together to produce the best product. There are a variety of different theories that attempt to explain group experience. These theories suggest similar trends to give us a general understanding of the patterns that most groups will experience. For our purposes, it is not necessary to cover all of the prominent theories of group work but to show those that best describe the trends in group research.

Most group communication scholars see four or five similar stages that groups encounter. Put these together and we get a clear picture of the patterns of group experience. These patterns can best be understood by looking at the work of famous group communication scholars: Ernest Bormann's (1990) *Recurring Pattern Model*, Bruce W. Tuckman's (1965) *Sequence Of Decision Making*, and B. Aubrey Fisher's (1970) *Theory Of Decision Emergence.*

Bormann's Recurring Pattern Model

Primary Tension → Secondary Tension →
Obstacles → Cohesion

All groups encounter stress. We know this to be true from our own experiences. Bormann (1990) called those stresses "tensions" and explained that every group goes through two types of social tensions—primary and secondary.

When we first gather, we normally feel the questions about who is in our group and what the interaction will be like. This is normal! (Even groups that have a long history can have primary tensions at the beginning of a meeting or new project.) Some signs of these tensions are feelings of caution, hesitancy in offering information, or even failing to engage in typical communication patters. If you have ever had a long awkward period of silence in a group then you know just what we're talking about. This is also a time of group members being overly polite and doing whatever possible to avoid controversy. Telling (appropriate) jokes and getting groups to laugh and talk about personal interests or individual experiences helps to reduce these tensions.

As groups move onto needing to make decisions then they encounter secondary tensions (e.g., when conflict occurs over what to do and how to do it). If your group does not have much tension over decisions, well, then your group may be exceptionally harmonious… or just bored and unmotivated. Your goals in a group are, so says Bormann (1990) to move past the tensions. Do not try to eliminate them because they are inevitable. Instead, allow tension to occur within normal limits and know that creativity causes positive tensions!

The final elements of this theory indicate that your group will face obstacles and reach cohesion. It would be nice to think that this is always the case—but even Bormann (1990) tells us that groups who remain caught in tension phases—and many groups do—can never directly address obstacles or opposing forces that they must overcome and they certainly can never reach cohesion. Some groups will move ahead and past tensions only to return to them when cohesion cannot be reached. This is why Bormann's model is not listed in phases but in a continuum that can keep cycling back. What we learn from him is that it is important to address tension if your group ever even hopes to move forward!

Tuckerman's Model

Tuckman's (1965) group model is equally useful for understanding our experiences in business groups. He describes five linear stages (which means one following the next… and not as cyclical as we saw above). These are forming, storming, norming, performing, and adjourning.

Each of these stages involves two aspects: interpersonal relationships and task behaviors, which means that in each phase we must give attention to both those in the group (interpersonal) and what we are charged with doing (the task).

In the first stage, **forming**, we take time to learn about each other and what we are supposed to do. (This phase tends to be when some folks are confused, not committed, and don't work really hard to listen to what's going on.) But groups don't get caught here. They move into the **storming** phase—or the time of engaging in brainstorming, getting emotional, having conflict, getting heard, and lacking cohesion. DO NOT AVOID THIS PHASE. If you are conflict avoidant then it might seem good to try and skip the storming… but without it then we end up making poor, single minded decisions that do not lead into the next phase… norming. **Norming** is when groups establish… norms! Group members will figure out the rules to having communication, achieving their goals, and eliminating (or embracing) tactics that distract them from their goals. If you can find healthy group goals (like brining pizza to every meeting… mmmm!) then you will have your best **performing** and be able to conclude your business (**adjourn**) successfully!

Fishers's Model

Fisher's (1970) model is linear like the model above. He offers up four phases that groups go through when they are trying to reach decisions. What is cool about Fisher is that he looked at change that happened over time. He saw that as groups figured out their choices and the choices became firm, groups would change their interaction process!

For Fisher (1970), we first come together much like we did as Freshman in college—through **orientation**. The orientation phase is a lot like primary tension. We all feel awkward and don't yet know the rules. We spend time during this phase to try to learn about others in the group and feel comfortable. Fisher sees that our first tensions will arise when we are charged with a task… like finding some campus scavenger hunt—or, at work, putting together a client proposal.

Tensions occur as we move into our **conflict** phase. We debate. We disagree. We are able to achieve the best results. Fisher reminds us that without conflict (a *positive* notion) that we come to decisions that are limited and less creative.

If we move beyond conflict to **emerge** then we have come to a place where our group's social structure (e.g., who leads, who adopts what roles, and how we make choices). We are now less tentative. It's like getting to your junior year! Some of our roles may be positive but others may be negative (yeah—we've all had that dude in our group who just wants to gab and can never focus on the work). If we choose to allow conflict to remain and we allow negative roles to go unchallenged then we emerge as unhealthy groups whose bad behavior has been **reinforced**.

While each theorists—and, thus, each model—uses different terminology and details per phase, it is important to recognize the trends. Groups show patterns in initial and later phases of interaction:

- **Initial Phases**
  - Primary Tensions – Initial Uneasiness
  - Secondary Tensions – Conflict Arises

- **Later Phases**
  - ○ Experience an Obstacle – Dress Rehearsal
  - ○ Experience Cohesiveness – Performance

The group's sense of itself emerges gradually, through a trial and error process, and there is no guarantee that a group will make it to that cohesiveness. In fact, some groups never get past their initial tensions while other blow up at the first sign of conflict.

Now that you understand the uncomfortable behavior of the group and why people do what they do, you are in a good position to help your group move through the stages. In the next few sections, we are going to look at how you can coach group members into taking effective group roles, as well as some strategies for productive conflict management.

LEADERSHIP AS ROLE EMERGENCE

For many people, including most of the early scholars of group dynamics, the most important role in a group is that of the "leader." There are countless studies and theories of leadership to help guide an adoption of this role—some of which have transformed how we understand leaders and others that have been discounted over time.

Initial Views on Leadership

Perhaps the most well known theory about leadership is **The Great Man Theory** (yes, they thought it was about *men*). The basic idea behind this theory was that great leaders were born that way. If that was true, then the best way to make sure you had a good leader was to hunt them down (consider the emergence of "head hunters" as the name of employee finders) and recruit them to your company/ group. After reviewing 287 studies conducted between 1904 and 1970, Ralph Stogdill, a psychology professor at The Ohio State University, Columbus, concluded that leadership success was not based on personality traits (Stogdill 1948, 1974). It seemed that certain traits were successful in some situations but not others, and that two leaders with different personalities could be successful in the same situation. Thus, **The Great Man Theory is today considered invalid**.

Today we know that being a successful leader is fairly complex concept to study. But for now, it's useful to STOP thinking about "the leader" as the superhero of the group who single-handedly saves the day to the applause of the passive followers. There is no leader in the world today who doesn't have a fleet of staff sharing the weight of the work. Your group should be no different. The more people in your group who pull their weight—who *do leadership*—the better your group will be. Consider applying your emotional intelligence to your approach to leadership.

Emotional Intelligence

One of the major parts in the leadership success equation is emotional intelligence, a concept made popular by Daniel Goleman's (1998) text. Emotional intelligence is defined through two models. First, the **ability model** defines emotional intelligence as "a set of abilities that involves perceiving and reasoning abstractly with information that emerges from feelings," (Mandell, & Pherwani, 2003, p. 389) while the **mixed model** defines it as "an ability with social behaviors, traits and competencies" (p. 389). What do these mean for business? Well, if your boss walks into the room where you and your officemate just finished yelling at each other (which you should never do) and he or she can't even tell that something is wrong... then either you two are fantastic actors or your boss has low emotional intelligence. Imagine the problems that arise or don't get solved when an employee can't read emotions!

Because these models describe traits that would seem quite important for leaders to possess (e.g., abstract reasoning, social competence, etc.), Mandell and Pherwani (2003) conducted an experiment to determine whether or not there was correlation between emotional intelligence and successful leadership. Not only did they find a direct relationship between emotional intelligence and transformational (visionary) leadership skills, but they also found that women scored higher on emotional intelligence tests than did men! (Sorry guys... you do some things better than women, too!) As you can see, leaders can use emotional intelligence to prioritize their corporate concerns—but all employees will have some varying degree of emotional intelligence that is a key part of the corporate equation.

So, for our purposes, let's define leadership to get away from the superhero. **Leadership** is influencing and guiding a group to go beyond its current status to achieve collective goals. This is something in which*all* group members can share.

Shared Leadership and Group Roles

Groups that are more successful are those where leadership is shared (and delegated) so that one person is not carrying the weight of the entire group. Recent research by management professor Eric Chong (2007) suggests that the distribution of tasks to those in a group can depend on the: 1) purpose of the group and 2) the stage of group development. What he tells us is that the success of the group is directly related to how effectively the roles are distributed!

Tasks and Relationships

Most research on role behaviors is based on the work of two influential organizational theorists, Kenneth Benne and Paul Sheats (1948). They concluded that there are two dimensions of work that occurs within a group: the **task dimension** and the **relationship maintenance dimension** (that should sound familiar from the above discussion on patterns of group experience!).

Task Roles

Roles that support the **task dimension** of group work are those that help the group directly to achieve its goals. The task dimension roles are obviously important because the group needs them to complete their job. You might have one person doing more than one role, or several people doing the same role depending on the task. These *helpful* behavioral task roles include:

- **Initiator/Contributor**: starts a process by offering suggestions, ideas, solutions, goals; suggests a way of moving forward
- **Information Giver**: may be an expert or have researched a topic, offers facts or experience for consideration

- o **Opinion Giver**: takes a position using values (rather than facts) to evaluate alternatives
- o **Information Seeker; Opinion Seeker**: asks for clarification
- o **Summarizer**: goes over the main activities or accomplishments, organizes what has happened
- o **Evaluator:** uses criteria (e.g. practicality, logic, speed, etc.) to judge the work of the group
- o **Procedural Technician**: performs necessary tasks for the group e.g. keep minutes, monitor financial budget, timekeeper
- o **Energizer:** stimulates the group to action, motivator

Relationship Maintenance Roles

The roles that support the **relationship maintenance dimension** of group work are equally important. These behaviors allow the group to feel comfortable working together. They do not directly help the group to achieve its goals (e.g., they are not tasks) but without them the group will ultimately fail. Such roles include:

- o **Encourager**: offers praise for good ideas or behavior, helps members to feel good about participation
- o **Harmonizer**: mediates disputes, helps members resolve differences or move beyond conflict
- o **Gatekeeper**: facilitates talk-time so that some individuals do not take over, or others do not contribute, calls on individuals to encourage/ discourage participation
- o **Tension Reliever**: tells jokes or finds other ways to relieve tension when the group gets frustrated

You certainly may have more than one task dimension role while simultaneously having a few relationship maintenance roles. Even more so, the role that you will play changes in each group, and you might combine different roles together. For example, you may generate ideas, ask questions, and harmonize the group. There might be other members of the group who overlap with your roles—it doesn't hurt to have two people harmonizing, or three or four people generating ideas. What is critical is that you pay attention to what roles are being done because if you see that a role is not being accomplished, you can (and should) step up to the plate and help the group by playing that role.

Coping with Dysfunction

A great deal of research has gone into cataloguing other roles in that sadly play out in too many groups. These are the **dysfunctional roles**— also known as **self-oriented roles**—that distract a group from its goal.

Self-Oriented Roles

No doubt you've been in a group with some people whose behavior has hindered the overall process. You may even have been one of those people. One of the roles that you or another took on could include:

- **Aggressor**: express disapproval of others, jokes excessively, attacks the group, shows envy
- **Blocker**: negative and resistant, disagrees and opposes beyond reasonable objections, takes discussion onto a tangent
- **Social Loafer**: acts indifferently; withdraws from discussion; fools around, daydreams, lets others take responsibility
- **Help-seeker**: expresses insecurity, uses position in group to address personal needs or gain sympathy
- **Special Interest Pleader**: comes to the group with a personal agenda to promote their particular bias

Remember that roles emerge through trial and error during the stages of group development. This means that if a group member does something dysfunctional and the other group members encourage (or don't discourage) the behavior, the person is likely to repeat the behavior. So, leaders… if you have a dysfunctional role players in your group,that person is there because the group allowed it to develop. Now, you must manage the situation.

Meta-Talk:

Once you've let someone form a dysfunctional role, the only way to stop it is to engage in **meta-talk**—talk that is about the *mechanics* of the group and whether or not the behaviors (norms, roles, etc.) are productive for the group. It is critical that if your group is doing something counter-productive, that someone (might as well be you) stops the group initiates meta-talk. You should address the behavior rather than the character of the person. Ask all members of the group whether they approve of the behavior or not and what alternatives they can suggest. If you do not stop a behavior, it will tend to become a *norm*.

Leadership "Styles" of Influence

Since we are talking about consulting your group about dysfunction, it seems apropos to address the means by which leaders involve their group in decisions and discussions. How we talk to groups in a work setting can best be described as our *'style of influence.'*

Four Styles of Influence

The below four styles of influence were first identified by Paul Hersey and Ken Blanchard (1969; Hersey, Blanchard, & Johnson, 2007) in a theory that explained how leaders manage their teams. Their popular management theory continues to be the basis for training future leaders to be successful! For our purposes, the following four leadership styles of influence can help guide you as you determine how to guide your group toward decisions.

Authoritarian/ "Telling" Style

A telling style works when the leader has information that other group members need and they are less motivated. In this case, you need to tell people what to do and closely supervise their work to ensure they do it (like being the 'boss' of a group). In a group of peers, it can be tricky to give orders, but sometimes people are happy to let someone else be in charge. Just remember what we said earlier about creating dependency.

Collaborative/ "Participating" Style

A participative style works when all group members have useful information and *shared decision-making* becomes a benefit. A result of shared decision-making is higher motivation among group members to carry through and do the work. When you use this style of leadership, you participate in the group as a co-member of the group.

Coaching/ "Selling" Style

A selling style works in similar circumstances as authoritarian leadership—selling is a bit like telling—but the difference is that the leader *persuades* other group members using <u>supportive</u> statements rather than telling them what to do. This works particularly well if the leader has less obvious authority in the situation, but actually is more knowledgeable than other members of the group.

Delegating Style

The style of delegation works when group members know what they're doing and can be trusted to work independently—making their own decisions and returning to the group with results. *Motivated* group members with skills and knowledge often appreciate this style of leadership.

We've certainly laid out a great deal of issues in regard to groups meeting goals: unmotivated group members, deadlines, timelines, emotions, differing styles. You likely have picked up on the notion that group work provides significant potential for conflict. That's not such a pleasant prospect. So, we need to learn about managing conflict to keep it under control.

ADDRESSING CONFLICT IN A GROUP

Too often group members report happily back to supervisors, bosses, co-workers (even professors) that there is no conflict in their group! Unfortunately, that's when we know that the group isn't going so well. Although you may not like it, *conflict is good for groups*. Without conflict, groups tend to make poor choices, have members who are less committed, and generally lose their opportunity for great achievements. It is critical that you learn how to manage conflict so that your group can have *productive* conflict.

Conflict, by definition, occurs when two or more interdependent parties perceive incompatible goals. We engage in conflict and disagree when we are dependent on that other person to meet our goals and perceive that he or she is blocking us from that goal—our competition for a job or promotion, a person who took credit for our work, a colleague who attempted to have our work not be published or presented.

These situations seem so negative that it might feel like a better choice to agree just for the sake of agreement. Sadly, that choice can be equally problematic.

Groupthink... a Bad Thing

Irving Janis was a psychology researcher at Yale University and is most famous for coining the term *groupthink* (Janis, 1972, 1982).**Groupthink** refers to the tendency to agree, solely for the sake of agreeing and occurs when a group doesn't engage in *productive conflict* during decision-making, thus the result is poor decision-making. According to Janis, there are particular *conditions* in which groupthink can develop and specific group interaction *symptoms* that signify its development.

Conditions
1. a high level of cohesiveness and attachment to solidarity
2. group isolation
3. time sensitivity

Symptoms
1. a group may overestimate its power
2. group members will think that they are right AND
3. assume their opponents are wrong

Groupthink is far too common and we can see how new groups would fall prey to it during forming and primary tension or early phases of interaction. How would this play out? Well, first, no one is willing to disagree (i.e., solidarity), then alternative solutions are not explored and concerns may not be raised (i.e., group isolation) especially in cases where groups feel the need to act quickly (i.e., time sensitivity) and the result may bepoor decisions or, at worst, *disastrous conditions*.

The real-world cases are too frequent. For example, the U.S. Senate Intelligence Committee reported that groupthink was responsible for the faulty decision by the Bush administration and Congress to invade Iraq in search of weapons of mass destruction before a coalition of allies could be built (see Porteus, 2004). As a result of this decision, the U.S. paid a high price not only economically but in terms of military deaths, civilian casualties, and diplomatic standing in the world.

In short—groupthink is bad. As you are working on your leadership skills in any business environment—including U.S. government work

– remember to encourage different opinions and to strive for the best solution, not necessarily the easiest or most popular one. Conflict, or not always agreeing, is actually good for groups. So, now that you are embracing conflict, you'll need strategies to keep it functional.

A Problem-Solving Approach to Conflict Resolution

Think about two people arguing. They're loud. They're using words to hurt one another and to try to 'win.' That attempt to hurt is an example of emotional or **affective** **conflict**. Affective conflict is what most people think about when they think about the concept of conflict. While conflict is not definitionally negative and emotional, it is this kind of conflict that destroys relationships and hurts groups.

Go back to the two people arguing. Imagine that 'John' goes all out and finally wins a verbal fight with 'Mike' (as we'll call them for this example). Is it over? Has John *won*? No, Mike goes and sulks and schemes about how to get even. Feuds can go on for several generations, so clearly emotional conflict is not good for groups.It is a very short step from fighting words to fisticuffs (that's an old British word for a brawl).

Behavioral conflict, or physical aggression, is destructive both of relationships as well as physical property and human injury. When it comes to small groups (and any interpersonal relationship), cognitive or substantive conflict is the only type of conflict that is constructive. **Cognitive conflict** is an intellectual disagreement that can be resolved rationally by careful consideration. The only way to solve affective or behavioral conflict is to turn it into cognitive conflict. To do that, you want to have a problem-solving approach.

The Reflective Thinking Approach

Problem-solving isn't just reserved for conflict. It also works well when an individual has a problem. This tried-and-true method for solving problems was developed by pioneer educator John Dewey (of the Dewey Decimal System!) in 1910, and forms the basis of most rational problem-solving models that are out there today (see Dewey, 1933, for an improved, revised version).

The advantage of Dewey's **Reflective Thinking Approach to Problem-Solving** is that it overcomes several typical mistakes that groups and individuals make. Communication professor Randy Hirokawa studied decision-making in small groups and found that the order of the steps was less important than making sure that critical functions were completed in a group's decision-making process (see Gouran & Hirokawa, 1996). In the following description, Dewey's six steps have been separated into two phases to emphasize the critical elements that Hirokawa studied.

(Items marked with an asterisk* are commonly overlooked in group decision-making, resulting in poorer decision quality.)

Problem Analysis Phase

1. **Identify the problem**: Make sure that you're focused the right problem. It can help to frame it as a question. ("Why are we losing accounts to our competitor?")
2. ***Research the problem:** Look at the problem from all angles, get more information, and understand the *whole* problem. ("Let's compile every sales report for the last two years.")
3. ***Identify criteria for an ideal solution**:Know what elements must be part of the solution—this will make evaluating for the best solutions far easier. ("Do we want the *cheapest* solution or perhaps one that is *quick* to implement?")

Resolution Phase

4. **Generate possible solutions**: This is the brainstorming phase and… more is better. Assume that it takes at least 10 adequate solutions to produce one brilliant solution. This is not the time to criticize or evaluate ideas. ("I think that we should only hire superheroes for our sales force!") A proven technique for brainstorming, developed by advertizing executive Alex Osborn (1953), calls for:
    - No criticism of ideas during brainstorming
    - Go for large quantities of ideas
    - Build on each others' ideas
    - Encourage wild and exaggerated ideas
5. ***Evaluate pros and cons of (the top) solutions**:Consider good and bad aspects—not just what you like and don't like. ("Hhmm… Superheroes, while amazing at their own deeds, don't tend to apply for sales jobs.")

6. **Select the best solution**: Vote or build consensus. Go back to your pre-determined style of influence to determine how you want to lead your team to the best solution.

(Note: Figuring out how to implement your solution creates a new problem…go back to the beginning and start over again. It will work just as well for this second step!)

The Reflective Thinking Approach is useful when a group (e.g., small team or even an entire company) has a decision to make or a problem to solve. Ironically, if you start out solving a problem without any conflict (e.g., we're all agreeable group members and we need to decide what to do for our project) then the decision-making process will naturally *create* conflict – and actually that's a good thing! Embrace the disagreements and conflicting research. Without conflict you are likely to generate groupthink. If everyone agrees it will be difficult to think critically about what is the best course of action.

Creating Conflict On Purpose

According to business consultants and management professors Kenneth Thomas and Ralph Kilmann, conflict is not a one-size-fit-all process (Thomas & Thomas, 2004). If you use the same conflict style in every situation then you aren't using the most effective strategy. Thomas and Kilmann created a conflict styles grid that helps guide conflict strategies. They suggest that the best strategy for handling conflict is to consider your goals on two dimensions: <u>concern for the task</u> and your <u>concern for the relationship</u> (again, this should sound familiar).

Thomas and Kilmann's Conflict Styles Grid

	Low Concern for the Relationship	Moderate Concern for the Relationship	High Concern for the Relationship
Low Concern for Winning	<u>Avoid</u> conflict		<u>Accommodate</u> to their goals
Moderate Concern		<u>Compromise</u>	
High Concern for Winning	<u>Compete</u> to win		<u>Collaborate</u> to find a win-win solution

Thomas and Kilmann's (2004) theory says that once you know how important the task (i.e. getting your way) and the relationship (i.e. still having one) are, then you can rationally select the best strategy.

Avoidance

Avoidance is often confused with accommodation. In avoidance, you don't address the conflict at all—you give up on *your* goal but you also give up on *their* goal (and thereby the relationship). Imagine you want to buy a unique item on eBay® and the seller really wants to sell it, but will only sell at a price you can't afford. The best solution is to walk away— neither party gets their goal and the relationship dissolves, but that's O.K. because the goal wasn't as important as the money and the relationship didn't matter too much either.

Accommodation

No doubt you've seen this one in action. Some people hate conflict so much they will give in rather than have conflict that would harm the relationship. Letting the other person win only makes sense if the relationship is very important and your goal isn't.

Compromise

Compromise is another misunderstood idea because our kindergarten teachers drilled it into us that compromise is best. In a true compromise, each party agrees to *give up something* so that they *can get something*. Since in this situation everyone loses something, you should only use it when your goal is not terribly critical (like whether you get one or two helpings of cake at the office party). It would be bad to compromise if the goal really mattered; like settling for a low paying, uninteresting job just to avoid looking for a new position.

Competing

Sometimes you want to win at all costs and don't worry if you make an enemy in the process. If you don't care about your relationship then competing is a great strategy for getting something you really care about.

Collaborating

Obviously a **win-win** is the ideal solution and many people will advocate for using this strategy all the time. Collaborating takes significant time, energy, and creativity to produce a truly win-win solution, so it may not be worth your while in every situation. If you really care about winning, but you don't want to lose your relationship, Thomas and Kilmann (2004) suggest that is when you look for a win-win solution.

By having some strategies for managing conflict at your fingertips, you are one step closer to having a functioning group. If your group can say that they regularly disagree with one another, but don't experience the negative effects of conflict, then you have a cohesive and effective group. This is the goal that any group member should work toward. When will you address these areas of conflict, in your group meetings! Meetings dominate how we do business or function as professionals.

WHEN GROUPS MEET

If you run a search for "meetings" on the Internet you'll find innumerable suggestions for how to run effective meetings along with a fair number of rants about ineffective meetings. Technology architect Craig Borysowich remarks on his blog that, "[b]oth the private and public sectors are a complete wasteland of time-wasting, soul-sucking, bad meetings. It needs to stop!" (Borysowich, 2005). To initiate a better system, consider writing formal agendas, keeping the meeting moving, and

Writing a Formal Agenda

The most important ingredient for an effective meeting is a well-written agenda. An **agenda** is a list of tasks that the group will undertake during the meeting, which is usually distributed ahead of time to group members. The agenda serves several functions for the group:

1. It reminds people to come to the meeting by telling them when and where the meeting will occur.
2. It forces the leader or group to consider what needs to be accomplished.

3. It tells people what to bring so that the resources needed by the group will be available at the meeting.
4. During the meeting, the agenda helps the group stay off tangents and complete its task in an efficient manner.
5. It provides information if someone were to miss the meeting, so that they can ask informed questions about what was accomplished.

Agenda Example

Project: TechSystem Redesign
Meeting Purpose: To identify risks for clients using TechSystem
Attendees: R. Johnson (Chair), L. Mannheim, J. Lake, S. Sawville, R. Jackson, T. Smith, J. Schultz, P. Talarico
Date and Time: Wednesday 11/17/2010 10:00 a.m.
Place: Meeting room 7

Agenda Item	Person Responsible	Time
1. Introduction, review agenda, meeting purpose.	R. Johnson	2 min
2. Review of risk management process Identify the basic definition of risk for this technology and consider the approach to risk management previously established for TechSystem.	R. Johnson	10 min
3. Risk identification brainstorming Produce an initial, expansive list of risks in all categories through active participation in a non-judgmental think-tank session. (The list will be assessed, prioritized, and maintained in subsequent meetings.)	All	60 min
4. Assign tasks, set date for next meeting, review meeting effectiveness	R. Johnson	15 min

Attachment: Copy of risk management standards and procedures.

Every organization and industry has a different way of doing agendas, so there is no standard for agendas that you can learn. In fact, some groups have the agenda format written into their by-laws or are legally bound to follow the agenda once it has been published. The outcome from this meeting could change the design of the technology and mean the success or failure of the product on the market.

So, as you can see, meetings can be very important—but too often a meeting is called with no clear goal in mind, is poorly managed, and wastes the time of all present. You want your meetings to be the good ones.

Agenda Common Elements

Although agendas can be written in a myriad of different ways, the good agendas do share some commonalities. You should consider the following features to see if they are relevant for the agendas you create.

- **Use a clear header**: It should be obvious to anyone scanning the document who, what, where, and when (time and date). After all, you want people to show up and if you find this document later you don't want to have to read the whole thing to identify it.

- **Identify objectives**: An objective is the outcome or goal of the meeting (not the process of how to get there). Good objectives are clear, positively worded, and achievable. This meeting will be over when X is accomplished.

- **Start with a warm-up activity**: Groups need time to get comfortable with each other, especially if they are newly formed. It is always good to have every member speak in the first 10 minutes to increase their participation later in the meeting. Ideally, the warm-up is related to the goal, not difficult to accomplish, and brief.

- **Clearly articulate each item on the agenda**: Sometimes it helps to use a verb in the header for each item. Be clear about who is responsible and how long you expect it to take. It is useful to provide additional information in the form of bullets or sub-headings to guide the group in performing the task.

- **Consider the time:** Groups tire easily, so put the most difficult tasks early in the meeting. Don't put too many challenges in the same meeting, it may be better to have another meeting or break the group up into sub-groups to hash out different items and bring a resolution to the larger group. Short meetings can also be a problem: If members have taken a lot of trouble to come to the meeting, there ought to be enough work to make it worth coming. Generally, 30-90 minutes are a good length.

- **Conclude with a wind-down period:** A group can feel like they accomplished nothing unless there is a meeting summary, assigned tasks, and the next meeting date is identified. It is also excellent to talk about how the meeting was run. This will improve the meeting skills of all involved.

Sending an Agenda

Now that you have an effective agenda, you are ready for your meeting! Right? Well, that may be the case for you but it is still crucial that you prepare your participants to do their part. Sending a meeting agenda prior to the day of the meeting helps those who arrive to be mentally prepared for discussions, bring critical materials, and even weigh in on the organization of the meeting itself. Almost all business scholars agree (see: Millard, 2007) that meeting agendas should be distributed in advance. When? Well, about three business days is a good start. Longer and the information can be forgotten (or give folks too much time to argue about meeting items and organization) and less time can lead to frustration and lack of preparation. Once your meeting is set, you must set the room! (Yes, walking in early and re-arranging furniture is part of meeting planning).

Adjusting A Meeting Environment

Have you ever sat in a lecture hall for one of your classes when your professor called on the guy in the last row to answer a question? Did you turn around to see who was talking? The lecture-style set-up does not exactly invite audience interaction, so if you are conducting a small audience meeting where want your coworkers to participate, a lecture style room may not be the most effective space.

Jean Rowan (1997), in the *San Antonio Business Journal*, offers up that "Seating arrangements should support goal of meeting" (p. 1). Whatever type of seating arrangement that you choose (from a rectangular table with chairs facing in one direction or towards the table; theater/ lecture style; a circular arrangement without a table) have distinctly different impacts on the participants and, thus, the meeting outcome!
Begin with a consideration of your meeting type:
- **Presentation**: speaker(s) in structured setting
- **Discussion**: informal swapping of information
- **Conference**: formal and structured collection of information
- **Seminar**: educational with moderate structure

Obviously, you cannot sit 100 people in a circle to watch a presentation and you cannot have a theatre seating style for a small problem-solving discussion. Rowan (1997) reminds us to make sure that chatty folks are not next to each other; vocal opponents are not be directly across from each where they can make direct eye contact; leaders can make direct eye contact with all. Setting your chairs, tables, and visual aids up ahead of time will ensure that you have the best space for your needs. If you cannot get in early— or are not the first speaker—don't let others intimidate you into using their set up. Ask everyone to stand and stretch… and then move to a better set-up. You will be remembered as the presenter who let people move!

Keeping a Meeting Moving

Moving is not just physical. It is important to understand that meetings will not always simply move *forward* as scheduled. Groups can get distracted (consider the roles discussed above), negative conflict can arise, or group discussion can go off in a tangent. Bormann (1990) observed that sometimes tangents served the group well but other times distracted the group from its task. It is fairly common for a group conversation to switch direction every 2 minutes. (That's pretty quick). Given this tendency, it is easy for a group to go off on a tangent—in fact this is quite normal.

This commonplace behavior means that the gatekeeper role is a critical one for any group. Most of the time, a tangent can be quickly re-directed back to the agenda topic but there are some times when Bormann (1990) suggests you should let the tangent run. If a group is frustrated or blocked sometimes a tangent can relieve tension and help them to build up energy. If the person who starts the tangent is particularly talented, the tangent might lead the group to be whimsical and creatively solve their problem by making an unexpected link between the here-and-now and some fantastical, unrelated idea. You will know if the tangent is productive because the group conversation picks up energy. Members' voices become animated and they interrupt one another as everyone tries to share in the story-telling. In this case, let the conversation go and it will have more positive effects than negative, although they may not be apparent right away.

LEADING & MEETING – YOU CAN!

This chapter has provided several models and theories to help you understand group dynamics. These include an Emergent Model for Group Development, Functional Role Theory, a Model for Leadership Styles, the Reflective Thinking Approach to Problem-solving, and the Conflict Styles Grid. These theories are similar in that they propose a rational approach to group work. You should recognize that these theories do not fully account for the emotional side of belonging to groups, but there is a U.S. American cultural bias towards rational behavior in business and the professions that is clearly visible in most research on groups.

As you develop your group meeting skills and your personal leadership style, it is good to rely on both descriptive and prescriptive models—just make sure you know which kind you're using. There is always more to learn about group dynamics, a field that is continually evolving in numerous disciplines. This chapter provides some core concepts to help you get started facilitating *effective* group work!

Chapter Five

Research: Having Ethos with Business Audiences

How Can I "Know"?

Where does the *meat* of your business presentation come from? This is a natural concern for those new to business – and even those who have been around the block a few times. It can be intimidating to be asked to get up in front of co-workers and give a presentation if you are unsure of your topic.

So, let's consider when you will be asked to speak. Will your boss come to you to lead a discussion on information produced in another department? Likely not. This is not your area of expertise and businesses tend not to ask non-experts to present ideas. Will your co-workers ask you to give the presentation if you are clearly the least informed member of the team? Again, it isn't likely. In order to be asked to give a presentation, someone has concluded that you have a level of expertise in the area. (This is a good thing! You want to be the person with needed information if you want to succeed). That being said, "expertise" comes in various amounts.

Your boss (or co-workers, for that matter) may very well ask you to speak about an idea or plan where you simply know *more* than they do. Does that make you an expert? In their eyes it might but respectable presenters know that offering up information in a public setting means that some type of investigation must go along with developing these talks. Presentation investigation involves delving into one's own background and knowledge as well as bringing together valid information from additional reliable sources. If we do this well then we are able to have **ethos** in the eyes of our audience—that high level of credibility gained from an honest attempt to present the highest credibility information!

This chapter explores just how you can build a foundation for your talk using available resources—including *you*. Whether you are in school with a library password or out in your first job, you will learn to:
- tap into resources
- analyze your audience's needs
- evaluate source credibility
- and build a foundation that will depict you as the expert in your subject matter!

WHY START WITH RESEARCH?

Imagine being asked tomorrow to give a speech on your college major or degree plan. You would undoubtedly know something about it but perhaps not enough to cover all of your bases without checking a few facts. You would not want to tell your audience something that you assume about your major (such as how it is the most popular at your school or one of the most difficult degrees to complete) only to have them tell you that they have read otherwise. Having a foundation for your ideas, before you begin to organize them or deliver your message, ensures that you maintain credibility with those listening to you. Research gives us effective evidence on which to base our talks.

Evidence is any external verification that you cite as support for your ideas. Without evidence the ideas that you offer are simply assertions, which means that they are nothing more than stating your own personal opinion. Regardless of your personal dynamism and sparkling personality… most audiences are not willing to give your opinion any more weight than their own. What's worse is that if your audience disagrees with you then your opinion carries *even less* weight than it would otherwise. Evidence can clarify your ideas by taking abstract notions and developing them into *confirmed* information for your listeners. Different audiences are swayed by different types of evidence (Bryman, 1998; Firestone, 1987).

QUANTITATIVE VS. QUALITATIVE EVIDENCE

Some people absolutely need to hear the hard-facts and statistics behind your arguments before they will even consider your position. Others will take note of your hard data but must have a developed illustration or story that shows the magnitude of a situation before they will be swayed. Thus, evidence will fall into two categories: quantitative and qualitative (Punch, 2005).

Quantitative *numbers + statistics*

Quantitative evidence is the information that you offer that demonstrates measurements or *quantities* (e.g., statistics, numeric comparisons, hard data, or other use of numeric measures). Generally speaking, if you are trying to *prove* a point, you need to present factual numeric evidence. Some experts even believe that numeric data is more persuasive with audiences than data in the form of illustrative qualifications and examples (Allen & Preiss, 1997). When considering the use of quantitative data, think about the options available along with their merit for grounding your claim. For example:

- **Statistics:** facts or pieces of data from a large quantity of numerical data that provide a general understanding of an idea
    - *Example*: "Crest™ continues to claim in their commercials that two out of three dentists recommend their product."
    - *Example*: "Karen Lynne, director of accounting here at Tri-Star™, informed me that as of Monday, sales are down by more than 20,000 units compared to the same period last year."

always use source! must be reliable

- **Numeric Comparisons:** use of numeric similarities or equivalencies
  - *Example*: "A *Post Intelligencer* study found that 30 percent of all material recycled in Seattle, Washington was glass or plastic as compared to only 3 percent in Austin, Texas – a city with generally the same demographics."

- **Hard Data:** facts provided as the basis of reasoning or calculation.
  - *Example*: "Given the spreadsheet analysis provided by our accounting department, for a 12 ounce latte with milk at $1.95 per gallon and espresso costing $12.78 per pound, it costs us $1.35 per serving for a profit of $2.31 per sale."

(Note how these examples provide quantitative evidence offered by cited experts. Because credit was given to the source of the information, the speaker has been ethical in the presentation. If you offer that information and fail to note that you did not crunch the numbers yourself... there's a problem.) *Basically*

Anything not numbers.

Qualitative

Qualitative evidence is qualities or characteristics (e.g., stories or narratives, examples, definitions, quotes, analogies, etc.). Numbers can be daunting and confusing for some audiences who will be convinced by *imagining* the affect of your ideas. They will want to visualize the arguments that you are offering. In these instances, qualitative evidence is necessary. The kinds of qualitative evidence that you can offer is vast but consider some of the more prevalent forms:

Cite the source

- **Stories or Narratives:** a spoken account of a series of connected events with a beginning, middle, peak, and conclusion; narrative illustrations may have greater impact than simple examples (Baccus, 1935).
  - *Example*: "One of the best stories that I have about interviewing comes from a time when we were hiring a new accountant at our firm. Normally, our process is to look over all résumés received and call in our top 3 candidates for an in-person interview. This had not always worked to

get us the best candidates so our managers decided to have a 15 minute interview with all candidates at a regional work conference. We were so excited to see that our first interview was with the woman whose résumé had most excited us. But when she walked into the room—things changed.

The woman who came into the room had an un-tucked shirt, uncombed hair, and, frankly, just looked a bit scary. We introduced ourselves and asked the first question, "Can you tell me about this project that you completed last year for (Smith's) accounting partners?" Pretty simple right? The woman reached over, snatched the questions and other papers out of my colleagues hands, and said, "What? Do you expect me to answer all of this stuff?!" Stunned, we looked back at her, told her that we would not waste her time with our silly questions and would get back to her later. She walked out the door and we never talked to her again. And, that is the reason to pre-screen <u>all</u> job candidates!"

- **Examples:** a single, typical case that is characteristic of its kind or illustrates a general rule:
  - ○ *Example*: "When I was new to this industry, I had a boss who insisted on micro-managing every detail of my work. After a networking event, he asked me to do the simple task of writing brief 'thank you' cards to all of the participants. I then had to bring them up to his office and he went through with a red pen and corrected any words or language that he didn't like and had me re-write them… three times! Now, *that* was micro-management."

- **Definitions:** a statement of the exact meaning of a word as it would be in a trade publication or dictionary; an exact statement of the nature, scope, or meaning of something
  - ○ *Example*: "To be more precise, what I mean by *accountant* is consistent with the OED dictionary definition of 'a person whose job is to keep or inspect financial accounts'."

- **Quotations:** a group of words taken from a text, speech, or individual's statement and repeated by someone other than the original author or speaker (also known as testimony).
  - o *Example*: "Because I lived up in the Bay Area of California, my favorite saying by Mark Twain has always been, 'the coldest winter that I ever spent was a summer in San Francisco.' And, that is sure the truth!"

- **Analogies:** a comparison between two things, typically on the basis of their structure and for the purpose of explanation or clarification; may be either **figurative** (comparing two items of different categories) or **literal** (comparing things of the same category)
  - o *Example of Figurative Analogy*: "He told her at the office party that her eyes were like pools of Evian™ water! We got the giggles!"
  - o *Example of Literal Analogy*: "As you can see, Generitek's advances in nano-technology will change the face of corporate processor usage and data storage much like touch-screen technology changed how we use computers today."

As you read through these examples of evidence, you may be tempted to use the type of evidence, either quantitative or qualitative, that is most convincing for *you*. Remember that you are already convinced so your needs are the least important at this moment. Instead, consider the needs of your audience. Will they be most influenced by numbers? Are they in need of a strong illustration to drive the point home? *If you do not know then you are best to choose liberally from both groups so that you are sure to address all reasoning needs.* The next step is knowing how to start looking for all of your evidence.

A Good Place to Start

There are so many choices to make in pursuing research—but don't make this harder than it is. Research can *sound* daunting. You may have disheartening flashbacks to a college research paper or your first big company report. These were learning experiences. As you read along, you will find resources that make the research process rather straightforward, and even enjoyable, to carry out.

Evidence collection is the most malleable (or not set in stone) part of speech construction. You will be gathering data at every point and revising both what you know and what you decide to relay to your audience. There are good steps to follow for collecting the information and critically selecting what to include as part of your talk… but know that research is <u>not</u> one-stop shopping. You might collect lots of information only to find out later that you are missing key facts and need to do another search. Once you have begun, the later searches are easier and far more productive. So, let's get started.

1. Start by knowing your topic

This is the easiest part of your speech but a good step to articulate. Ask yourself (or the person who asked you to speak), "what is my topic?" Perhaps you will speak on advances in technology in your industry, discuss necessary accreditation tests, give a status report for a current project, or other information. But, you cannot know what to research if you don't know what topic you are to discuss!

2. Know what elements you want to discuss

Some topics are broad and others are quite narrow (e.g., *biology careers* versus *evidence assessments made by chemical forensic biologists*). As you begin to organize your topic into a full-fledged speech, you will need to broaden or narrow the information to suit the needs of the situation. We will discuss "speech topic breadth" more thoroughly a bit later but, for now, start with more general ideas so that you have enough information to later make decisions on breadth.

3. Outline what you already know

Yes, you already know some stuff! It was for this reason that you were asked to talk. You might be surprised at what you know when you get into the process of writing it down. These steps can even help to guide your research process.

4. Start a record

Perhaps the most crucial part of your research will be to start and keep track of where you have searched and for what you have searched in each location. This record will become vital for a) *saving time*, b) *getting help*, and c) *returning for subsequent searches*. For example, if you were exploring the idea of teaching, you might have an initial search chart that looks like this:

Source	Search Terms	Findings (+/ -)
NPR (National Public Radio)	- teachers - students - testing	- teachers (3 stories +) - students (nothing) - testing (assessment story)
Google®	- education - school - teachers - students - testing	- education (vague) - school (org websites) - teachers (individual stories; some strategies) - students (not useful) - testing (examples and types; some assessment)
EBSCO databases - Aca. Search Complete - Education Abstracts - Sociology Complete - Psychological Review	- education - school - teachers - students - testing	- education - school (vague) - teachers (LOTS – mostly teaching strategies) - students (not useful) - testing (lots on assessment)

This chart will be useful when a colleague or librarian (yes, you should still make use of librarians even after college), or even a professor wants to know where you have <u>already</u> looked. Rather than guessing, you can explain exactly where you have searched and even document what you have found. If you were to take such a chart to a librarian, that person would not need to suggest that you use the *EBSCO database Academic Search Complete* because he or she can see that you have searched this resource. You may be told to search *Google Scholar®* and include *teaching* and *classroom* as part of your search terms.

You can see how charting (even on a scrap paper that you keep in with your research) be useful not only when you go to get help but also consider how useful it will be to make sure that you do not repeat previous searches and that you save time by streamlining your process! (Yea charts!)

5. Collect data

This part is pretty self-explanatory… but read on in the chapter for clues on where to look and how to critique what you find.

6. Strain data

As you go about your search, know that you don't want to keep everything. No matter what your topic, there is likely far more information that you could ever fit into your allotment of speaking time. For your initial search, you may keep whatever seems interesting but, as your narrow your speech, you will delete some information and go out to find more on other details. Remember that this is a work in progress—and you cannot find all that you need to know in a single sitting.

7. Fill in the holes

As you develop your speech, be sure to _go back_ and fill in the holes where your evidence is thin so that your ethos for the final presentation is strong throughout. You might have six sources to support one idea but no sources at all to support another notion that you… "just know." Read on to figure out just how much research your speech will need.

HOW MUCH RESEARCH DO I "NEED"?

While many public speaking instructors might assign you a specific number of sources to include in a given presentation (e.g., "you need 6 sources in this 5 minute informative speech."), the world outside of a classroom is not like that. No one will tell you how much research to do or what will provide you with "enough" credibility to have established ethos with your audience. It will be up to you to figure out how to develop and deliver a strong foundation. Your choices will have your audience believe that you are trustworthy—or that your information is a bit suspect.

Your friends and family probably know you as a trustworthy person—that's great! This means that they generally believe what you tell them. Hopefully, your colleagues will or do feel the same way. If you continue to give presentations at work with no backing for your ideas, your wonderful personality and general air of confidence will start to fail you with your audience. In a professional setting, we must to prove that our ideas are trustworthy by showing that they are backed by experts other than ourselves from the most credible sources.

Utilizing these guidelines as you collect evidence will help you to show audiences that you are ethical, credible, and… that you know what you're talking about! So, it needs a source:

1. If it's a number

Numbers come from somewhere and that somewhere is a *source*. If you convey a percentage (e.g., "30% of all people….") then tell your audience where you learned it. If you give a date (e.g., "… in the 1986 merger between….") then cite it. (These standards do not apply for commonly known numbers and dates (e.g., "the Twin Towers fell on September 11, 2001.").

2. If it's a quote

People make statements. These words do not appear out of thin air but can be attributed to those who were wise enough for us to quote. When using a quotation, be sure to give credit where it is due. Doing so will actually increase your credibility and gain you the esteem of those who also respect your source.

3. If it's evidence

Both math and speeches have "proofs." This simply means that as you talk to your audience, you will likely need to show data, substantiation, confirmation, and support for your ideas. For example, if you are explaining to a group of interns the difficulty of passing the CPA exam to become accountants, you may want to tell them how many new hires (*according to your Human Resources Department*) your company had to let go in the last few years because they failed the exam. This citation helps to show that you are not guessing or exaggerating—no, instead you show your ethos.

4. **If it cannot be verified by you alone**

As you put together your speech, you will want to provide a source for any information that did not come from you or is not common knowledge for *this* audience. No, you do not need a source let folks know that you have been with the firm for 6 years. This information comes from you and is about you. Yes, you do want to cite your boss when you explain why the company changed its mission at that particular time… because you were not part of decision-making group—you had to find out the details from your someone else. See the difference?

Even if you are the source and have personal experience, it's important to realize that some sources need support as well. You know that your experience alone may not hold enough weight to be persuasive. Consider that some sources will be seen as more valuable when they are part of a group (i.e., one source, even a credible one, may not be enough to convince us that video games lead to poor social skills but seven credible sources make it seem far more plausible!)

Hopefully, these steps will help you get a good feel for how much research to have in your speech—and you will begin to track in your research from which sources your data comes.

Cite it... Don't Steal it.

As you begin to collect data for your presentation, you will be, as Issac Newton said, "standing on the shoulders of giants." Being up that high is a great benefit to you as a speaker because you don't have to be an expert at everything—you just have to know on whom you can rely! You have the ability to garner your ethos by aligning yourself with the ethos or credibility that others have! However.... if you stand on those lofty shoulders without *citing*, you are stealing. That's right—stealing. The result is a total loss of credibility.

If you present someone else's information as your own, without telling your audience who said it first, you have technically stolen someone's work—it's their intellectual property, or their ethos.Regardless of the form of evidence you use to support your ideas, it is important to give credit to the source in order to avoid **plagiarism**. Why? There are three good reasons not to steal.

1. It's not ethical to steal

Regardless of your moral code, you would not like others to take your words and pretend that you had nothing to do with creating them. Plagiarism is the same—along with not being fair to others, most people would say that it just isn't right (see the Ethics chapter).

2. Citing makes you look better

Citing sources lets the audience know that others agree with the idea or position you are taking, which bolsters your argument. This is a fantastic means of enhancing your credibility by showing the listeners that you have thoroughly researched your topic and know what you're talking about!

3. You'll get caught

Plagiarism can be particularly problematic if audience members are aware of where you got the information you are presenting.

They might realize in the moment or have suspicions that are later confirmed. Either way works against you. <u>Take this real life example</u>: A business woman attends a conference to improve her technical skills. She sits down to hear the hired keynote speaker begin his talk… only to realize that the talk is pulled right off of a lecture that she saw the week before on YouTube! Not only did the speaker lose all credibility in the conference but his actions cost him all future jobs.

From the classroom to the conference room, your ethos will increase when you cite and it vanishes when you do not. (Any college or university will explain quite clearly what that specific institution means by plagiarism, including specific penalties and processes. When you leave college and your presentations are outside the classroom, remember that the penalties are just as harsh and can be even more permanent.)

There is a significant discussion of ethics at the end of this book. It might seem like our text should begin with such a discussion. But, until you have a good idea of which materials you will want in your presentation and where to find them, it is often difficult to imagine citing them or giving them an ethical amount of credit. As you read on, you will learn where to look for sources. If you continue to give credit to your sources throughout your career, then you will find that you stand on the shoulders of giants and are placed well ahead of your colleagues. For now, let's look at how to analyze your speaking situation to determine what evidence you will need!

Contemplating Your Rhetorical Situation

Just as every speaker and audience is unique, each time that we try to influence a situation with our words, we must consider that each speaking situation is unique. Effective speakers take this uniqueness into account when evaluating what arguments, claims, and <u>evidence</u> will be most valuable. Just as you will want to use support that is either quantitative or qualitative depending on your audience, you will want to collect evidence that can influence not just any group that happens to be in earshot but the specific audience in front of you that are in a very particular situation… a *rhetorical* situation.

Lloyd Bitzer (1968) was the first to coin the phrase **rhetorical situation**. For him, this idea references all of the elements of a time in which a speaker is *called to respond*. You see, Bitzer didn't believe that we start talking without reason—that would just be making noise! He argued that when we are moved to speak, it is because a situation occurred that needs a response. For example, you might have a sudden dive in sales for the past fiscal year. If no one at your company addressed this issue, the stockholders would be completely confused. In this case, someone must say something! But not all responses are appropriate. If you called a department meeting to discuss the viability of a product that was no longer produced and well past its time (e.g., dial up phones or the pet rock… yes, old folks had these in the 80s!), then people in the room would wonder what the heck you were doing. After all, there is no need for such things and your *'response'* would seem pointless. How do you craft an appropriate response? You understand what information or evidence is appropriate to the particular rhetorical situation that you will address. We do this by looking at the *elements* of the rhetorical situation.

The Three Elements of the Rhetorical Situation

1. Exigency

Exigency (or exigence—depending on usage) is the most crucial part of the rhetorical situation and refers to the need or urgency to address the situation. Bitzer (1968) would argue that communication does not occur between speakers and receivers unless the speaker is reacting to a *need* for a message. For instance, that pet rock? Bitzer would say that such a presentation does not <u>communicate</u>—it's just noise. C'mon… you've been in presentations that are just noise, right? Did you sit on the edge of your seat waiting to see what you could learn or do? Not likely. When there is a time to speak, step up, and respond to the exigence— the result will be an engaged audience.

2. Audience

Bitzer (1968) tells us that the **audience** in a rhetorical situation consists of people who are capable of *mediating change*. We would not attempt to give our sales pitch for why one must install new windows in their home to the 5-year-old girl playing in the front yard. No—we would need to knock on the door and talk to her parents, the homeowners, about such a task.

Bitzer asks us to consider these <u>agents of change</u> as part of our communication. If they do not exist (e.g., no one can do anything about the information that you give them, won't understand it, or feel that it was useful to them in some way), then true communication does not occur.

3. Constraints

A final element of any rhetorical situation is the element of constraints. **Constraints** will <u>limit</u> or <u>open</u> opportunities to have effective communication. Elements that constrain the rhetorical situation include (but are not limited to): the speaking occasion, the speaking surroundings, and the speaking context.

Most groups to whom you will be speaking will have gathered for a reason—an occasion. Because of this, your audience will have a set of expectations based on *why* they have gathered. An effective speaker understands and adapts his or her evidence (and delivery style… but that is addressed in a later chapter) to the occasion in which he or she is speaking and the constraints that go along with that occasion. For example, consider:
  • would you give lots of technical numbers to a group gathering before their morning caffeine jolt?
  • would you tell a group of tech savvy, number crunching administrators a sappy story of how their policies made someone in your group sad?
If you are not in touch with constraints specific to your speaking/ rhetorical situation, especially in any business context, then you limit your potential for success!

Now, to be fair, there are some scholars who do not believe that a need must exist before a speaker can use rhetoric to influence the situation but that speakers instead create that need (e.g., Vatz, 1973, or Foss & Foss, 1994) . Other texts that you read might reference this idea—and knowing all sides to an argument is a great way of determining what you believe.

This being said, all of these authors acknowledge that it is crucial to vary your evidence to: 1) meet the needs of your audience, 2) meet your needs, and 3) match the context of your talk. So as you address exigency (or create it), be sure to gather the best evidence possible!

GATHERING EVIDENCE

We have come to the part of research that you have been waiting for – actually collecting your evidence. You have determined your topic, thought about what you know, analyzed your rhetorical situation, and even determined if you will want to collect quantitative data or qualitative illustrations. The only thing left is to do is pick up a book… or in this day and age, look to the Internet!

We would be remiss to ignore the fact that search engines such as Google™, or Ask™ or Dogpile®are likely your initial tool for finding information. You will not find any discouragement here of those sources! You will find, however, a bevy of other sources to build your resource pool as well as a means of analyzing the information and sources that you find online. With all of these tools together, you should be able to quickly and efficiently provide your particular audience with the details that they need.

Audience Analysis

As you begin this search, it might seem odd that the first place that you would look for evidence is to the very people that you will hope to inform or persuade. Actually, your audience can be your best resource for both qualitative and quantitative evidence—as well as a great resource for determining the scope and direction of your talk. Audience analysis sounds rather formal but there are actually numerous means of understanding and gathering data from your audience. You likely have completed audience analysis prior to previous speeches without even knowing it!

Informal Audience Analysis

Informal audience analysis is a means of gathering information about your potential listeners without any predetermined and set procedures. These are the natural steps that we take on a regular basis to figure out who's in our audience and whether or not our information will be good for them. Think of it this way… have you ever told a joke to a group of friends where they howled with laughter but you decided later not to tell the same joke to family members or co-workers? This is because you had prior knowledge that the other groups would have a different response. You did an *informal analysis* of the rhetorical situation! There are a few different ways of going about this analysis.

- **Prior Knowledge**
  Information known about the audience—given past experience or interactions—can help you to know what will work the next time. Prior Knowledge Example: walking into a room and recognizing several former employees from another company who had told you complaints about their past jobs

- **Common Readings**
  Information that you have read or observed that you know will be familiar to your audience because they have been exposed to the same information. Readings Example: a) using a story from *New York Times* that you know the employees have read or heard about, b) sending an agenda or briefing materials ahead of time

- **Asking Others**
  Contacting business insiders can help you to understand the needs of your *specific* audience. Asking Others Example: speaking at a business that where your aunt works—who has told you that the executives do not associate with lower management at all (i.e., a tall organizational structure)

- **Direct Observation**
  You can use face-to-face means of using your senses to comprehend an audience's needs. **In-Person Viewing** is an observation of what you, yourself see your audience do or what you personally hear them say. **Stereotyping**, which is often used negatively, can in this context be a useful (albeit, not always accurate) method of drawing conclusions about a group from a single or few examples. In-Person Viewing Example: you walk into the room to see that your entire

audience is female and decide to cut out almost all of the examples geared toward men.Stereotyping Example: you know an accountant who is only convinced by direct numbers so when you ask, during your speech, and find out that all members of this audience are accountants, you decide to focus on quantitative reasoning because this is more likely convince such a group.

Informal audience analysis is likely the most common type of "investigation" that you will use before beginning communication with an audience of one or of many – and it should not be discounted. This is a valid and useful means of focusing your message and connecting with your audience without having gone through the more rigorous means of formal analysis. While you may see the ease of informal audience analysis, a more formal analysis can provide rich details that will help to give a foundation to your talk.

Formal Audience Analysis

Formal audience analysis is, shockingly, a means of gathering information about your potential listeners by using predetermined and set procedures. These methods are the ones with which speakers tend to be more familiar— even if they are less often used. The reason that these methods are not typically used is that they are more time consuming than doing nothing. Yet, if you have ever had a salesperson try to pitch you something then you know that the person who knows more, knows you better, and seems generally more informed is going to get the sale beyond the one who just uses the information that you provide in the moment. For this reason, formal audience analysis is recommended whenever and wherever possible.

- **Published Research**
  The calculated and planned means of finding published materials regarding your topic (i.e., may also include Internet searches and other source material produced by a third party). Publication Examples:
  a) company or employee websites
  b) company annual reports
  c) 3rd party stock reports
  d) newspaper articles (current and those in historical context)

e) magazine articles

f) televised newscasts

g) documentaries – or other media

h) brochures

i) blogs

j) specialized trade dictionaries

k) journal research articles

l) and many others!

- **Interviews**

  Interviews are conversations between two or three people, either face-to-face or mediated, for the purpose of a topic specific consultation. This is a big fancy way of saying that you get the most **rich data** (or detailed and nuanced information) from interviewing someone. Interview Example: calling the company CFO to ask about financial policies before speaking to the company regarding new investment strategies.

- **Focus Groups**

  By gathering a demographically specific group of people (i.e., either diverse or a chosen homogeneous set) to participate in a guided discussion about a particular product or idea is to hold a **focus group**. This is another **rich data** source; while not as rich as a personal interview, this is a great means of getting quality feedback from potential audience members! Focus Group Example: December 2010 advertisement, "*EA Sports*: Electronic Arts in Burnaby is looking for local gamers of all ages to participate in focus groups. If chosen, you will be invited into the EA studio located in Burnaby to play games like: Need for Speed, NHL, FIFA, NBA ELITE, Fight Night, and many other EA titles. Get the chance to provide game design feedback to the producers and designers."

- **Surveys**

  Most of us have taken a survey or two—even if it was delivered by a telemarketer in the middle of dinner.**Surveys** are measurement instruments used for data collection that are later analyzed to reach **generalizable** conclusions (or something that you can show as applying to a larger group… such as your whole audience or even bigger!). These instruments are also handy because they can use a variety of question types. Surveys do not provide as **rich data** as the other methods but they make up for it by being generalizable. For example, an interview can tell you that one person in the audience had a horrible interaction with the new boss but it can't tell you that 65% of your audience can't stand the new boss! (Surveys can!)

In order to make the best use of this tool, you must consider what information would be useful to find out about your entire audience and then consider what questions you can create to get the information. It is not always good to come right out and ask something. This can create barriers with your audience. For instance, if you wanted to convince your audience to work an extra hour each day, you may not want to come right out and ask them: "Would you work an extra hour each day?" They might start to think of a million reasons why this is a bad idea! (Wouldn't you?)

Questions should, instead, be directed to every consideration that would impact their position. For instance, ask questions about how much they like their work, how dedicate they are to the company, and what they might offer to save the company from going under. If you have this information then you would be able to talk (hopefully) about the high percentage of people who care enough to save the company by offering something very little! (See how this works?)

As you prepare your questions, first start by considering what you want to know and then what question formats could help you get that information as well as what issues your questions might bring about. Once you have a draft, be sure to **pilot** your survey (or have a small group—perhaps a focus group—take it to see what issues come up before administering it to your whole audience).

Formal Audience Analysis Question Formats

It is not enough to simply ask your audience questions. A crucial element to this is planning out the questions ahead of time so that you get the best information from whatever answers that you obtain!

Survey Questions Formats

Survey questions have many different purposes and will, of course, take on a form to help them meet their individual purposes. You must consider all of the various types of question so that you are best prepared to get the information that you want from those who you are asking!

Closed-ended: Questions that are closed will have a pre-determined number of answers that is set by the survey. They are not always 'yes' or 'no' responses—as many folks think. Instead, think of closed-ended questions as ones where if you had to list out all of the possible answers… you could.

Examples:

1. What is your gender? (circle one) Male   Female

2. Who is your supervisor? (circle one)
   John Smith   Mark Daly   Mike Willis   Alicia Jones

Open-ended: These questions have an unlimited number of answers—or allow for interpretation from the survey taker. You might never be able to guess just how a person would answer.

Examples:

1. What questions do you have for management?

2. How many hours do you work per week?

3. What is your favorite type of ice cream?

Problem: This last question may appear closed-ended or at least that it has limited response options—in fact, consider some of the following response options that are not the flavor answers that you thought would get: "I don't like ice cream", "Ben & Jerry's", "I am lactose intolerant", "LOTS of ice cream". Be sure to pre-test questions to see what you are getting yourself into!

Scale: A scale question will allow the respondent to select from an array of options. While technically a closed-ended question, the scale provides more rich data that can be used to determine not just the existence of something but the degree to which that thing exists. The most common scale options come from Likert scales. Likert (1932) came up with the notion that we could research the intensity of a person's feelings about a particular concept using the five response options of: Strongly Agree, Agree, Neutral, Disagree, Strongly Disagree. If you have seen 'intensity' scales that do not use these particular options or have more or less than five choices, we call these Likert-type scales.

Examples:

Likert
1. I enjoy my work: (circle one)
Strongly Agree - Agree - Neutral - Disagree - Strongly Disagree

Likert-Type
2. I enjoy working in groups.
Groups Rock – Groups are OK – Groups Stink

Filter: The purpose of a filter question is to eliminate unnecessary responses and categorize your respondents into groups. The problem with a filter question is that it can eliminate all or many of your respondents—so be sure to do enough preliminary research to make sure that you will have ample answers to for all option categories.

Example:

1. I have smoked in my lifetime: (mark only one answer)
____ Yes (go to question 2)
____ No (go to question 6)

Audience Analysis Question Issues

Survey questions have many different purposes and will, of course, take on a form to help them meet their individual purposes. You must consider all of the various types of question so that you are best prepared to get the information that you want from those who you are asking!

"push"

Leading: Any question that pushes the respondent to a particular answer is leading. The means of leading the audience can be subtle or obvious but, if you intend to get a real understanding of your audience, be sure to avoid this common issue.

Example:

> 1. It is incredibly important to vote regardless of how much information you have on the candidates. (select one):
> _____ Strongly Agree
> _____ Agree
> _____ Neutral
> _____ Disagree
> _____ Strongly Disagree
>
> *Problem: pushes respondent to think favorably about voting*

<u>Bias</u>: Survey questions that assume that a respondent has a particular background or experience are bias questions.

Example:

> 1. What was your favorite Biology class at Avery University?
>
> *Problem: assumes both that the respondent goes to Avery University and has taken at least one Biology class*

<u>Double Barreled</u>: When a single question actually asks more than one question, it is referred to as double barreled.

Example:

> 1. Have you had a friend or family member that has gone bankrupt?
> ____ yes _____ no
>
> *Problem: does not allow the survey to differentiate between responses that are in regard to friends as opposed to family members—or vice versa*

Gathering your evidence can be a fascinating process. Putting together a list of questions and actually picking up the phone to call a CFO will help you feel empowered when you speak! If you are able to provide your audience with specific numbers about what *they* think and feel (and even quote your audience back to them) then your ethos can skyrocket!

So, enjoy collecting all of your information but be sure that you always take everything with a grain of salt. Inspect and evaluate your evidence!

EVALUATING EVIDENCE

If you assume that the information that you gather is correct, well, we all know what that does to "you" and "me." So, to avoid that particular issue, you must always double check the credibility of your evidence just as much as your audience will be evaluating yours! If you are collecting the data yourself (e.g., surveys, focus groups, or interviews) then you know the accuracy of your information. You, however, will be just as likely (if not more likely) to be gathering information from others and, thus, need to make sure that those sources are valid.

All published materials have some type of credibility! This means that they have a level of integrity that ranges from none… to significant. Immediately, you must be thinking, "I want all of my evidence to have the highest credibility!" Good for you. This is a noble aim. However, it is important that you know that not all levels of sources will cover every topic. Be sure to "aim for the stars and you will hit the moon." (Confucius said that!) What this means for you is that you must try to get the most credible information in every case possible while knowing that in some cases you may have to use the second or third best level of credibility in order to have a depth of information.

Published Material Credibility

Published materials are those sources that are put out for general consumption from some source. These can be your friend David's website or the *Wall Street Journal* or even… Wikipedia™. If you can find out there in the world then you must evaluate how much ethos or credibility the information has.

- **No Review**
  The lowest level of credibility comes from those sources that have been published without any review (e.g., nooutside source has proofread or verified the information). Consider how the following don't have anyone to check and see if they are valid or reliable:
  - the "Learn Accounting Free Online" website,
  - John Atherton's "How to Teach—Mind Map" URL
  - Bernie Madoff's blog

- **Audience Review**
  The next level of credibility comes from sources where the *readers* determine the validity of evidence and decide to edit the details. The notion of such websites is that if enough readers contribute then the information collected from a large group is likely to be correct. This can work or it can truly backfire. For example, let's say that you wanted to know the history of President Obama. If you looked him up on Wikipedia, there are enough readers of information that incorrect details are quickly changed. The problem is if you read something before it has been changed—or if you go to a topic where few visitors participate and wrong information can be left up for quite some time… and even correct information can be deleted and substituted with wrong information. *Be careful* with using these for anything more than your own general reference.
    - Wikipedia™ (all wiki websites) *not reliable!*
    - The Internet Movie Database™ (IMDb) *not credible!*

- **Editor Review**
  An editor is typically an expert in the field of the publication who determines the accuracy and applicability of information for the
  not always credible.

publication as well as serves as a gatekeeper to keep out irrelevant materials. Within the category of editor review, publications have their own hierarchy (such as: the *New York Times* is more credible than your local town paper even though the both have editors) and some publications just work better than others (*The Christian Science Monitor* and *Vogue* are both credible but if you are speaking about industry changes in fashion then the latter is a far better choice). Editors review each of the following before they are sent to print:

- *TheWall Street Journal*
- *The Chronicle of Higher Education*
- *Vogue*
- *People Magazine*
- *OK Magazine* (see how the credibility drops?)
- About.com™ (see how the credibility *really* drops? be cautious of edited information that only checks topic applicability and not accuracy or validity.)

- **Peer Review**

  The highest level of credibility in published materials comes from sources that have multiple experts in thefield who pre-screen an article before it is given permission for print. These are **peer reviewed** (or **refereed**) sources that contain articles specific to a topic or industry and, like editor reviewed work, they have their own levels of hierarchy depending on how strict the review process is and how high the levels of expertise are for the reviewers. In short, they are the most scrutinized publications and if your topic is in one then you want to use or gain information from these sources (plus, they will also have an editor who pre-screens the article even before it is sent out to experts!). Such as:

  - *Journal of Banking & Finance*
  - *Journal of Public Affairs*
  - *Quarterly Journal of Speech*
  - *Administrative Science Quarterly*
  - *Industrial and Labor Relations Review*

Website Credibility

Much like you would review a book or a journal, you must give equal attention to websites. Some of the above review steps would work—but not always. Websites bring on their own unique set of challenges. Using this checklist can help you to make sure that you did not stumble upon the perfect information… that's just wrong!

The Website Credibility Checklist

✔ **Author**: What is the credibility or ethos of the person/ people who wrote the materials? By searching for that person's résumé or credibility, you can understand how credible the information might be.

✔ **Date of Publication**: How current is the information? How current does it need to be? Web material should be the most up-to-date but obviously a webpage on Aristotle's writings do not necessarily need a current publication date.

✔ **Publisher**: Who is supporting and offering this information? Are they a reliable source? Are they relevant to the area (e.g., is a medical website putting out information on financial strategies?)

✔ **Evaluative Reviews**: Just like print materials, website information can have experts who review their information. This is most likely to happen with organizations that publish research but is also useful for general information.

✔ **Reference Credibility**: Does the website offer references for its information? Are the facts cited? What is the credibility of the references offered?

✔ **Cross References**: Who cites this website? Do credible websites or printed publications also refer readers to this information?

✔ **Bias**: Does the information clearly take one side over another? Does it ignore obvious arguments or counter arguments?

✔ **Tone**: Could the page or site be ironic, such as a satire or a spoof? Is it something that you should not take seriously?

What to "Know" Final Ideas

These initial evaluation tools can help you to decide what information to include in your presentation and what to keep out. (There are some interesting postings on Wikipedia... but does your boss really want to know that you got your information there rather than *The Wall Street Journal*?) Also, be sure to weigh review credibility with availability. (You may be trying to convince investors to fund a community skate park in your area and find few peer review articles but a slew of edited articles. This is great. When you add in the supplemental information you get from talking to the experts and interviewing potential users, you will be on fire!)

Don't be daunted by the process. Research is actually easier than you may think and can be the most fun part of your presentation process—no lie! You shouldn't just turn to the Internet because you *can*; widen your grasp on the information that is out there on so many business concepts! You will find far more interesting, valuable, and potentially audience engaging details when you go beyond the basic search. Even the most knowledgeable speaker can benefit from getting the perspectives of other people.

By consulting others, you fill in the gaps of your knowledge and, as they say, two heads are better than one! By collaborating with others (in person or through published works), you can feel confident about being the true expert that can be trusted to present. Your next step is to organize and structure the very valid information that you have collected.

Chapter Six

Organizing Your Thoughts for the Ideal Business Speech

FRAMING WHAT YOU KNOW

Once upon a time, a girl lost a glass slipper. She had lost it at the ball that her Fairy Godmother transformed her for and where the Prince had fallen in love with her. But, it all started when her father died and left her to live with her stepmother. That was ok because they all lived happily ever after and she found her shoe. The End.

Most people know the story of Cinderella. This is a classic story from our youth—or at least a fun cartoon produced by our friends at Disney. However, even with a story so well know, re-ordering of the parts means that the message of the story, the moral, and the point to which the audience would otherwise be naturally led—is lost. Speeches are the same way. No matter how well you think that your audience knows the point of your message, the path must be clear!

Speeches' effectiveness hinges on the logos of the message. Logos, as discussed early in your readings, is the appeal to a sense of logic and order that a speaker makes to the audience. Logos asks the question, "does this make sense?" If your message does not makes sense to your audience then you have not properly selected evidence and placed it into the best order.

This chapter leads you through the steps of speech creation so that you might do your best to make sense to your audience and achieve your purpose. You will learn to clarify your purpose, create your arguments, place your evidence, lure in your listeners as well as lead them along and bring them to a final appeal. This…. is speech organization!

SPEECH PREPARATION

Before you begin to write a word (yes, speeches are written—but differently than a paper or an essay), you must have a plan. By articulating a clear plan of action, you are able to best move your audience to the place that you would like them to be. And, if you recall the idea of the **rhetorical situation** (see Chapter 5) then you know that speeches happen for a reason. Speakers are moved to react to a need, whether it be a need to direct sales tactics, respond to investor concerns, inform new employs of company policies, push for financial investment, or simply provide details about an industry—speeches are created for a purpose. The first steps to achieving that purpose are about planning. Once you have a good plan then you can more easily create the elements of your talk.

Selecting Your Topic… If You Can

In most cases, your job in the organization will dictate the topics on which you speak. For example, if you are a sales representative, you are likely to be selling a particular product your company produces; if you are a CFO, you are likely to be offering internal and external updates on company finances; if you are an event planner, you are likely to be directing volunteers and coordinating efforts. Make sense?

Why Talk About Topic Selection Now?

In the last chapter, you learned about the strategies of collecting evidence and you might be thinking, "Why talk about topic selection now?" In fact, topic selection is malleable. It will change given circumstances and what you find out in your collection of evidence. For example, you might be asked by your team to explain at the company retreat all of the ingenious ways that your group has learned to cut the company budget. Only, you find out during the research you have done to increase your speaking credibility that another company used the same strategies and failed. Thus, your once strictly informative speech must now convince fellow employees that you are not like the other company and that these practices will work for them! Yes, topic selection is a process rather than a decision. So let's start from the beginning.

In some instances, you may have to the freedom to select the topic on which you will speak. For instance, you might be asked to speak at your organization's annual retreat on a topic of your own choosing. You may be asked or even choose (as speech making becomes second nature) to make presentations at regional or national conferences in your field based on your area(s) of expertise. In cases like this, you have a great deal of leeway in what you talk about. As you advance in the organization, the variety of occasions on which you might be asked to speak will broaden, both internally as well as to external groups—and your topic selection will become more autonomous.

If you have the luxury of choosing your own topic for a presentation, your choice should be guided by two key considerations: 1) _your knowledge and interests_, and 2) _your audience's interests and needs_.

- **Considering You:** First and foremost, you should choose a topic that you care about—one that you find interesting and about which you are knowledgeable. As a professional in your field, you will have accumulated a valuable body of knowledge. Not all of this knowledge is fascinating stuff, though, even to you. An appropriate topic means should be one that you know quite a bit about and find interesting enough to want to find out more!

  Presenting a speech is not an invitation to explore a completely new area of interest or a time to try to develop a new area of expertise. Talk about what you know. Yes, you will want to supplement your knowledge with information from other sources, but you should already have a good working knowledge of your chosen topic… even if you have just acquired that knowledge through research on a more general topic.

- **Considering Your Audience:** Second, you should choose your topic based on what you believe to be your listeners' interests and needs. For instance, if you are invited to speak to a group of business students who are nearing graduation, you probably don't want to discuss how they can manage the *initial* stress of college (they know and have been there!). By the same token, a group of accountants probably would not be interested or need a presentation on the latest trends with internet marketing. You must figure out what is or what you can show to be interesting, useful, and needed by your potential listeners.

  Meeting the needs of your audience does <u>not</u> mean that you should change your position or opinion to meet an audience's needs. If you are about to give a talk to a government group about the merits of abolishing the death penalty, do not change your position to be in support of the death penalty just because that group's members are in support of it (you wouldn't do that!). Similarly, do not give up your topic because the audience has no information on it or a different stance. If you are part of P. Diddy's *Vote or Die* campaign and encounter a group that is not ready to cast votes, you can still believe in voting but just shift your information to be about the merits of voting—and save the push to register until your next encounter.

Effective topics are located at that nexus between your knowledge and interests and your listeners' interests and needs. Consider both needs and the final result will be a topic that both you find interesting and your audience will want to hear!

Creating a Path

Once you have your topic, you may be wondering, "now what?" There is no particular set process for putting a speech together. What you must do is to consider all of the elements of a speech and how to put them together in the most logical order as to not skip crucial elements or create extra work for yourself. Following these steps can help you be sure to cover all of your bases—and not repeat effort! The details of each element are discussed in depth throughout this chapter.

1. General Purpose
2. Specific Purpose
3. Thesis
4. Main Points
5. Claims
6. Evidence & Support
7. Rephrased Thesis
8. Intro & Conclusion
9. Transitions:

Are these steps set in stone? No. There is no single approach to producing a presentation. In fact, the last three (rephrasing the thesis and creating transitions and the intro/ conclusion) can really be produced in any order. These guidelines will simply give you an indication of the elements that you will need to include and complete. So…. let's discuss them in detail!

Determine Your Purpose

Now that you have a fantastic topic, your next step in this process is to determine your purposes—yup, more than one! This means deciding on your general purpose as well as crafting your specific purpose. These are critical decisions because they will help you make sure your presentation stays focused. If a piece of information doesn't help you advance your purposes, then it doesn't go into the presentation.

General Purpose

"What the heck was that about?"
"Wow! That talk was all over the place."
"What was her point?"
If you have ever responded like this to a talk—or heard others whispering it in the crowd, then you have heard a speech without understanding its general purpose. A **general purpose** is the overall aim of your presentation. Every speech has a primary general purpose: to inform,

to persuade, or to entertain. Many speeches have a secondary purpose (e.g., I want to persuade my audience to adopt this business strategy so I must first inform them of all of its elements so that they can appreciate its merits).

1. To Inform

Speeches that aim to inform will layout a new understanding of your topic for your audience. This presentation does not sway an audience or have them change to see a topic in a new way but simply gives them new knowledge (from little to more—or from nothing so some).

For example, if you are training your peers (or subordinates!) then you can provide them with instruction on how to manage company software. If the group already knows how to use this software then the information <u>does not inform</u> them and is likely to bore them to tears. That being said, if your company is about to drop its existing software in search for another, your presentation purpose could very well be to provide employees with a new perspective on the existing software—such as recognizing the glitches and limitations of the existing software. This way the group will be understanding of the reasoningwhen management makes the change.

2. To Persuade

Speeches that aim to persuadeare designed to change the perspective of your audience on some particular topic. Persuasive presentations have the goals of trying to change:
- a) **beliefs**: what one considers true or not true (most difficult to change)
- b) **attitudes**: a positive or negative association
- c) **values**: socially set regard for something
- d) **feelings**: one's emotional state or reaction
- e) **existing actions**: particular present behavior

How does this happen? Persuasion will aim to either: **strengthen or weaken a listener's commitment to the topic.** For example, a salesman of a particular product can worry that existing clients are thinking of going to a competitor and, thus, must strengthen commitment to the current product. Conversely, you may not be able to get a new client to purchase your product instead of a competitor's… but through a speech to weaken commitment to the product they currently use, you have planted a seed that will create an opening for a future sales pitch!

As you can imagine, it will be more difficult to change a person's belief system than their attitude. After all, beliefs are truths in the mind of the audience. It's like trying to convince the audience that they do not breathe to live. Easy? Perhaps not. This will take quite a bit of evidence and solid argumentation! So, should you avoid attempting to change something that is difficult? Heck, no.

Much like our discussion regarding informative general purposes, you can alter your take on the topic without changing the topic or your position on it (e.g., asking an audience who is not ready to 'act' on voting to have a good 'attitude' on the topic instead). Promoting a set of beliefs and urging action are two distinctly different goals; because of this, they place different demands on your presentation. Read on to figure out how to best strategize this change!

3. To Entertain

Business are far more amenable to comedy than you might expect. Retirement parties are great places for humorous looks back and even a CEO presenting the annual report to stockholders might ask someone to do a quick presentation beforehand to ready the group for the longer discussion. In fact, there are many examples of business speeches to entertain in movies and television shows. Jim Carrey's movie, *Liar Liar*, offers up a great example of a speech to entertain. A roast…

> **Walking into a management meeting, Carrey's character, Fletcher Reede, is asked what he thinks of his boss, Mr. Allen.
>
> *Miranda*: Well, what do you think of him?
>
> *Fletcher*: He's a pedantic, pontificating, pretentious bastard, a belligerent old fart, a worthless steaming pile of cow dung, figuratively speaking.
>
> [a moment passes and Mr. Allen starts laughing. The other board members follow his lead and start laughing also]
>
> *Mr. Allen*: That's the funniest damn thing I've ever heard. You're a real card, Reede. I love a good roast! Do Simmons!
>
> (IMBD, 2010)

While you likely won't (and shouldn't) have the chance to publically scrutinize your boss, you may be asked to engage in any number of presentations whose purpose is solely to entertain the troops! **Speeches that aim to entertain** are largely ceremonial and primarily designed to amuse an audience on a special occasion. Their primary purpose is _not_ to either lay out new information or change the perspective of the audience even if they secondarily do either of these.

Specific Purpose

Once you have determined the overall aim or general purpose of your presentation, you need to focus on what you want your listeners to get out of your presentation. In other words, you need to construct a specific purpose. Any presentation you give should have a **specific purpose** that *focuses* you into a <u>single</u> central goal. (If you have multiple goals you want to pursue, you probably should be giving multiple presentations!)

Consider this: if you were to give a speech on the topic accounting and knew that you wanted to solely inform your audience, what would you talk about? Some options may include:

a) tests required to become a CPA
b) currency differences between countries
c) the financial workings of the American Cancer Society
d) how recession affects the USA
e) tax tips
f) etc.

If you tried to give a speech on all of these topics then your speech (besides being painfully long) would have very little focus and not have the logos that your audience craves. What your specific purpose will do is allow you to clearly articulate what your speech is about—and what it is NOT about.

So, let's move ahead with an actual speech. Let's select accounting as our topic and begin to do some research. Based on what we find, there are some rather discouraging stories in the paper about poor accounting practices (e.g., Bernie Madoff's multi-billion dollar ponzi scheme!). This leads you to think about your rhetorical situation. You know that as you begin to talk about accounting, your audience will already have an idea about how accounting practices can be deceitful. You know that there will be a level of urgency—a need or exigence—for information about how to avoid being caught in one of those schemes! In reaction to that, you decide to <u>specific your topic</u>.

Example:

> _Topic_: Accounting
> _General Purpose_: To inform
> _Specific purpose_: To teach my audience how to avoid financial fraud through strict accounting strategies

As you can see, once you have established your specific purpose, you have a clear and concise gate-keeping device to help you determine which ideas to allow into the presentation and which ones to keep out! This can help you to go on to articulate the argument that you will make; it can direct your subsequent research; it can help you to craft strong logos in your speech that will have the audience saying, "Wow… that makes sense!"

Your Primary Argument: Crafting The Thesis

Now what? It may seem that once you have focused your topic well enough that you are in a good place to begin to go about ordering information and organizing your qualitative or quantitative support. Not quite. Speech preparation is for *you*—it is not for your audience. Now that you have planned, you need to begin to craft the parts of your speech that will be shared with your audience. Now is the time for speech creation and this starts with your thesis.

Speech creation begins with your most important speech element, which is undoubtedly the thesis. Your **thesis** is the primary argument of your speech. Without knowing what it is that you wish to argue, you are not in a position to select what types of evidence you will use, how you will organize your presentation, or make any other crucial decision about your speech. Should all speeches have an "argument"? They should!

Why Argue?

Whether it is your task to offer an informative presentation or a persuasive speech or any other general purpose, you must offer an initial argument. Some people are uncomfortable with the notion of putting arguments in informative speeches; after all, don't arguments ask for a change? Aren't arguments specific to persuasion? For our purposes here, arguments are offerings of specification. Think of arguments as saying to your audience, "hey, think about this," (rather than something else related to the topic).

Like much of speech creation, your thesis will differ from the thesis that you may have written for a paper or other written material. Verbal communication differs from written communication because of how the audience can receive it. If you have ever read a mystery novel, and gotten to the chapter where the detective says; "If you were at the meeting last week then you are the killer!"—do you flip back to see if the suspect was there? (Many readers do!) The point is that written communication allows the reader to take in information at his or her own pace and to both go back and to skip ahead. Verbal communication does not do this. It must be structured so that the audience and take in the information the first time and retain it. We use a **simplified structure** in verbal communication so that the audience can: a) follow and b) recall. This does not mean that verbal communication is simple. Hardly! Crafting an excellent speech is an intense task with a great deal of evidence and intentionally intricate detail. Only the structural elements use this type of focus, which begins with your thesis.

Elements of the Thesis/ Primary Argument

1. **From You:** A thesis statement is the verbalized idea that expresses conclusions that <u>you</u> have drawn from what you know. It is *your* idea. This is not a place for quotes, statistics, or evidence from another; develop your thesis on your perception of all that you know! (Remember from the last chapter that much of what you know comes from other sources. That's ok. You can't be an expert in everything. You can and should be the person who draws conclusions from all that you have read and offers your position statement.)

2. **Single Idea:** Unlike a written thesis, multiple ideas and concepts in your verbalized argument create confusion or can be mistaken for a preview to a speech but a single idea will direct your talk. It can be difficult to specify just one idea but don't over think it. If you come up with your thesis before trying to imagine all of the claims, ideas, and evidence that you will add—the thesis will be far easier to create. If you try to pick the main ideas first then you may be playing a logical game of *Twister*. (That's the old game with colored spots on a mat and someone would say, "Left foot— yellow! Right hand—blue!"). You might be trying to pull together ideas that are difficult to connect when you let the ideas determine your thesis rather than the other way around.
   a. Some common "connector" terms to avoid include:
      - and
      - which
      - that
      - "," (the comma – or any other punctuation)

3. **No Questions:** Having no questions as part of your thesis is another crucial means of making yourself clear and understandable to your audience. As such, it consists of two elements:

   a. **Your Thesis Should Not _Be_ A Question**: "How should our sales staff work to find the best results?" Er, uh, I don't know. Shouldn't you? You're the one talking!

      - Remember that you are the one in charge of your talk. When you are asking questions of the audience (a great means of audience involvement during the speech but not in offering your arguments) then you are never sure which way their minds will go and you are in a position to confuse and fail to meet needs.

   b. **Your Thesis Should Not Lead Questions**: "Sales is about the many aspects of relationship maintenance." How many? What exactly is "relationship maintenance"? Before you even start, your audience is perplexed rather than eager to hear your ideas on a clear concept.

      - If your audience is confused by your thesis then you are off to a rocky start; it is important that the people to whom you direct your message are not given terms that they do not understand or ideas that will leave them scratching their heads.

These might seem like rigid rules for just the creation of one simple sentence—but they are the rules that will help you to be articulate and succinct in a way that sets up all parts of the rest of your speech! These steps will make it far easier to determine what to include and not include in your speech.

How can you craft a strong thesis? Easy! Thesis creation begins with your general and specific purposes. If your specific purpose is clear then your thesis statement will naturally flow out of it.

Example:

Topic: Accounting
General Purpose: To inform
Specific Purpose: To teach my audience how to avoid financial
fraud through strict accounting strategies
Thesis: Strict accounting strategies can help you to avoid being taken
in by financial fraud schemes.

Example:

Topic: Football
General Purpose: To inform
Specific Purpose: To show the cultural impact of the Superbowl
Thesis: The NFL Superbowl has become an American cultural
phenomenon.

As you can see, once you have established your specific purpose, you
can easily lead yourself, and subsequently your audience, through your
clear and concise argument. While arguments must be concise, you must
be sure to avoid some common issues.

Common Thesis Issues:

Topic: Management

Thesis: I will talk about management.
(Problem: no argument here)

Thesis: My topic is management.
(Problem: a topic statement – not a thesis)

Thesis: Management styles help leaders to guide and control their employees.
(Problem: more than one idea - as indicated by the word "and")

Thesis: Contingency theory is the effective management style, which lets leaders change according to need
(Problem: more than one idea, indicated by the word "which" that connects the two parts)

Thesis: Carter McNamara shows how management decision-making is contingent on managers' ways of thinking.
(Problem: evidence and not from the speaker)

Thesis: How can managerial sense-making help you to become a more effective leader?
(Problem: thesis is a question)

Thesis: Post-modern management styles are true forms of effectiveness.
(Problem: leads to a question – what are "true forms of effectiveness"? and for that matter, does anyone really know what "postmodern" actually is?!)

Avoiding these common issues will help you to make more sense to your audience (that's what good logos is all about!) and to achieve your purpose of informing, or persuading, or entertaining much more effectively. To offer you some further help on this important element, notice how removing issues from these thesis statements have improved them.

Thesis Fixes:

Problematic: "Let me tell you about Product X."

Better: "Product X is on the leading edge of information storage."

Problematic: "There are two kinds of sales people in this world: aggressive and poor."

Better: "Aggressive salesmanship is your key to career success."

Problematic: "Who was "Mary Kay" Ash?"

Better: "Mary Kay Ash's frustrations with male favoritism in the workplace led to an empire of female empowerment."

Problematic: "You must put your business information on LinkedIn."

Better: "LinkedIn widens your existing network of trusted contacts."

An effective thesis statement, as you can see, does more than tell your audience what you will be talking about—it also tells them why you are talking at all. Once you have that argument laid out, you can move on to determining what ideas will be support it.

ORGANIZATIONAL PATTERNS

Determine purpose – check!
Understand rhetorical situation – check!
Craft thesis – check!
Conduct research – check!
If you have come this far then you have a superb foundation for an effective business presentation. Your diligence in completing the initial groundwork is about to pay off. From here on out you are in a position to organize your arguments appropriate to your purpose and audience as well as fine tune your delivery. You will begin to fill in the elements of your speech like coloring inside the lines of a picture. It's easy—but it still allows you to have lots of creativity and individuality.

Organizing Ideas

If you have ever been in a presentation and thought, "Huh, how does that make sense?", then you have likely witnessed poor organization. Take yourself back to our earlier discussion of ethos, pathos, and logos. (Those three appeals keep coming into play, don't they?). If the speech does not make sense, then it is violating Aristotle's sense of logos. If your speech has poor logos then it is possible for your audience to doubt that you know what you are talking about—and then you have encountered a loss of ethos! It is vital that you make strong organizational decisions so that you keep your audience attuned to your every work and you can achieve your goals!

Patterns of Organization

Patterns of organizations are more than just how you group ideas together as they make the most sense to you—they are the sequence of your ideas so that they bring your audience to the informed, persuaded, or entertained point that you want them. Yes—your speech sequencing actually helps you to *realize* your specific purpose. It has a reason! While there are any number of means of patterning your talk, you should realize that certain patterns fit with particular general purposes and only a few overlap. If you wish to inform, then certain organizational structures will work for you and others will not. The same goes for persuasion. Speeches to entertain may fall into use either informative or persuasive structures depending on your particular needs and that of your rhetorical situation. Read through each pattern description closely to see which fits your needs!

(Note: You may read in other texts that a particular organizational pattern meets a different general purpose or that some patterns listed specifically in one area in this text will in other texts meet the needs of a different general purpose. First, it is GREAT that you are reading up on how to communicate—yea you! Second, research adds to our knowledge all of the time. What you find listed here is based on current research. Be sure if you make alternative choices that they, too, are well grounded and current rather than just an idea that you or someone else *thought* might work. You have worked hard to get this far, don't blow it on a hunch!)

Informative Patterns of Organization

Informative speeches lay out knowledge for the audience. They do not lead audiences to a new belief or to take an action. Since this is the case, you do have the options of several patterns of simply offering up your information.

- **Chronological:** This is the time sequencing of information that offersparticulars or events from most recent to least recent—or can build from the past to the present.
    - Example: New employees can be curious about promotion processes. It might be your job to take them through the timeline from new employee to company CEO from the start of what they must do through the subsequent steps.
    - Example: Many companies have a corporate narrative that traces the history of the company and you may tell this narrative to visitors or new employees from where the company is now back to where is all began (this is **Reverse Chronological Order**).

(direction)

- **Spatial:** This structure deals with relationships between physical or structural parts like geography, anatomy (parts of the whole) or magnitude (large to small, small to large).
  - o Example: You might give a presentation indicating regions to which your company has grown and expanded from one and then to the next that takes listeners from the East Coast to the middle of the U.S. and then out to the West Coast.

- **Categorical (or Topical):** Categorical structures are sometimes called topical structures because they focus on key groupings or linked concepts within the main topic.
  - o Example: A speech on the key criteria for a successful career in Sales could group concepts of: building relationships, remembering to "close," and knowing the product (these could go in any order within the speech).

    What you have when there's no real order.

- **Causal:** This structure looks at the <u>relationship</u> between catalysts and consequences (effect to cause or cause to effect).
  - *Cause +*
  - *Effect*
  - o Example: BP, Halliburton, and Transocean were all trying to explain the reasons why the U.S. had a catastrophic failure at the Deep Horizons oilrig in the Gulf of Mexico in April, 2010. Each showed how their particular acts did (or did not) lead to the disastrous results.

- **Contrast:** This structure explores the differences and/or similarities between ideas or items.
  - o Example: Coke Zero® must differentiate between its product and the previously developed Pepsi Free® by showing key differences between the two products in elements of taste, calories, nutrition, and cost. This speech may be organized with the product being a main point and the elements of comparison being the subpoints or it may be organized with the elements of comparison being the 4 main points with the two products as the subpoints for each.

Persuasive Organization Considerations

Persuasive speeches lead audiences to a new belief, to take an action, or make a change. As such, their structures must _move_ the audience to a desired new position… not simply lay out information. The relationship between your audience and the topic (_not between your audience and you_) will help you to determine which pattern best fits your rhetorical situation.

Types of Audiences

There are three types of audiences that you might encounter when delivering a speech in a persuasive situation:

Hostile Audiences will primarily include listeners who are firmly set against your topic (e.g., speaking to new employees about the benefit of foregoing annual bonuses and vacation time to help the expansion of facilities).

Supportive Audiences primarily include those who are firmly for your topic (e.g., speaking to accountants about the benefits of strict financial policies).

Wavering Audiences may include either:
a) those who have not yet developed a position on your topic (e.g., speaking to new employees about a potential change in the existing sales software).
b) a group who is divided on their positions (some hostile and some supportive) (e.g., speaking to existing employees about a potential change in the existing sales software).

One or Two-Sided Arguments

Most literature on persuasion will tell you to choose your organizational pattern based on your type of audience. Particular audiences need to hear one-sided or two-sided arguments (Perloff, 2003). A **one-sided argument** provides only one view on the topic and is generally better suited to a group that shares your idea. A **two-sided argument** provides more than one perspective on the topic and is best suited for those who are hostile to your position (and, therefore, want to see that you recognize or do not discount their position) as well as those who are undecided on a position.

There has been much discussion and research regarding the pros and cons of **one-sided arguments** versus **two-sided arguments**. And while it has been supposed that one-sided arguments *always* have a greater effect on audiences who share your ideas, and two-sided arguments are better suited for audiences who oppose your ideas, there is a bit more to the issue.

Two-sided arguments have been found to have better persuasive effects on *any* type of audience in comparison to one-sided arguments, **but** be aware—there are two types of these two-sided messages (O'Keefe, 2002, p.220).

1) **Refutational**: A message that presents two varying opinions but attempts to *refute* one of them.
2) **Non- refutational:** A message that presents two varying opinions but does not actually try to refute one of them (just tries to make it look pretty bad!)

Persuasive Patterns of Organization

Persuasive patterns of organization offer either one or two-sided arguments and must be selected to have the greatest impact on the specific audience type. A few of the informative patterns may also be applicable for persuasion because they can be developed to both lay out information and to lead audiences.

- **Problem/solution/(action):**This structure defines a problem and offers a way (or ways) to solve it and can sometimes suggest action to the audience when they are prepared to take an action; this pattern often includes the action step as the last main idea
  - Sidedness/ Audience: one-sided/ supportive
  - Example: A presentation to discuss the revenue problems your company faces due to an economic downturn and ways to attract new business in a more austere economic environment.

1) Attention

- **Monroe's Motivated Sequence:** The Monroe's Motivated Sequence (MMS) structure is the only organizational pattern that is named to acknowledge the person who changed persuasive formats so that the *audience's perspective* is highlighted over the speaker's perspective; it has four main points that include: **1)** highlighting an audience need, **2)** clarifying what will satisfy that need, **3)** offering a visualization of life with or without the need satisfied, and then **4)** directs the audience how to act to realize the visualization (Monroe, 1935).
    - Sidedness/ Audience: two-sided/ hostile or wavering
    - Example: most sales pitches are motivational speeches (i.e., the need is to feel young and alive, the satisfaction is a new sports car that can make you feel fast and energized, the visualization is the picture of you zipping down the road with all admiring eyes on you, and the action… is to visit the dealership!)

- **Causal:** uses information that highlights the positive or negative relationship between catalysts and consequences alters a causal speech into persuasiveness
    - Sidedness/ Audience: one-sided/ supportive (but can sometimes be used for wavering)
    - Example: BP, Halliburton, and Transocean are all trying to show how the other is responsible for the catastrophic failure at the Deep Horizons oilrig.

- **Contrast:** uses information that illuminates the positive or negative differences and/ or similarities between ideas or items
    - Sidedness/ Audience: two-sided/ all audience types
    - Example: Coke Zero must show how their product is superior to Pepsi Free.

Example:

> To make this clear, let's put all of these issues together. If you are, for instance, a strong advocate of pulling all of your companies manufacturing plants out of Asia and placing them in the United States' mid-west region, you must pattern your talk to the needs of the audience... NOT the topic.
> Topic: plant relocation
> (Your position: supportive)
>
> **Option 1:**
> Your audience position/ pattern: supportive/ Problem-Solution-Action
>
> **Option 2:**
> Your audience/ pattern: hostile/MMS or Contrast

Choose your pattern purposefully rather than just assuming that you should follow a certain pattern solely because of the type of speech you are giving. You must consider the audience (part of the rhetorical situation), your goal, and your purpose. Once you have this pattern chosen, you are able to move on to crafting the content of your speech – the main points.

Laying Out Your Main Points

You have superb argument (your thesis) and have collected all sorts of evidence to support that argument. You have next figured out what type of audience you have and know your general purpose. You may be thinking that your next step is to plug in the right type of evidence into the right spot so that it best supports your thesis... and you would be right! You must develop your main points.

Main points are the cluster of ideas, concepts, arguments, and evidence that are gathered together and organized to fit the pattern that you have selected for your speech. **They are not stated in the speech but are simply an organizational tool for you that will help you develop your arguments and place evidence.**The number of main points you have in your presentation should develop organically. There is no perfect number for how many main points to have except that there should be enough to support your thesis. If you need 17 main points—so be it! If you need 3 main points—fantastic! If you do not have enough information or time to fill 17 points, or even 2, then you must go back and reconsider what goal you can meet in the time that is allotted and revise the number of main points to meet that goal.

Matching Main Ideas with Organizational Patterns

As you may have guessed, some patterns of organization will pre-determine a base number of main points for you. For example, if you are giving a chronological speech then you need at least two main points in order to show a movement in time. If you are giving a motivational speech then you will have at least the four points of need, satisfaction, visualization, and action (some folks may have more than one main point for any given element… but you cannot fully motivate if you *delete* steps along the way).

You may hear that the ideal number of clusters (main points) that you should end up with is three to five. This is because research has shown that this is the number of items that can be kept in working memory, and the number of interrelationships between elements that can be kept active in reasoning (Halford, Cowan, and Andrews, 2007). If you want to maximize assisting the audience in processing your reasoning, three to five main points or arguments is one way to do this. In reality, though, phenomena and experiences do not always parse neatly in three to five areas. Remember to have as many (or as few) main points as are necessary to support your argument.

Main Point Creation

To determine how to create main points, let's take a classic (albeit – not business related) example: football! Football is something to which most

U.S. citizens have at least a passing understanding (no pun intended). If your topic were football then you may have collected evidence about teams, rules, players, history, playoffs, college and professional differences, mascots, injuries… this list could go on and on. Your specific purpose will have allowed you to focus your ideas but you will still have much to consider. Apply the steps and guidelines discussed above to start laying out the major clusters of ideas that you will develop.

Example:

> *Topic*: Football
> *General Purpose*: To inform
> *Specific Purpose*: To show the cultural impact of the Superbowl
> *Thesis*: The NFL Superbowl has become an American cultural phenomenon.

Option 1:
Organizational pattern: categorical
Main Point ideas: definitions of culture, product advertising, jargon creation, general population behavioral change

Option 2:
Organizational pattern: chronological
Main Point ideas: history of the Superbowl, early sponsorship, viewership changes, later product advertising, modern day viewer-product relationship

Option 3:

Organizational pattern: causal
(** alas, we would need to change our thesis to make this pattern work because there is no causal relationship shown in the current thesis)

New Thesis: The NFL Superbowl has led to the celebration of sport as a pervasive part of American popular cultural.

Main Point ideas: changes in advertising (before Superbowl/ after Superbowl), changes in viewership (before Superbowl/ after Superbowl), changes in popular behavior (before Superbowl/ after Superbowl)

As you can see, you will develop your main points based upon your thesis, purpose, and the evidence that you have collected. Begin to (even on the floor with piles of printed evidence) layout where you have significant details and, again, read through your information to see what it is that you know about each area so that you can develop a central argument per main point.

Claims

Just like with your overall speech, you main points cannot just "start." They need to have some type of foundation that ties them together. In a speech, we call this the thesis. In your main points, we call this a **claim**—or the primary argument of the main point. (Think of this like writing a topic sentence in a paragraph for an essay!) You have already worked through writing a thesis so writing the claims will be easy.

Take the main point idea and just write a sentence! Because this sentence is part of verbal communication and it is an argument, you should follow the same rules as with writing your thesis. Claims should
- **Be from You**
- **Be a Single Idea**
- **Produce No Questions**

Elaboration of Previous Example:

Topic: Football
General Purpose: To inform
Specific Purpose: To show the cultural impact of the Superbowl
Thesis: The NFL Superbowl has become an American cultural phenomenon.

Organizational Structure:
Organizational pattern: categorical
Main Points:
1. definitions of culture
2. product advertising
3. jargon creation
4. general population behavioral change

Main Point Number One: definitions of culture
Claim Number One: Cultural definitions help us to understand how changes impact our society.

This speech has FOUR main points so it will have four claims. Let's take main point number one and create a claim:

You may find that, like with a thesis, you run through five or ten or more attempts at a claim before you find just the write wording that can be the launching point for all of the wonderful evidence that you have collected. Don't feel the need to get it perfect the first time. Write one. Wait a day. Write two revisions. Work on the next point. Come back to it – and revise it so you love it!

Incorporating and Organizing Your Evidence

Your claims come *from* your evidence – so now you must match your evidence to those claims. You have already clumped all of the evidence together so now it is just a matter of organizing what you have and fill in the holes.

Take every element of your research (your statistics, interviews, examples, analogies, hard data/ facts, etc.) that is separated *per main point* and begin to group these into smaller categories. These smaller categories or areas of discussion will become your sub-points. Your notation of what you will discuss in sub-points does not need to be full sentences because these elements are evidence rather than *arguments*. The **sub-points** are the cluster of ideas that will "prove" our claims (ok – prove is not a term we use in social science but you get the idea). Remember that it is in your best interest to place both quantitative and qualitative evidence as support for your claims—to best connect to any audience type. How many sub-points as many as are needed to support your claim! (Research suggests that 3-5 ideas are the easiest number to retain for most audiences.)

Example:

> Claim Number One: Cultural definitions help us to understand how changes impact our society.
>> Sub-point 1: Defining "patterns of experience" (Yip, 2002)
>> 1. Definition (Derth, 2008)
>> 2. Active observation—example (Yip, 2002)
>> 3. 30% change based on observation (Jones, 2010)
>> 4. Personal narrative

At some point you may decide that a piece of evidence needs to be moved to a different main point or that an example should be removed from the speech or that a new idea, statistic, narrative, or piece of data needs to be added. Your content is very flexible. The most important notion to remember is that you select and include the evidence that is best fit to your particular audience!

LINKING IDEAS

Ever heard a speaker who spoke for ten minutes and at the end of the talk… you had no idea what his (or her) main ideas were? The speaker may have had incredibly clear claims and great evidence but these all ran together. Statements that link but differentiate your points are **transitionary statements**. These will help you not sound like your six main point speech is just one big speech; they will help you to not abruptly launch into a subsequent main point – or subpoint; they will help your audience to follow along and recall! (hmmmm… that's seems like something we've heard before!)

There are several places within your speech that will need transitionary statements. In each place, you will need them to tell your audience what is to come and to remind them what has already passed. These connections should come between all main points (**external transitions**) and are effective within main points (**internal transitions/signposts**) so that the listener has a rubric for understanding the information.

Some folks think that their transitionary statements begin to stand out more than their facts—and this bums them out. Indeed, it should. Transitionary statements should not be the focus of your talk. They should be the scaffolding that holds up the rest of your speech! Practicing clarity and fluidity will allow you to have effective (but not obnoxious) transitions!

Organization Between Main Points – External Transitions

Your first transitionary statements are the most obviously needed and perhaps the easiest thing to produce—these are your external transitions. You will have three kinds of external transitions:

- **Preview**
- **Between Each Main Point**
- **Review**

Once you have written your claims—voila! Your external transitions will come naturally out of these!

- **Preview:**The preview is a verbal checklist for your audience. Just like a checklist that you would take to the grocery store (e.g., milk, cereal, coffee, pasta sauce), your preview should not be a complete picture of your speech (e.g., Nature's Promise Organic milk, Kellogg's Frosted Flakes cereal, Pete's Decaf ground coffee, Trader Joe's Organic Marinara pasta sauce). That's way too long and hard to remember— and you have your grocery list written down!

  You want to keep it short and to the point (after all – your main points are for arguments... the preview just tells them what general ideas are coming!) How do you do this? Keep your preview simple by <u>labeling your main points</u> with a few key words from your claim—the exact words as to not confuse your audience.

  Example:

  > <u>Way Too Much</u>: In order to understand why you will want to own Product X, let's take a look at its storage capacity—both in terms of its shear volume as well as how it compares to similar products; then, your ability to access information efficiently will be our next area—from how user friendly the program is as well as how quickly it responds to your requests for information; and last, I want to zero in on savings—including both initial costs and then just savings accrued through using this system.
  >
  > **No one is ever going to remember all of those details to stay on track during your presentation.**
  >
  > <u>Much Better</u>: "Product X has three advantages over the system that you are using now: capacity, efficiency, and savings—let's look at how each can effect your bottom line."

Just about any listener who is paying attention can remember these key concepts and will wait for them to come along as destination points in your speech. This makes you speech much easier to follow and recall!

- **Between Main Points:** The statements made in-between major concepts are transitions (yes, like in an English essay). **Transitions** summarize the idea that was just discussed and provide a logical link between it and the next idea. *This notion of logical links is crucial.* If the preview is a checklist then the transitions allow the audience to put checks next to each item and remember to grab it off the metaphorical shelf!

Example:

> Transition with No Logical Link: Now that I have talked about fraud, I will talk about audits.
>
> Transition with Logical Link: As you can see, financial fraud is crippling our company, but, with keen attention to details through regular audits, we can change our financial future.

In this way, the relationship among the main points of your speech is highlighted. We know in both sentences that the first main point is about fraud and the second main point is about audits. If you have difficulty showing a relationship between main points then.... alas, you may not have the best (or most logical) structure for your speech. Rethink it. Speeches are living creatures that are continually shaping to make strong connections to your audience: ethos, pathos, and logos!

Also, know that CLAIMS AND TRANSITIONS ARE NOT THE SAME. (Sorry. All caps can sound like yelling but in this case, we're just trying to make a point.) Remember that claims provide arguments. Transitions do not. Transitions provide links and help the audience to follow and recall. You will need both statements in your speech—and they must be clearly different to effectively serve their individual purposes!

- **Review:** You previewed. You should review. Your **summary** (or **review**) is the counterpart to your preview. The idea here is that just as much as an audience needs to have a mental checklist for where you will go, they need that same mental checklist to see if indeed you went to all of the places promised. You give them this in the review of your main points, which serves as a fantastic means of reinforcing your ideas for long-term recall. Like your preview and transitions, the review cannot be cluttered or complicated.

Example:

> Way Too Much:
> You have spent the last ten minutes hearing about Product X in order to understand how it gives you: greater capacity, increased efficiency, and substantial savings.

You will need to make sure that you use the samekey words for the preview, review, and transitions so that the audience will not think that you are introducing new ideas. now that's a good checklist!

Organization Within Main Points: Internal Transitions

You are sitting in your company's annual employee meeting. Your CEO is hoping to get folks on board with the move from one location to the next. First, she details the problem with the current location. Second, she somehow lays out how the new location will fix the problems. Finally, she asks that you help in the process by giving details of…

Oh gosh. You tuned out. Sure, you could tell what the main points were but after that – all of the details just ran together and, suddenly, you found yourself creating a grocery list in your head. (P.S… you're out of milk.)

One of the most forgotten notions of speech giving is that not only must we have patterns of organization for our entire presentation (between main points)—but we must have organization *within* each main point. If not, the audience may lose focus and have difficulty *listening* or they may think that we are just babbling. Internal transitions help to maintain clear logos for each major concept/ argument in your talk. We call these signposts.

- **Signposts:**The strategic, audience-centered verbal transitions between sub-points or details are called **signposts**. A signpost should include words or phrases that cue the audience that you are moving to the next sub-point and that there is a thought out organization of those sub-points. In other words, don't just throw the details into your speech haphazardly. Organize the information and then verbally cue your audience in to the fact that you have.

  To make it easier, organizational patterns that you will use for the details of the speech are the exact same patterns that you have used to order your main point ideas. Once you know how information is organized, the signposts directly correlate with that organization.

  If you use this pattern, then you will verbalize this signpost:
  - **Chronological**: First, Second, Third, etc.
  - **Categorical**: Next, In addition, Moreover
  - **Causal**: A leads to B,
  - **Contrast**: By comparison, In contrast
  - **Spatial**: Next to this, As we move to
  - **Problem/Solution**: The initial issue, Which was fixed by

You will know you are finished organizing the body of your speech if the ideas flow clearly and smoothly; if your main points don't overlap, but logically relate to one another; and if all key aspects of your topic are covered and your purpose is fulfilled.You have an argument, information… and logical steps, yet, your speech is not finished. You must pull your audience in – and then send them on their way.

GETTING IN AND GETTING OUT

Imagine hearing a speech that began with, "Today, I will talk about (insert topic)." Are you intrigued? Fascinated? Of course not; and why would you be? Even if the topic is something about which you already have an interest (such as video games or breakfast cereals... yum!), this sentence does little to make you want to hear what *this* speaker has to say. You likely feel the same let down when a speaker finishes a talk with, "that's it." Can you feel the disappointment? Beginning and ending your presentations can either engage or disengage your colleagues. The great thing is that you get to decide which they will do.

Opening Your Talk

The reason to create your introduction *after* the speech content is complete is so that you can tailor your opening remarks to that content of the speech. If you develop the introduction first, you will tend to try to force the speech to follow the path set by the introduction (rather than the argument or the thesis). The body of your speech should not serve your introduction; it's the other way around. Opening your speech begins by grabbing the audience's attention in a way that effectively draws them into your thesis.

- **Grabbing Attention:** A CEO walks into the auditorium full of 400 employees. He moves to the lectern, picks up a stack of the company's annual report, and proceeds to hurl them at the audience. The idea: that we are throwing out the past and moving to the future! Good idea? Well, not if you are sitting in the front row. Not if you just got hit in the face with a 60 page bound document. Are you thinking about his message? No. Likely you are thinking about medical attention or how not to get hurt if this guy tries that same theatrical trick again.

Contrary to popular belief, **gaining attention is NOT the sole purpose of your introduction!** Grabbing attention is not about shock value or drama for drama's sake. It is about making your audience truly believe that what you are about to say is of value to them. While most listeners will look at you as you get up to speak, most will be preoccupied with other issues (e.g., planning their dinner, wondering if the kids got home from school yet, or "Wow, what on earth is that speaker wearing?"). A myriad of thoughts that can distract audiences from speakers. You want everyone to refocus their attention on your message, so you need to give them a reason to redirect their thoughts toward you. The **purpose of your introduction** is to draw your audience into your thesis—or primary argument.

You may wish to use a quantitative introduction (shock them with the numbers that impact their lives) or a qualitative introduction (pull on their heart strings with a narrative that could happen to them) or both. However, *your introduction should be focused so be aware that using numerous ideas will actually work against you.* Consider the following useful techniques:

- **Audience Identification**: Audience members can connect to speakers with whom they share an experience, which includes acknowledgement of the particular occasion ("we are together in these troubled times"), past experience ("so I've talked to each of you and know that we have all lost someone to cancer"), or even shared reading ("who remembers reading '*A Catcher in the Rye*' when they were in school?")
- **Story / Narrative**: The telling of an amusing or powerful story that relates to your purpose can bring life to hard data or basic information
- **Analogy**: Relating current circumstances or data to similar and perhaps more well known or other significant scenarios can enhance understanding ("So, we all know that we are on the same path that led to the oil spill off the gulf coast last year…")

- o **Rhetorical Question**: This type of question does not expect an answer but serves the same purpose as a persuasive statement ("How many of you want to reach your sales goals for this year?!")
- o **Significant Quotation**: Sometimes others are better able to say what we mean ("Issac Newton said that we become great by 'standing on the shoulders of giants.' I come here today as your CEO not on my own but humbly and appreciatively because of your great shoulders.")
- o **Humor**: Telling jokes and amusing stories is a great way to produce an emotional response from an audience but *must be used with caution!* Humor can engage but it can also offend, not be understood, or… just not be funny.
- o **Demonstration or Visual Aid**: Showing images, actual models, and even providing a brief demonstration of your topic or something associated to your topic produces instant audience buy-in; you must, however, keep these elements brief, focused, and introductory rather than visuals that are best developed and used to support claims.
- o **Hard Data**: Numbers and facts can be dramatic and work best to involve quantitatively-oriented audiences ("70% of you here today are at risk of losing your jobs; 10% actually will; and 100% of those who follow the process that I outline here today will be able to remain with our company in a successful capacity").

The bottom line here is that your choices are limited only by the limits of your own creativity.

- **Providing Significance – Why Should I Care?:** After grabbing your audience (NOT by throwing things at them), listeners tend to wonder why your topic is important to them. Most people are very busy. We can always find something else to do instead of listening to you speak. So, it is crucial that your audience knows why they should care!

Example:

> Significant Quotation Attention-Getter:
> Isaac Newton said that we become great by 'standing on the shoulders of giants.' I come here today as your CEO not on my own but humbly and appreciatively because of your great shoulders…

> Significance that Leads to Thesis:
> You have asked me to choose a direction for this company and that direction will impact every aspect of your jobs. It will change the way that we interact with our customers and the outcomes of our long term future. If you give me your attention for just a short time… I can help you to move seamlessly into a better, brighter, and personally more profitable future!

Aha! Now your audience wants to know what you have to say. They are ready for that primary argument (which will answer the "how will we move me into a more profitable future?" question) and hear your evidence. They are ready for your talk! Once you have finished that talk, it's important to do a bit of reminding of these same ideas that we've just discussed.

Closing Your Talk

How many times have you heard speakers end with "I'm done;any questions?" This can be abrupt and does nothing to make a positive final impression on your audience. An effective conclusion should pull the key ideas of your speech back together and refocuses your listeners' attention on your specific purpose. Finally, to give your speech a sense of unity and your listeners a clear sense that they are fully and comprehensively empowered, you always want to add a clincher that ties directly back to your attention-getter—a "style match."

- **Returning to the Purpose – A Rephrased Thesis:**
  You have spent a great deal of time talking. Anything from two to ten minutes gives the audience a chance to forget the primary

argument of your speech. They are rehashing ideas and evidence and mulling over the stories that you have told. Since this is *always* the case, it is *always* your job to refocus them on that purpose as wrap-up. This process is simple because it simply involves you going back to the idea of your thesis.

Now is not the time for new information. A **rephrased thesis statement** or the same idea in different words offers your audience a revision of your purpose. Why not just say the exact same thing? Well, on the one hand, your audience may think that you have just had a mental hiccup! ("Uh… didn't she already say that?") And while **redundancy** (the repeating of ideas in new language to help with retention for all audience types) is useful, **repetition** (the exact and word-for-word restatement of language) can be result in a lack of understanding by folks who didn't understand the first time—and confusion by folks who think that you are making a verbal error. So… <u>after you have reviewed and before you conclude</u>, rephrase!

- **Wrapping it All Up – Clinchers and Style Matching:**
  You reviewed! You rephrased! Yippee—you're finished, right? Not quite. Speeches that just end leave audiences feeling abandoned and ill-prepared. *Your final words to the audience should serve the function of a last appeal to accept your information or be persuaded.*
    o **Clincher**: Clinchers are verbal moments that offer deciding factors for your audience. Such as, if you have given a persuasive speech that asks for someone to buy your product, give them a final sentence that encapsulates their newfound reason to do so. If you have provided new information to a group then offer them a final appeal of how that information matters. Think of this not only as a clincher but as a verbal zinger!

    o **Style Match**: With this final appeal and feeling of inspiration in the room, don't leave your audience hanging. Pull it all back together with a style match. A **style match** ties your conclusion directly back to how you began

(Sprague & Stuart, p. 166). If you began with a story, return to that very story by giving them the positive (or negative) result. If you started with a reference to the listeners/ audience identification, refer back to that statement and leave the audience knowing that you truly do *get* them. If you begin with a demonstration, return to it(or at least say something about it). *The most effective presentations end where they began.*

A Final Frame on Organization

Once upon a time, a little girl lost her father. She then lived her life as a poor and ragged servant to her scary stepmother with no hopes of a bright future. But… when the prince of the land threw a ball looking to take a bride, her Fairy Godmother appeared and transformed her! She went to the ball, fell in love with the prince, and, even when she slipped away at the stroke of midnight losing one of her beautiful glass slippers and transforming back to her former self, the prince found her and they live happily ever after!

Ideas that have order make more sense. We know it in our fairy tales and know we know that the same ideas are true in business presentations. However, just as in fairy tales where we are captivated by engaging and descriptive language (and likely the great voices our dads used to tell these stories!), how you say your message will be just as important as what you say in your message. It is with this in mind that we will next turn our attention to the words, voice, and movement of presentation delivery.

Chapter Seven

Words, Voice, Movement: Business Presentation Delivery

TALKING THE TALK

Have you ever heard a presentation and thought, "wow, that guy (or gal) is amazing!"? Sure, we all have. There are presenters in many walks of life who really impress us with their dynamic delivery styles. This may leave you thinking that if you do not have a dynamic style that you cannot be a captivating speaker—or that speaking is mostly about style. It is not.

Consider some of the most memorable public historic figures—the ones whose messages changed people, nations, laws, and social values:
* Mother Theresa
* Mahatma Gandhi
* The Dalai Lama
* Desmond Tutu

These are amazing speakers who affected their audiences—but none of them had dynamic (and by that we mean vibrant, energetic, and lively) speaking styles. They also may not have been the speakers that first come to mind for you. Your list might have included Malcolm X, Rev. Martin Luther King, Richard Branson, Warren Buffet, or Stephen Covey; a far livelier and vocally passionate group. They key here is that both groups have commonly used their own individual ability, style, and effective argumentation to make changes. What we can take from this is that you can be quiet and effective *or* dynamic and effective—as long as you speak in a means that is true to you and expresses your passion and ethos. These two ideas are crucial to speaking in a business context.

They mean that once you have compiled all of the ideas on which you want to speak and you have organized them effectively, you'll still need to find that "style" that makes _you_ successful!

In this chapter, you'll learn how to embrace your own style by realistically assessing and managing your nerves, understanding the modes of delivery available to you, utilizing verbal and nonverbal delivery strategies alone or in a group, and (of course) seeing just why practice will dramatically improve your speaking technique and just how to do it.

Addressing the "Nerves" Issue

Let's start with the elephant in the room. Because every speaking situation contains a level of uncertainty, it's pretty natural to get even a little bit nervous despite our best efforts to be thoroughly prepared and be totally psyched up. This state of anxiety, no matter how large or how small, is referred to as **communication apprehension**. Communication apprehension can come before, after, or during a speech; it can be those small butterflies in the stomach all the way to full fledge panic (which… is far more rare than you may have been told). In fact, Jerry Seinfeld once lamented, "According to most studies, people's number one fear is public speaking…if you go to a funeral, you're better off in the casket than doing the eulogy!" (Seinfeld Scripts, 2010).

OK—a bit of an overstatement along with the total misrepresentation of those 'studies' (see Garber, 2009, for how these rumors started); however, it is true that almost everyone experiences some type of small to moderate nervousness when preparing a speech. And, even when some professionals' careers depend on it, they don't want to give public speeches. Why? Most professionals do not have the training to know what to say, how to say it, and be confident in their presentations. Being an effective presenter requires developing the right mindset and understanding the nature of and how to overcome those nerves.

The Right Mindset

The first step toward giving a successful presentation is to develop a positive mindset about public speaking. So much of our ability to effectively reach our presentation goals depends on getting into the right frame of mind. For many folks (not quite as many as Jerry Seinfeld imagined), giving a speech can be anxiety provoking even for the most outwardly confident and dynamic individuals and even more for the more natural introverts. (Remember this: Gandhi was a soft-spoken, engaging introvert who inspired millions.) What throws people off is the erroneous belief that speeches can be perfect. In this pressurized condition, even the smallest mistake can feel like a monumental gaffe. It's no wonder Seinfeld's pun strikes a chord with so many people. Eek— the pressure!

Instead of expecting perfection, we need to set a more realistic expectation. The standard that we should strive to achieve **is** *effectiveness*. If you are effective in achieving your purpose then your listeners will understand what you intend them to understand, accept the point of view you want them to accept, or act the way you have convinced them to act. That's success!**In fact, you should probably know that there is no such thing in presenting as perfect**. Practice makes… better! And we should strive to become better every day. How so? There are practical steps.

Practical Steps

It sounds very easy to just…. BE POSITIVE about speaking. "Oh, great – I'm positive!" But we can't just make the change with the snap of a finger. Changing your mindset can and will happen with time but the first part of your change will be to take very practical (and sometimes even tangible) steps toward an ease of anxiety.

- **Visualize the Good:** As you prepare to deliver your speech, you will be more successful if you visualize yourself presenting it effectively (Ayres & Hopf, 1999).
    - The key here is to imagine with as much detail as possible. Imagine yourself giving not just a good speech; imagine yourself giving a great speech! If you can imagine it this

way, you are in effect, creating a mental model to guide your actual presentation. The **self-fulfilling prophecy** simply means that if you believe *it*, that *it* is more likely to happen(Merton, 1948).

- **Visualize Fixing the Bad:** Bad stuff can happen. What throws presenters is when they are not prepared for it. Imagine the issues (slide show doesn't work, someone walks in during the speech, you get the hiccups, etc.) but then… imagine what you would do to fix them
  - If you imagine that the slides don't work then imagine having handouts—but also be sure that you bring handouts to your *actual* presentation just in case. If you find yourself too attached to the mental model of mistakes during the presentation, *never* let this be the end of your visualization. Be sure to have imagined the fixes because the self-fulfilling prophecy works for the good and the bad!

- **Examine Nonverbal Impacts:** Some speakers visually show when they are nervous (shaking, red blotches, sweating in usual—and unusual—places, etc.). If you know yours then you can take steps to hide them (if you do not know yours then ask someone who has seen you speak or video tape a test run!).
  - **Clothing** (if you get red, avoid V or scoop neck; if you sweat, wear dark clothes and layer, etc.)
  - **Actions** (if you have shaking hands, don't hold papers; if you have dry mouth, keep a bottle of water with you, etc.)

- **Roll a Paper Corner:** Nervous energy needs a place to go. Tear off a small corner of a piece of paper and roll it up between your thumb and index finger. Continue to hold it and roll it back and forth between your fingers during your speech.
  - The rolled paper cannot be seen by your audience but allows you to have a focus other than your nerves and a physical outlet for that energy.

- **Have Water:** Whether it is before or during a presentation, some liquids will enhance your ability to speak well and diminish nerves. Water works!
  o Having water with you will help with dry mouth during a speech. Water will not stain clothes if spilled (which inevitably will happen; it's ok, water also dries). Water will not develop a film in your mouth or throat.
  o Caffeine will work against you. Colas or coffee or energy drinks will all lead to an excess of physical action that is difficult to control in a setting that requires ease and a relaxed physical state. Avoid this both during and even within any close time to your speech!

- **Do a Dress Rehearsal:** The first time in your new shoes should not be as you plan to walk with confidence. Movement should be natural and your audience will know when you are not comfortable in your attire. (This includes guys who do not regularly wear a sports coat and will be fidgeting and having hands in and out of pockets or tugging at lapels just because they are novel!)
  o Practice your <u>entire</u> speech while wearing exactly what you will wear when you deliver the actual talk! This will help you appear relaxed and natural.

- **Warm up Your Vocal Chords:** It is not necessary to walk around outside of your presentation room saying "meee meee meee" or repeatedly verbalizing "rubber baby buggy bumpers." It is, however, important to have your vocal chords be adequately stretched and prepared before you speak.
  o If you have an early morning talk, be sure to call your best friend in the morning and chat all about your weekend plans. If you typically sit quietly all day and your talk is just before lunch, this is a good time to actually go up and chat with the person in the cubicle next to you (you will be focused on something other than your speech or nerves and may even make a friend!).

While none of these tactics are world changing, they each have their very own practical means of managing nerves. This will give the appearance to your audience that you are confident and you will find that they will respond with positive feedback! (To borrow a phrase from a 12-step program: fake it 'til ya make it! The results will follow.) Once you are feeling the good vibe, you'll need to select the right mode... mode of delivery that is.

Modes of Delivery

Imagine the President delivering the State of the Union address just... off the cuff. Picture the CEO of Valero Energy (the tenth largest company in the United States) reading word for word to his shareholders off of a bunch of note cards. Now... imagine your college professor delivering her 50 minute lecture from memory with no interaction at all. While you may be impressed that she can do that (and has the time), the way that she is speaking and the way that the others are speaking does not seem suited to the situation. **Modes of delivery** are the methods of operation by which presentations are conveyed. There are four basic modes of delivering a speech: **manuscript**, **memorized**, **impromptu**, and **extemporaneous.** Select yours intentionally!

Linking Delivery Style to Rhetorical Situation

Each speaker must determine the mode of delivery that is best suited to the speaker, the environment, the constraints of the situation, and the audience. That's right! Modes of delivery are specifically linked to the Rhetorical Situation (see Chapter 5). There are particular circumstances that will call for particular means of delivery. Since you analyzed these circumstances as part of your research for this speech, you are in good shape to select your mode.

- **Speaking from Manuscript:** If you are giving a presentation in which precise language is critical in order to convey exact meanings then you may want to deliver a speech from a manuscript. **Manuscript** is just as it sounds—a fully written out, word-for-word version of your speech.

  Situations for Manuscript Speaking: One situation where use of a manuscript is important would be when you have any type of legal wording—where even one word difference can be detrimental. Most of us do not have to meet such stringent standards for the content of our speeches. Demands for this level of precision are usually reserved for people who are in the upper echelons of management, criminal justice or legal industries, and politics.

  Problems with Manuscript Speaking: As you probably have seen with others' speeches, this mode of delivery can produce some of the most boring presentations you have ever heard! Manuscripts speakers come across more like they're doing an oral reading than a connected presentation. To avoid this you have to get off the page or teleprompter and connect with your listeners.

  You can avoid some of these manuscript speaking problems by:
  - Practice as much as time permits
  - Use a font size and style for notes that is large and very easy to read
  - Space out ideas so they are easy to see
  - Mark up your manuscript in a way that highlights critical or key ideas
  - Gesture and add some animation to your delivery

- **Speaking From Memory:** Similar to the manuscript speech is **memorized** speaking, which includes a word-for-word delivery of a speech with no notes. This mode has all of the benefits of the manuscript but without the pages! You eliminate the need for a lectern or place for your notes (which helps to remove a physical and psychological barrier between you and the audience) and still get the wording just right.

Situations for Memory Speaking: At some point, you may find yourself in a position in which you have to give essentially the same presentation on multiple occasions (e.g., if you are traveling around the country to train employees for your company or if you are providing company status updates to various divisions) and whether you have intended to do so or the repetition simply results in it, you may get to the point of memorization.

Problems with Memory Speaking: Just like actors in a play, memorized speeches still need to be dynamic in order to hold the interest of the audience. After all, if you begin to sound like you are giving directions to the same place for the millionth time—the audience can tell! Even more problematic, if you have memorized your speech poorly, you can lose your place and not be able to move forward. The words become like links in a chain; drop a link and the chain is broken, and you cannot continue along the chain until you have repaired (recalled) the missing link. If you don't have to give the same presentation on numerous occasions, don't try to memorize your speech.

- **Impromptu Speaking:** Impromptu speeches are those that are given with little to no preparation. This does not mean no organization! If you got up to talk with no preparation *and* no organization then you would not be giving a presentation as much a babbling out loud. Impromptu speakers do well when they know and use the basic speaking organizational structure (i.e., intro, thesis, preview, main points with transition, review, rephrased thesis, and style match).

A manuscript that is written out word-for-word involves a serious time commitment—even more if you plan to memorize each word. While, it would be nice if we always knew well in advance when we are expected to speak, unfortunately, we won't. If you are called on suddenly to give a presentation, use impromptu speaking, don't babble.

Situations for Impromptu Speaking: Consider, for example, that you are sitting in a departmental staff meeting and the department head asks you to bring the group up to speed on a your team's project. It is unlikely that this is a request that you can decline. Instead of saying, "Yeah… I'll pass," (or pretending you did not hear your boss – that might work once but it's a risk!), you will need to gather your thoughts quickly and present a clear and cogent speech.

Problems with Impromptu Speaking: You should use impromptu speaking only in circumstances like this—when you have no advance notice AND you have a good working knowledge of the topic. Never just wing it!

- **Extemporaneous Speaking:** At this point, you may be concerned that none of these speaking modes sound like regular everyday circumstances for you. You won't have time in accounting to write out your reports word-for-word so manuscript is unlikely. As a corporate manager, your job will change too much to memorize a repeated script. Certainly, in any position you will need to give the occasional impromptu speech, but you will try to have room for a bit more preparation. What mode seems most likely?

For the most part, the professional presentations you will give will allow you a moderate amount of advance notice. **Extemporaneous** speeches are prepared well in advance and based off a speaking outline rather than word-for-word script. These speeches must be *practiced* for clarity and fluency, and delivered from limited notes. Your limited notes will provide you with a skeletal flow of ideas using key words to jog your memory for what comes next in the speech.

Situations for Extemporaneous Speaking: Speaking extemporaneously lets you present your ideas in a dynamic and engaging way similar to what you could achieve in a well-memorized speech.

Selection of Speaker's Extemporaneous Notes

Claim 1: Cultural definitions help us to understand how changes impact our society.
sub-point 1: defining patterns of experience (Yip, 2002)
1. Definition (Derth, 2008)
2. Active observation (Yip, 2002)
3. 30% change based on observation (Jones, 2010)
4. Personal narrative

Because you refer to your notes only occasionally, you can spend most of your time connecting directly with your listeners. At the same time, your notes keep you organized and on track by providing you with a prompt of what idea comes next as you are speaking.

Extemporaneous speech notes are easier to handle so you can gesture freely. You can anticipate the need to refer to your notes and bring your hand up to create an instant temporary lectern. Once you grasp the idea, you can put your hand down and go on gesturing normally. Your notes should become totally unobtrusive—almost as if they disappear in the eyes of the audience.

Problems with Extemporaneous Speaking: The most basic reason to avoid extemporaneous speaking is if you have not adequately read through and understand your research. Extemporaneous speaking isn't about faking it… it's about knowing your information and not getting bogged down in notes. If you aren't there, audiences can tell.

No one mode of speaking is inherently better than the others. The mode you should use depends on the situation. Choose a mode after you have thoroughly pondered the demands placed on you by your speaking situation. Once you have, you are in a position to work on the verbal and nonverbal parts of your talk!

VERBAL AND NONVERBAL CONSIDERATIONS

In May 2005, Tom Cruise jumped up and down on Oprah Winfrey's couch to declare his love for the woman who was soon to be the mother of his child. The passion was unmistakable. The jumping is unforgettable. The act, well, perhaps it was something unwise. Why? It's difficult to fault anyone for falling in love and be enthusiastic enough to show it publically. What was problematic in this public declaration was that the jumping became more memorable than the idea behind it. Tom Cruise made one of the crucial errors in public speaking—he let his verbal and nonverbal communication overshadow his message.

Think that this doesn't happen in the refined world of business? Think again. Microsoft's Steve Ballmer screamed and ran back and forth on the stage (to the point of not being able to breathe when he began to speak) as he kicked off his company's 25th Anniversary—spawning several YouTube videos and brought him the nickname"Dance Monkeyboy." Apple's mega-presenter Steve Jobs was so unprepared for glitches while attempting to show off features of the new iPhone 4 that his standard responses throughout his speech included: "ah geez," "whoops," nervous giggles, and some serious eye contact avoidance.

So, even the best presenters have verbal and nonverbal gaffes. How do you avoid such things, well, first you make sure that you consider the delivery options available to you and practice with what suits you best. When you read on, you will find tools for speech presentation. Remember that word – tools. Just like a hammer is a great tool, it does not work for every job. Not every tool mentioned in the following discussion will be useful to you in every speaking situation and you will need to find your own style to use those tools. Not all speakers, just like not all speeches, are the same (remember Gandhi and Mother Theresa versus Malcolm

X and Richard Branson). There is not one way to vocally or physically deliver your speech so be sure that you are matching <u>your</u> style to the range of options listed below.

Verbal Effectiveness

Vocally, an effective presentation expresses your ideas in their full intellectual, aesthetic, and emotional dimensions. That's a mouthful. Basically, it means that delivering a speech is more than just getting the words in the right order out of your mouth. There is a world of difference between *reciting* and *delivering* a speech. **Recitation** gets all of the ideas out in the right order, but robs them of their full meaning by reducing them to a mere arrangement of words. Verbal effectiveness means selecting language that expresses meaning and using vocal qualities so that you words engage your audience.

Language Strategies

Anytime you give a presentation, you want to choose language that both holds the audience's attention and clearly communicates your ideas. This means using an effective style of speech. Politics aside, if you look at Presidents Barack Obama, George H. W. Bush, and Bill Clinton—the importance of style is immediately apparent.

Example One :

> *Change will not come if we wait for some other person or some other time. We are the ones we've been waiting for. We are the change that we seek.* (**Obama**)

Example Two:

> *America is never wholly herself unless she is engaged in high moral principle. We as a people have such a purpose today. It is to make kinder the face of the nation and gentler the face of the world.*
> (**Bush**)

Example Three:

> *There is nothing wrong with America that cannot be cured with what is right in America.*
> (**Clinton**)

If the names were not with the quotes, most likely you could still differentiate their style even if you weren't sure which was which. Once you become a veteran speaker, your style will also become distinctive as well. Like fashion style, style is how we clothe our ideas in words. (Are you Nordstrom? Forever 21? Kate Spade? Burberry? Target? You decide.)

Common Elements of Oral Style

While style is unique, there are some speaking elements that work for every speaker. We call these **common elements of oral style** (compared to written style). The reason they work for all speakers is that the enhance langue clarity.

Simplicity
Effective speakers realize which, unlike the written word that can be revisited, they only get one shot for an audience to understand their message. Oral style is necessarily simpler than the written word: sentences are shorter and less complex (hhmmm… sound familiar? see Chapter 6 for cues to an effective oral structure). Readers can go back and read an idea over and over until they get it, but listeners can follow the thread of an idea only so far before it becomes frayed. So, keep it simple.

Repetition vs. Redundancy
Yes, these ideas have been mentioned a few times in this text, thus far. The reason? Audiences don't always get what you have to say the first time so speakers must be skilled in sending messages more than once— without sounding like they are having verbal hiccups. So, to reiterate:

The repeating of ideas in new language to help with retention for all audience types is **redundancy** (a good speech tool) whereas, **repetition** is the exact and word-for-word restatement of language. When going back to ones thesis, repetition can work against you. When giving a speech, some (sparingly used) repetition can drive home a point—think of Martin Luther King's "I Have a Dream" speech. This catch phrase was repeated for emphasis.

Conversational Tone

You are not giving directions on a Disneyland ride, you are interacting with audiences. As such, your style should be more informal than a written style but still professional. You would not speak to your boss at work the same way that you would your friends during a Super Bowl party but you should adopt a style that invites audiences to feel spoken with rather than at. Your voice should sound as natural as it does on a daily basis.

Limited Non-Fluencies

On the challenging side, oral style can get cluttered with oral garbage such as "like," "you know," "um," and "uh." A conversational tone will make these *less* noticeable but your job will be to limit such breaks in style. As you practice your speech, have a few catch phrases that you can insert. When you begin to say "uh," change it to "in other words." The first few times that you try this, you will feel awkward and the catch phrase will stand out more than the non-fluency. Two things will happen: (1) you will begin to naturally insert your catch phrase or (2) the insertion will become such an interruption that you will start to phase it out for more fluid speech!

Individual Elements of Oral Style

Beyond the basics of what *all* speakers must stylistically achieve, you can differentiate yourself with your own unique flair (Yes! Flair in the office!). The following strategies do apply to all speakers but *how* they are implemented is a matter of personal choice.

Word economy

The skill of saying exactly what you want to say but in a few words as necessary is called **word economy**. This is the hallmark of good speaking style but *how* brief you will be is entirely up to you. In the 19th century, audiences were accustomed to speeches that lasted for hours but, today, lengthy speeches (your rhetorical situation will determine what constitutes "lengthy") can create hostile audiences. Why? Well, digital media has given us a broad span of attention for what kinds of content we take in, but a short attention span for how much we take in (Hart, 1994). So… are you a one word wonder? Do you tell elaborate stories that are contained in simplified structures? You decide.

Concreteness

You should strive for your own level of concreteness. **Concreteness** is the opposite of abstraction—it means solid and real. Renowned semanticist (meaning 'a guy who studies words') S. I. Hayakawa (1949) developed the *Ladder of Abstraction* (see examples on this page). The ladder described the levels of language that we use that go from conceptual to precise.

> **Ladder of Abstraction**
>
> **Level 4: very abstract**
> (Examples: life, activity)
>
> **Level 3: classes of nouns**
> (Examples: enterprise, business)
>
> **Level 2: categories of nouns**
> (Examples: news outlets)
>
> **Level 1: specific nouns**
> (Examples: Cable News Network, Reuters News Service, Philadelphia Inquirer)

Individuals must decide where on the language ladder they belong based on personal style and per rhetorical situation. For instance, you may experience times in which being more ambiguous may be to your advantage. If you tell an audience, "We have taken initial steps toward fixing the problem," heck, you can mean just about anything! Such an expression may give you some wiggle room, but it does not have a whole lot of meaning. Being ambiguous is rarely to the *audience's* advantage—if they want answers, and then lower down the ladder into more concrete expressions will be expected. To avoid this backlash, you should avoid ambiguous language when possible.

Jargon

Words are specific to groups. **Jargon** is the specialized language particular to a specific profession, field of study, or distinct group. If you use jargon that *you know* but that your clients do not then you disconnect yourself from your audience! Too often, speakers try to establish their credibility by loading their speeches up with acronyms and other specialized expressions that are not part of the ordinary language of their listeners (they are trying to <u>sound</u> smart). Unless this jargon is the 'language' of your audience, you will be more effective if you use words that can be decoded!

Modifiers and Qualifiers

We use **modifiers and qualifiers**, or terms that are not synonymous but that basically serve the same function, to give scale to elements of your discussion. These are the terms that we put in our talks when we are trying to be SUPER EXCITED!! But, actually they can serve to complicate speeches and serve as non-fluencies.

Think back to your last trip to a restaurant to know how tedious excessive modifiers and qualifiers can get. Since when did a "bacon cheeseburger with fries" become:

> *"A subtly seasoned, open fire grilled, one-third pound angus beef patty topped with aged baby Swiss cheese and a rasher of maple smoked pepper bacon served on an unbleached flour, sesame seeded Kaiser roll, with locally grown heirloom tomato slice, shaved red onions, a leaf of romaine lettuce, with a dollop of fat-free mayonnaise, and accompanied by a generous side of Cajun batter-dipped, Idaho Blue Potatoes quick fried in canola oil?"*

Huh? This does sound yummy but an audience will never remember this and likely miss the main idea. ("Oh, it's a hamburger?!"). Like condiments, which are great in some conditions and ruin a meal at other times…use them selectively!

As a final thought on selecting language, remember that some concepts are universal but most are individual to speakers. Your speaking style should reflect who you are; you should always use **your authentic voice**… be yourself. This is the same idea when you are actually turning your good language into good oral communication.

Verbal Speaking Strategies

To deliver a speech is to be fully engaged with the ideas. This means you have to 'get into' your speech. Getting into your speech lets audiences get more out of what you have to say and affects your credibility in their eyes (Pearce & Conklin, 1971). What is commonly called **vocal variety** (or animation) is the process of infusing your ideas with life and with energy. Have you ever seen the movie *Ferris Bueller's Day Off* (or if not the full movie, the clip of teacher Ben Stein calling roll)? *"Beuller? Beuller? Beuller?"*

Can you imagine listening to that man give a 50-minute class lecture? Bleck! Do you want that monotone speaker to be you?! Absolutely not! Vocal animation means bringing the full range of expressiveness to your voice and can be accomplished through four basic strategies.

Projection

How loudly or how softly should you speak? Well, projection isn't about just being loud. Vocal **projection** is _supporting_ your voice so that you are speaking with enough volume and strength in voice to be heard easily by your entire audience. You should project enough to '*fill the space'* in which you are speaking as well as the number of people in the room (i.e., if you are in a small but full conference room then you will raise your voice over the noise; however, if you are in a practically empty hotel ballroom then you will not need to force out a space filling voice).

None of this means that your voice should boom to be heard down the hallway. Too many speakers think that good delivery means being loud. Just the opposite. Do you like to get yelled at? Do you want your boss to think that you are yelling at him? Noooooo! Too loud of a volume often wears your audience down or even make them hostile. The problem is that, if you project too softly, your voice can sound small and be easily ignored. To be sure you are striking a good balance, try to always talk in a space before you begin your presentation so you know how you sound in the space and can adjust.

Articulation and Enunciation

Are you an articulate person? Most folks actually don't know what this really means. **Articulation** is the precision with which we say the words that we speak. Slurring words, dropping syllables, or simply mumbling are some forms of poor articulation. Oddly enough, many associate being *articulate* with being smart. That association is a **connotation** (the sentiment attached to the word) rather than a **denotation** (the actual meaning of the word). Both notions help us to establish ethos in our speeches but they are not in fact the same.

When we do not speak clearly, we force the audience to work harder to understand the ideas we are trying to communication. This can be very frustrating to listeners who may opt to tune us out rather than having to struggle and guess at what we are saying. For instance, in the greater Philadelphia area the expression "yanaamean?" is difficult to decipher for the person not well versed in "Philly-speak." What this is actually saying is, "Do you know what I mean?" No listener should ever have to work hard to extract meaning from what you are saying. This does not mean that you have to be *overly* distinctive in your verbalization (you don't want to sound snobby, after all), but you should say the word clearly to help it be understood.

Articulation is often mistaken for enunciation. **Enunciation** in speech, according to the Oxford English Dictionary, is "the action of giving definite expression" (versus articulation, which is the utterance of the <u>distinct</u> elements of speech). In speaking, enunciation is the range that most of us experience when we are engaged in a lively conversation or friendly debate. Our inflection rises and falls, our pitch varies to reflect the emotional content, and we embrace verbal emphasis to stress key words or to convey different meanings. For example, all of the phrases below use the same words, but they don't *mean* the same thing:
   o   asking an expert (even in your company)
   o   Key sales figures in the fourth quarter (strict information)
   o   **Key** sales figures in the fourth quarter (these figures are vital)
   o   Key ***sales figures*** in the fourth quarter (the figures are from sales and not another division)
   o   Key sales figures in the ***fourth*** quarter (the figures represent only one period of the financial statement)

Pronunciation
Pronunciation is saying a word using the accepted and recognized standard. Mispronunciation can lead an audience to discount your ideas because it may seem like you don't really know what you are saying (poor

ethos!). If you are ever in doubt of how to say a word, find options that don't include: "er, I think that's how you say it." Consider:

- o asking an expert (even in your company)
- o checking online (most online dictionaries will verbalize the word so turn on your speakers and click on the icon; most smart phones can do this, too!)
- o selecting another word when possible and appropriate

Pausing

Making your ideas accessible requires silence as much as it requires words! **Pausing** is a brief verbal hesitation. "Brief" is the key word in this sentence. Dramatic pauses are for finding out who got kicked off of *Top Chef* but not for business presentations. An effective pause gives your listeners time to process what you are saying and, at the same time, it gives you time to think about what you are saying. Running sentences together robs both you and your listeners of much needed reflection time. Ineffective pausing can also be distracting. Vocalized pauses/ non-fluencies (such as "um," "like," "you know, "and so," as well as "or whatever") can also rob your listeners of necessary clarity. In both cases, a little bit is acceptable; a lot is unforgivable.

Presenting to an audience is not simply an oral or vocal exercise. When you speaking in front of others, *you communicate with your entire self!* Your whole body should work together to deliver your ideas to the audience.

Nonverbal Effectiveness

Do you know people who 'talk with their hands'? Is this you? If so, try to sit on your hands. It becomes difficult to speak! By embracing who you are as a physical speaker, you fully realize your speaking style. To do this, be sure to consider: your appearance, posture, facial expression, and gestures.

Appearance and Attire

Physically, before you arrive at the venue where you will speak, you've already made a very important delivery choice—how to dress. Your appearance communicates volumes before you even open your mouth (see Interviewing Chapter for specific examples). The rule of thumb for any interaction where you will be evaluated is that you shouldn't wear anything that can **distract** the audience from your purpose in your presentation! While appearance and attire are culturally and regionally specific, some general guidelines include:

- **Link to the Specific Industry**: A three-piece suit may work well for an attorney's office but could distract for a construction management office; select appropriate attire that offers the *best* look (not everyday wear) for your specific audience.

- **Dress One Level Above Your Audience**: Select appropriate attire that offers the *best* look (not everyday wear) for your specific audience. If you show up to an office of folks who typically wear khakis and button-downs wearing khakis and button-downs then the employer will assume that this is the best that you can do. They won't know that when a client comes in and the team wears suits that you have one and know when to wear it.

- **Be Groomed**: Iron clothes, bathe and smell fresh, shave anything unkempt and visible, remove flashy or peeling nail polish, and generally look as if you care about your personal appearance.

- **Look Like A First Interview, Not A First Date**: Keep the sexy at home during interviews and presentations. And don't show cleavage (or.. plumber) in a presentation setting. Be sure that what you have on fits rather than baggy or too tight clothes. While jeans may work once you are the CEO, when you are on your way up it's better to be overdressed rather than underdressed.

- **No Distracting Colors/ Patterns**: Hot pink, bright orange, bold stripes, and holiday patterns can be more memorable than you on clothes, accessories, ties,

- **Selective Jewelry and Accessories**: Avoid excessive, distracting, or potential to 'fidget with' jewelry whether you are a man or a woman. Understand that some industries and regions will expect limited and tasteful jewelry if any at all—and men should be more selective than women. Accessories such as large earrings, bangles, cuffs, pins, belt buckles, or headbands can draw focus away from your message. (If interviewing, avoid backpacks and opt for a professional carry-all).

- o **Limit… or wait, Don't Use Cologne Or Perfume**: A scent should linger on you but not be smelled before or after you enter the room and only slightly when leaning in.

- o **Don't Smoke**: Smoke becomes part of your attire—even if you didn't smoke in that particular outfit. Be aware and avoid being known for the lingering odor of tobacco.

Posture and Stance

One of the biggest distractions a speaker can create during a presentation is to have poor posture. **Posture** refers to how you carry yourself from the waist up. Good posture implies confidence, trustworthiness, and persuasive appeal. Lots of people have a very relaxed stance and might rest their weight on one hip; this is too lax for a presentation and can give off an unprofessional image. Keep your feet underneath your shoulders (guys, be aware that your shoulders may not be as wide as you hope… sorry!)

Your posture and stance can alter dramatically if you are speaking from a podium or a lectern on a table. When asked to speak in this setting then stand close enough to be able to reach your notes while standing far enough back so that the lectern does not become your <u>excuse</u> to lean rather than stand up straight (White, 1964). *Lecterns are sooo irresistible. Resist.* When you have a choice, come out from behind any tangible barrier between you and your audience!

Movement and Walking

Have you ever looked at the United States flag for more than 30 seconds? *Really* looked! Try it. Now look away. What you will see is an optical imprint of the flag. Yes, it makes an impact on your eyes but there is no connection with the actual object. The same thing happens for speakers who select to stand in one place for an extended time.

First, non-moving speakers have voice and voice alone to carry the audience connection. That's a lot of pressure! Second, these speakers lose connection with an audience who is both mentally and physically engaged in following the presentation. **HOLD! Before you take this as an excuse to wander aimlessly and never plant you feet, remember that movement should be used sparingly.** Yes, moving into your audience's space and in sync with your verbal transitions can captivate a group, but constant movement (even within a small spot) will keep attention on your feet rather than your message.

Third, movement includes moving to a close physical proximity to your audience. Again, if you are far away then your voice much reach further and do more. Movement is like physical intimacy with new acquaintances. If you keep really far away, they may think that something is wrong with them (or you!). If you get way up in their grill then they may think you are kinda creepy. There *is* a happy medium. (hint: Take note of the location of the previous presenter. When you begin to present, take one step closer to the audience to help imply a greater level of intimacy and lack of nerves!)

Gestures
Good physical delivery means incorporating meaningful gestures. **Gestures**, or the movement of part of the body such as a hand or head, to express an idea or meaning, are considered so important that they have been called co-verbal, on equal footing with the words we use (Wachsmuth, 2006). In fact, gestures can alter how an audience interprets our message (McNeill, Cassell, & McCullough, 1994).

Yet, for some reason, when we get in front of an audience, these very useful appendages that we have attached to our shoulders (arms with hands!) become alien objects that we have no idea how to use. We try to hide them behind our backs, clasp them in front of us like a fig leaf, jam them into our pockets, turn them into hair rollers, or turn them into word rollers to help us pull the words out of our mouths. Gesturing constantly can be worse than not gesturing at all because gestures are such a powerful means of communication (Maricchiolo, et. al, 2009). Therefore, you may want to follow a couple of basic guidelines:

- o **Keep It Simple**: A few gestures go a long way—they should emphasize *key* ideas, not every idea.
- o **Avoid Repetitive Mannerisms**: An overused gesture will render all of your gestures meaningless and trivial.
- o **Avoid Distracting Mannerisms**: Eyes are drown to movement so stay away from gestures that get more attention that your message

For those who don't know what to do with your hands while talking, remember that you should not force yourself to behave in a way that is foreign to you. If you are comfortable gesturing—do it! If you are not, simply avoid doing anything distracting. Drop your hands to the side and hold (not wave around) your note page with one hand.

Facial Expressions

As you stand in front of your audience, you are literally 'facing' your listeners. Your face speaks volumes about your message and how you feel about your message—what is on your face will also influence how your *listeners* feel about the message, too (Sato & Yoshikawa, 2007). Since this is the case, it is crucial that you do not look like you are in pain while you speak!

Your face should mirror the emotional content of what it is that you are saying. If you are talking about something sad, don't smile… that weird (and even disturbing). If you are excitedly promoting a product then your face should *show* enthusiasm. If you face connects to the information, it is as if you are adding another visual aid to your talk that can help with audience understanding. Moreover, if you have engaging facial expressions, your audience will look you in the eyes!

Eye Contact

Strong **eye contact**, or the act of looking directly into one another's eyes, is essential to an effective presentation. In fact, some presentation scholars will suggest that you look at every individual in the eyes for 3 to 5 seconds per person. Ok… so let's think about this. Try to go up to even a person that you know and make direct eye contact for (one thousand one, one thousand two, one thousand three). Uh, creepy! That's just too long.

The key is to have sustained and substantial eye contact long enough to create a <u>connection</u>.

The best guideline for eye contact is to present a complete thought to an individual before moving on to someone else. Remember the communication model about feedback? This is your time to send a complete thought and then wait for feedback! Because you are most likely, in a business setting, to be speaking extemporaneously—feedback will allow you to make changes as you move through your talk to suit the needs of the audience. If you are looking at your audience and they have the expression of "what the heck is she talking about?" on their faces, you can rephrase, clarify, and adjust as needed.

Strong eye contact will:
1. help you relax as a speaker
2. have a series of 'mini-conversations' with members of your audience
3. help you build a bond with the audience
4. acquire feedback

If you are speaking to a large audience (e.g., a company retreat or a share holders meeting) then eye contact with every person is impossible, however, you still want to appear to connect with as many people as possible. The means of doing this is through the use of anchors. **Anchors** are select individuals spread out in a large space with whom you make eye contact (i.e., one person in the front middle, another person in the back left, a person in the back right). You can select one anchor in a group of 10-20 people and connect with him or her. The people around that person will also feel as if you have connected with them (Bill Clinton uses this trick!).

If you are speaking and you do not receive feedback from an audience member (we've all be given the… deadpan stare), don't belabor the point. Move on. Come back to that audience member for another idea and see if you connect. If you spend all of your time with one person then the rest of the audience will feel neglected and your ethos will diminish as they seeing you losing your mastery of the situation.

Considering Your Space

What is that situation? Where are you speaking? Where do you look? Well, it depends on the space. Adapting to your space and (more importantly) adapting your space *to you* will help you best connect with your audience.

Every space is different—each offering its own set of opportunities that can be exploited as well as its own set of limitations that you must overcome. The more you know about the venue in which you will be speaking, the better you can tailor your presentation to take full advantage. For example, consider speaking in a room next to cheerleading tryouts for a local professional football team, consider speaking in a room where the technology is only as fancy as a flip chart when you have painstakingly designed effective PowerPoint slides, consider that <u>any</u> speaking setting will not be perfect and that perfect is never our goal.

Effective speakers manipulate their presentations to meet the needs of their rhetorical situation which includes the speaker, the audience, the constraints, and the environment. Therefore, you must consider as part of that environment (and the constraints) elements. While many of these were discussed in the Leading and Meeting chapter, remember to consider:

1. The size of the space
2. The shape of the space
3. The acoustics of the space
4. The accessibility of the space
5. Lighting and sound options
6. Technology options
7. Sources of ambient noise
8. Room temperature (and ability to adjust that temperature)
9. Seating arrangements and whether or not seating is flexible or stationary
10. The amount of room you have for your presentation
11. Whether or not there is a lectern
12. Available storage (to stow items out of sight until you need them)

While this list is not all-inclusive, it gives you an idea of some of the variables that effect what is possible or not possible for your presentation in a particular venue. You will need to make sure that you <u>arrive at the room early</u> and adjust your speech to the constraints of these elements. If you arrange your room and the previous speaker or group changes what you need, do NOT let their arrangements stand. Own your room! Move their notes out of the way (courteously) and reset the room as <u>you</u> need it or… as your group needs it.

Presenting With a Group

Wouldn't it be nice if we never had to rely on anyone else to achieve any of our goals? If we were alone all of the time with no one off whom we could bounce ideas, share the work load, brainstorm, and bond? Ok, group work can have its problems but it also has numerous benefits (see Chapter Four). What's more…. group work and presentations are an almost inevitable part of business.

When you are presenting in a group, coordination is the key. You will need to pay special attention to details in order to make sure that your presentation is cohesive, not just a series of individual presentations that happen to be on related topics. To make this happen, in addition to practicing separately (yes, still do this!), you should also run through the entire presentation as a group to make sure the individual parts flow together smoothly.

Group Organization

Designate one person to be the presentation's coordinator—much like an administrator for the group. It can be tough in our careers to give power over to another person, especially an equal but this is necessary to make sure that you *all* look good in the end. Create a plan together, assign individuals their own research and specialty areas to research (alone or as two or three), and then send information to the coordinator so that this person can assure a cohesive look (as in for visuals) and cohesive language.

Each presentation should also have a strong structure—again, to be one presentation rather than several concurrent talks. One person may be assigned to be the emcee of the talk by verbalizing all structural elements and even introducing and concluding the talk or running the questions section (He or she should not have more *prominence* than those people offering the substance of the talk).

Group Language

If you handed your speech to a colleague and asked that he or she deliver the second main point, the audience might wonder who this person is and why he or she is jumping up in the middle. Audiences need clarity and group presentations ask for additional verbal clarity. Offer it to them! Include all of the following language in your presentations with others:

- o **Full Names**: After your introduction, be sure to tell folks who is standing there. Give full names (and even areas of specialty or position titles).

- o **Group Preview**: When previewing your talk, which happens especially in group presentations, you will want to give first names associated with each coverage area (e.g., *"John will layout the needs that you have identified for us, Marcy and Greg will then go over possible options to satisfy those needs, Tom will introduce a new product, and I, Sally, will talk about the steps available to you."*).

- o **Speech and Group Oriented Transitions**: Never "hand it over" to the next presenter. Ugh. This is not professional. Have the person that is stating your transitions, just as they would be in an individual speech, add in your names (e.g., *"As you can see, the financial fraud that Karen discussed is crippling our company, but, with keen attention to details through regular audits, we can change our financial future. Lynn will tell us how."*)

- o **Review**: Look back using the names of who talked about what.

- o **Q&A**: While one person should 'run' your Question and Answer session, it is important for ethos that each team member be able to interject answers. The coordinator should ask them to do so (e.g., "Finley is our sales executive. Finely, would you like to address that question?").

If your audience knows each of your names then they are more likely to connect with you than with others… think of the benefit of this for sales presentations!

Group Look and Movement

You should also be aware of how you *appear* as a unit! Yes, this means coordinating your attire— not matching! You are not the Rockettes or a boy band; you are professionals who should all appear to have the same level of professional appearance without wearing the same outfits (i.e., all black pants and red button down shirts… perhaps a bit over the top and distracting).

With group presentations you should do a dress rehearsal together. Without even thinking about it, did three of you wear pale blue shirts and one person showed up in yellow? Did you all wear shades of green but, yuck, some of them clash? Will the audience see four people in suits and two people in khaki slacks with polo shirts? All of these things would visually distract an audience—and you can't afford that in business.

Similarly, you and your whole team should have coordinated movements (Again, not the Rockettes.). There are a few useful strategies for coordinating movement in a group speech:

o **Spread Out, Select and Move to Speaking Areas**: Many groups will come into a room and flank either side of the PowerPoint projector screen. This looks awkward and ill planned. They then will walk up in front of the slides when speaking and back to their designated spot when finished. You might be wondering, *"Where else should we stand?"* Good question. Consider your space. Would it work to have the first main point speaker begin while in the back of the large auditorium and have the audience turn to become physically involved? If you can be unique without distraction then you stand out. Some presenters might wish to sit until it is their time to speak. Again, figure out if this will work and not distract.

o **Give One Another Full Attention**: Your audience is only as interested in your team members as you are! Reviewing your notes to make sure you're ready is important; so, do it before the group starts! If group members look inattentive during one another's presentations, why should the audience be attentive?

o **Control Facial Expressions and Distractions**: Someone messed up—and we all know it because your face looks so appalled that you might actually pass out! Not a good choice in a group presentation. You may as well be rifling through your briefcase or getting up and leaving the room. Avoid drawing attention to anyone but the speaker. Do not read your own notes, shift in your seat, make audible comments, or pull away from the speaker. Give attention to that person because if you can't be bothered, why should the audience?

o **Be Polite with Necessary Interruptions**: Someone messed up. You keep your face attentive and respectful but in your mind you are thinking, "Oh no! He just gave them the wrong sales figures!" Don't panic—but also don't just let it go. At the end, you may have lost the client because someone gave the wrong details. Instead, **_politely_** interrupt and offer a change. (e.g., "Tom. I do apologize for interrupting but just noticed that we may have pulled up the wrong figures for last year. Can I just shift slides for you?"). Notice the use of "we" rather than the blame of "you." If you don't work together, you all end up looking bad. This tactic also works well with nervous speakers who tend to go over time (e.g., "Mary. I'm so sorry to interrupt but noticed that we are limited in time. Can I distribute those handouts for you?").

Ultimately, your physical and verbal delivery, whether it is individually or in a group, should be relaxed and engaged. It should connect to the audience and show that you are comfortable enough to have an organized conversation but informed enough to have strong ideas that you express well and without distraction. To get there … practice, practice, practice.

PRACTICING FOR EFFECTIVENESS

Practice makes better (Not perfect – remember?). If someone told you that practice makes perfect then they were both wrong and setting you up for failure. We have already talked about the notion of perfection and you know that you can be extremely effective without being perfect. So? Let it go and get down to practicing for *effectiveness*!

When you practice your speech you should have **two key goals** in mind...

Become One with the Ideas

Because you are speaking extemporaneously, you won't be memorizing your speech word for word. So, you need to practice to make sure you are comfortable with phrasing ideas in the moment. This should sound like a conversation that you are having with a peer about a subject that you know like the back of your hand. Try out different language choices as you practice. As you practice, you will settle into wording that is vivid and fluent without having to commit to specific words or be completely dependent on notes.

The idea here is to reduce your notes as you become comfortable with the flow of the ideas in the speech. As you move from session to session, cut your notes down. By your final practice (yes, there should be more than one and even more than three practice sessions!), you should be able to use that key word outline to jog your memory of the order of stories and data that you could not know better. If you find that you are bound to your notes, you need to keep practicing.

Go Beyond Visualization

As you started this speech, you visualized. You thought of yourself doing everything right—and of any issues that could go wrong and how you would fix them. This was the **self-fulfilling prophecy** that means that if you believe *it*, that *it* is more likely to happen (Merton, 1948). Now that you have crafted every element of your presentation, you need to see how it actually *is* done and adjust to those discovered needs.

These final sessions of practice are best done in front of an audience rather than in isolation (Smith & Frymier, 2006). You should run full 'dress rehearsals.' Yup, this means putting on the shoes and the suit (or other appropriate attire) so that what you are wearing is not a distraction for you as you address your important audience. You should also practice every element of your *technical* presentation.

Your actual, day-of presentation is not the time to discover you have technical difficulties. The Visual Aids Chapter (see Chapter 8) will talk you through the elements of visual aid creation and delivery but if you have not practiced that delivery then you may as well guess as to what will happen.

Your audience will not care why your planned presentation went sour. They will simply assume that you are not capable. Practicing your speech fully can let you know where the potential glitches are so you can avoid them or, if they are unavoidable, you can develop a contingency plan. NO presentation ever goes exactly as planned—some go better! What matters is how you handle whatever happens *during* your presentation.

YOU ARE READY!

You are going to see a lot of job advertisements in your life. You may apply to jobs based on these ads or even write them yourself. In case after case, these advertised jobs will want—expect—good communication skills (Morreale, 2001; Morreale & Pearson, 2008; North & Worth, 1996). Can you do it? Well, with practice you can and will get better. You must put yourself in the place to try, flop, try again, get better, get really better, and ultimately, be able to advertise your own fabulous communication skills. With practice, you may even find that you enjoy making presentations! Moreover, if you want to become a hot commodity— and who doesn't?—you will want to get past any reluctance you may feel and embrace your ability to connect to audiences. Remember, we do not have to be perfect but we do strive to be effective!

Chapter Eight
Aiding Business Presentations with Visuals

CONNECTION AS THE FOUNDATION

If you are giving a presentation in any business setting, it is not only likely that you will <u>use</u> a visual aid but that it will be *expected*. In fact, we have become a society that is both drawn and attached to visual support (Genard, 2005). We want handouts and PowerPoint® slides and graphs and charts—and anything that impresses and wows our audience. The problem, of course, is that using a visual aid is not always a good choice. Almost every expert in public speaking will tell you tell that visual aids can distract the audience (Grice & Skinner, 2007; Lucas,1992; Zarefsky, 2004), hurt audience connections (Tufte, 2003, 2006), or even inhibit your audiences' abilities to understand or retain your messages (Carroll, 2007)! So, if they are so bad, why use them? Good question.

We use visual aids because they have the ability to engage your audience and increase both comprehension and retention (Heap, Burill, Dewey, & MacDonald, 1994; Rotman, 2009). You will certainly find that using visuals can be an effective tool for when your role is to 'present' information in a formal way (such as a CEO giving annual report information to stockholders, a saleswoman outlining product benefits to a potential client, or even an in-house demonstration of your team's current work product), but visuals are even useful when you are simply trying to help a small groupto understand your point in an informal setting. As professional trainer Ethan Rotman (2009) reminds us, "*The potential of visual aids is great, yet we often ignore this tool with small groups such as at staff meetings*" (p. 32).

The application of visual aids in specific industries will differ because each group will have distinct norms about what is appropriate and what is not. Lawyers and those in advertising will typically avoid the technological approach of PowerPoint®or Keynote®or Prezi®presentations, but financiers and teachers will actively employ each. Industries will decide not only what kind of aids should be used, but also what elements can be on them. It is your job to understand what tool to use and then how to use that tool effectively (aha… we're back to the sending and receiving of messages… and audience analysis!).

You don't always have to use a visual aid but, when you do, it is your job to ensure that you have selected the appropriate aid, are using it in the correct setting, in the correct manner, and for the correct audience. It's tricky business (no pun intended), but appropriate visual aid use is a trained skill.

A Communication Model: Aristotle?

Aristotle's teachings are the basis of much of what we use to develop modern speeches. It almost seems strange that the words of someone who lived in ancient Greece would still be part of our modern day teachings – especially in the development of modern day visual aids. And yet, his direction is crucial in this area.

Consider our discussion from earlier chapters in this text that Aristotle wanted our speeches to contain:
- **Ethos**: which means that our information should be of the highest quality and credibility
- **Logos**: which means that our information should be organized in a manner that supports our argument and makes sense to the audience
- **Pathos**: which means that what we present should have emotional resonance, or connection, with our audience

In each of these elements (which he called the "**3 Appeals**"), Aristotle told us to make what we say, show, and do *about our audience*. Can you imagine if we did not use these standards in visuals? What if our audience didn't think that our PowerPointÒ slides were of high quality? What if our posters were disorganized and difficult to follow? Imagine that we showed a video that repulsed the audience so much that they couldn't listen to another word! Would you be in trouble? Absolutely!

Visual aids communicate. Following communication guidelines helps your aids to communicate well. So, when considering any of the information in this chapters—know that considering Aristotle's appeals and, thus, your audience, will help you to determine what should be on your aids and if you need them at all.

For This Audience – At This Time

Have you ever been to a concert where the singer came out onto the stage and shouted, "What's up…" and then the wrong city?! Britney Spears and Lady Gaga both did it in 2009. Kid Cudi got booed in 2010 for forgetting what city he was in when he performed at SXSW in Austin. The Alice in Chains lead singer got the city wrong three times during a concert in Alabama. And the list goes on. The response was the same each time. The audience feels like they are not meaningful to the performer.

When you present with visuals that are not linked to your audience, you are that singer who hollers, "What's up, New York?!" when you are at a venue in Philly. Therefore, it is just as essential for you to make a visual connection with your audienceas well as a verbal one. How so? By representing your actual audience, the one who will be sitting in front of you, on your visual aids. This can happen in a number of ways—and perhaps even all of these methods together if the setting calls for them:
- Put the name of your audience your visuals (e.g., the name of the university and class to which you are speaking, the name and logo of the company whose business you want, etc.)
- Show images from that group (e.g., people in the class, members of the group, pictures showing events or ideas that have been part of your discussions with them)
- Keep the "feel" of your slides consistent with that of your audience (i.e., if their corporate image is relaxed and laid back like Disney or

Ben & Jerry's then have your visuals match that *tone*—just like a bank or medical organization might have a more conservative tone or feel to match their corporate image)

Some may argue that it is not necessary to have your visuals actually list the name of your audience on them. That can be true. Similarly, a singer can walk out onto stage and just perform without ever stating the name of the city. The performance may be fine... but the connection is lacking. Even rock stars know that acknowledging the exact audience in front of you seals the deal!

VISUAL STRATEGIES

There are about as many visuals available to you as there are arguments that you can make. **Visual aids** are just that—they are *visuals* that *aid* a presentation or talk. If we were to send out our slides on their own, then these would not be visual aids—they would be the actual presentation (and some visual aid software can be used to create printed or emailed stand alone graphic information). Images or visuals that go out alone would need to convey all of the information necessary without relying on you to speak, explain, or connect them to an idea. Instead of helping to clarify your argument, they would have to both make it and explain it. Whereas, visual aids will fulfill only a supporting role.

Is there a time for visuals without a talk... indeed! Think of the online Flash presentation of images that your college or university has on its homepage. Think of those beautiful coffee table books that you have flipped through at someone's home. Think of every wedding that you have been to where someone has put together a slideshow of the bride and groom from babies through present day (groan! Alright, yeah, they can be cute.) These visuals convey messages on their own that are determined by the audience rather than the speaker. They do not need to follow the guidelines described here because they are not serving the same function. When, however, you are giving a talk and using visuals to help illuminate the areas of your talk or connect with your audience, the guidelines that are discussed below will help you to have your aids serve their function well!

Usage Overview

As noted above (and, yes, we are almost beating a dead horse at this point), not every talk needs an aid. Before deciding what visual aids to use, your first decision must be whether or not you need them. If you do not have information that will be better explained by the use of a visual aid – then do not use a visual aid. (It's like that person who puts every animation and every sound on all of his or her PowerPointÒ slides. Just because you *can* doesn't mean that you *should*!)

At the same time, do not use visual aids to hide a poor verbal presentation. Too many speakers think that if they spend all of their time on amazing visuals that these supplements will 'sell' the talk. They won't. If your presentation is lacking then audience will notice and attribute you with low ethos or credibility. Spend most of your time on your talk and then look to see what *needs* visual support. This will help you to make strategic time choices and, ultimately, have a better presentations. In deciding what to use, consult the following checklist.

Your "To Use or Not To Use" Checklist:

- Will I <u>need</u> aids at all?
- If I have aids, how few can I use to make my point?
- What specific arguments, ideas, or examples would require a visual?
- What medium (or type) of visual would be best?
- Is the medium that I want available (i.e., if I want to use slides can I get my hands on a projector?)
- Who is my audience?
- What is the set up of the room?

Without knowing the content of your message, the audience, and the environment (basically, all of the components of your rhetorical situation), it is impossible to give you specific details on what you should use for your exact presentation. Instead, the information here is an overview that will help you to make good choices about visual aid use when the time comes for your to select what to use, how to design your aids, and how to present them.

If you have decided that visual will help you to make your point, then you will need to know the **Four Golden Rules** of visual aid use:

1. **Keep visuals simple**
2. **Keep the number of visuals reasonable**
3. **Have someone else proof read your aids**
4. **Bring back-ups**

If you follow these golden rules then you are well on your way to using visual aids that will be effective support for your talk.

All Visuals Can Distract

As a student, have you been in a classroom situation where the instructor showed a video that was, well, seriously out of date? The clothing on the people is now considered 'bad fashion' and the hairstyles are just laughable. And, what if they use words like "rad" and "fer sure"? You start to focus far more on the quality of the video than the message it wants to send. Visual aids need to avoid elements of distraction and they will distract if they:
- Draw away from your point
- Becomewhat is remembered (rather than the message)
- Disconnect you from your audience

The only way to avoid distractions is to make strategic choices with both your medium and content such that you keep the focus on <u>you</u> and retain the purpose of your visual aids!

Avoiding the "Boomerang Effect"

Visual aids can actually do more bad than good. This kind of result in persuasion is called the **boomerang effect**, which refers to ideas, arguments, or visuals that unintentionally encourage audience members to do the opposite of what you want – or do nothing at all.

There is interesting research about how the boomerang effect plays out in business contexts - especially during efforts to persuade the public. Man and Hill (1984) looked at these effects within consumer research. They specifically looked at how advertisers attempt to get the public to buy products; and they found that some campaigns that had a positive influence would actually dissuade audiences from taking the desired action when they were combined with other positive campaigns! Think of it like food… "I like this and I like that… but when I eat them together – YUCK! I don't want to eat either one of them ever again." The same thing happens in persuasion and with visual aids. One intense picture can make a point, but a few more makes us ignore your side altogether.

Too many situations give us the opportunity to shoot ourselves in the foot. Your job is to always consider *both* sides of a visual's possible emotional impact!

Content vs. Medium

Consideration of visual aids involves strategic planning of not only the type of aid, but also what is on it. This is the difference between the **medium** and the **content**. If you will recall, Chapter One discusses communication models that have both medium and content. *The medium is the channel where as the content is the message. They are different.* You are not limited to sending your message through one channel. You can choose your medium along with your content. Thus, consider that as you add the visual aid medium to your oral presentations, you must consider what they contain just as much as deciding what type of visual to use—low-tech, high-tech, or both!

Visual Content

When we think of visual aids, it's easy to imagine presentation slide shows, handouts, or even flip charts (yup – these are still getting heavy in lots of business settings). But, before you even begin to think about how to display an image or element, it is crucial to consider what it is that you might wish to display.

Does your audience need to see a graph of dipping sales figures? Would a picture of the needy residents sway investors to give more money to a women's shelter? Can you best demonstrate your strategies for effective product distribution with a map of production sites across the country? These are the questions that will allow you to "show" your information in the best way.

Content: The Stuff that Goes on Aids

You have a plethora of options by which you can demonstrate your ideas to your audience. You might choose a graph or a picture or even a few words (which are also "visual" when displayed). Each of these has its own intricate design elements that you should consider as you use them.

Text and Font

Words? Yes, words will be a part of your visual aids. They are useful in helping audiences to follow the organization of your talk and to highlight key elements. When selecting words for any visual, you should be guided by what will help you to achieve your purpose and not distract.

Font Typeface: If you are driving down the road, take a look at a traffic sign. Does it use Times New Roman font? Likely not. Most traffic or road signs that use text will use the text that takes the least amount of time for our brains to process. These fonts tend to be **sans serif**.

Serifs are the little 'feet' or hanging chads at the bottom of letters. If it has them then it is a **serif font**. If it does not then it is "without" or **sans serif**. The feet on serif fonts work to guide the eye from letter to letter and have been thought to best engage readers in a written text. Thus, when you open up a new document and begin to type, you will likely see:

Cambria (on a Mac), or

Times New Roman (on a PC).

These font typefaces are those that a reader can mull over. They tend to take longer to absorb, which is great if you have time to read. Other serif fonts include:

Baskerville
Garamond
Century
Lucida

When you open up a PowerPoint® slide show and begin to type, your words will likely be displayed in the sans serif (or 'without feet') typeface:
Calibri (Body)

This font can be processed quickly so that those looking at words on a projection can then return their focus quickly to a speaker. Other sans serif fonts include:
Tahoma
Arial
Lucida Grande
Century Gothic
(Note: the best list of serif and san fonts online is through Wikipedia. Yes, not the best reference but, upon last check, most of those listed were either sans serif or without *distinct* serifs).

Font Style: If you have your font typeface chosen, you should next consider the style of font that you would like to use. By font style, we are referring to the bold, underline, capitalization, sizing, or other modes of altering the appearance of a font to add emphasis.

Consider the difference between the following:

Visuals can be enhanced by the use of text. (century gothic)
Visuals can be enhanced by the use of text. (bolded)
<u>Visuals can be enhanced by the use of text.</u> (underlined)
Visuals can be enhanced by the use of text. (italicized)

Visuals can use text. (font size 8)
Visuals can use text. (font size 10)
Visuals can use text. (font size 12)
Visuals can use text. (font size 14)
Visuals can use text. (font size 16)
Visuals can use text. (font size 18)
Visuals can use text. (font size 20)

Which is easier to read and in what context? Which one draws the eye? What style gives what impression—as a title, emphasis, or even to draw your attention? Similarly, the capitalization of a font can change its impact.

New Yorkers don't like to be yelled at!
NEW YORKERS DON'T LIKE TO BE YELLED AT!

New York Daily News writers, Andrew Phillips and Pete Donohue (September 20, 2010) describe in their article, *New Yorkers outraged as bureaucrats order city to change lettering on every single street sign*, how all New York city signs (that have always been in all caps) will have to be changed to sentence case style in order to meet federal guidelines. The cost to the city will be $27.5 million. Ouch!

Wait. Does this mean that New Yorkers don't want to get yelled at… or that they want to be able to yell?

Font Location: Much like a street sign has to be placed where it will draw the eye of a driver, text on a visual aid should be laid out such that it guides the eye of the audience. You should know where to look first and then in what direction to look after that.

Slide	Handout
	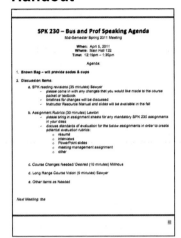

Numbers

Numbers are the reason that many visual aids exist. Presenters want an audience to not only hear the numbers but to absorb them and reflect on them. Visual aids are an excellent way to do this.

Because numbers in visual will be typed out, their use should follow all of the same guidelines as with text. Make them big enough to be seen, in a legible font, and guide the eye from one number to another. It can help to make your point about a 50% drop in revenue simply by having a huge 50% flash on the screen behind you. Let folks take that in for a minute and see if they all gasp!

Visual aids, however, are not the place to number dump. In fact, a descriptive visual or image can actually explain numbers without the need of the numbers themselves (Garcia-Retamero & Galesic, 2010). Imagine that your company is facing an annual loss of 50% revenue—this is the same amount of money that could be used to (alright… these are the pictures that you would show) build a brand new on-site state of the art gym, offer company-wide day care, or provide all employees with another week of vacation. Audiences may not remember a big **50%** on a poster

– but they will remember that gorgeous gym or other visual links. So, it is important to consider when and how to use numbers.

Most often you will not have a number on a visual aid all by itself but you will guide the audience's eyes by putting your numbers into a format such as a chart or table…

Charts, Diagrams, and Tables

Charts, graphs, diagrams, and tables are means of organizing data into a visual form. There are many different kinds of charts (pie, line, bar, graph, flow, organizational, etc.). Some industries even have charts that are specific to the type of work that they do such as open-high-low-close chart (investor and financial industries), stock (financial industries), Gantt chart (construction industry), and more. Most industry specific charts have standard settings in PowerPoint® software.

Chart Options in PowerPoint (for PCs)

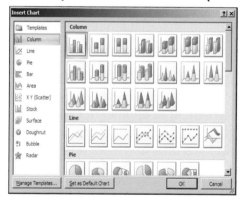

Selection of Chart Options in PowerPoint (for Macs)

Diagram

Have you ever tried to put together furniture that you bought at IKEA? Can you imagine trying to figure out what all those little metal pieces and wood blocks are for without the diagram of the stick figures putting it together? Scary.

Diagrams are visual representations of an actual thing. These representations are useful when a verbal or written explanation will not capture the complexity and intricacies of the object. They also help when intercultural or language barriers may make the selection of terms difficult.

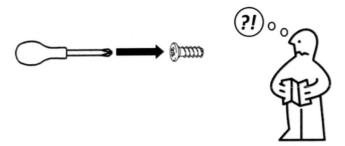

Table

A more linear representation of numbers can come in the form of a table. **Tables** are used to demonstrate categories and allow for comparison. While you may wish

Sales 2009	Sales 2010	Sales 2011	Sales 2012
6,334, 291	5,924, 834	3,778, 469	6,334, 291
+ 6%	+ 4%	- 3%	+/- ? %

to use a line graph to show decreasing sales over time, a table can allow you to list out those numbers next to each other so that we see actual figures and how they relate to one another.

Graphics and Illustrations

When you use the computer to draw or create visual depictions for you then you are using graphics. When you display a hand-rendering of an objection, place, person, or thing then you are showing an illustration. Both can be useful to demonstrate a fully-fleshed out idea to an audience without having to take or find a picture of the item. For instance, if you are talking to a group of new employees about the fantastic healthy options in the work cafeteria then you don't have to run down at lunch to take pictures but can insert a computer graphic or even (if you have the skill) draw an image to display.

Computer Graphic

Illustration

Images (Pictures)

Not liking these images? Sometimes graphic or drawn objects can have less appeal and less clarity than the real thing. Certainly a picture of an apple would leave no doubt as to the identity of the object whereas the fruit tray above may illustrate an apple… or is it a California Holly, a Red Pear, or perhaps a Quince?

Actual pictures give the most professional appeal to your visuals with the least amount of room for interpretation.

Dog?

Dog!

Are image-based aids with NO text a good idea? Well, they can be. The result of picture-based visual communication is improved learning and recall. Levie and Lentz (1982) looked at 46 experiments comparing pictures included with text, or text used alone, and found that 45 of the studies—all but one—showed that including pictures improved memory or comprehension. In one case, a group following directions that were given in the form of text illustrated with diagrams did an amazing 323% better than a group following the same directions without the illustrations. WOW! What we learn from this is that showing people meaningful, content-based visuals, as opposed to text alone, lessens their cognitive exertion (how hard their brains have to work) and improves overall experience (Chabris & Kosslyn, 2005).

You may at this point want to drown your audience in visual support—but be careful! Most research states that, in terms of audience engagement and retention... less is more! (see: Beaver, 2007).

Color

Your last consideration of visual content must be color. How can color be used to help you illustrate a point? Color can help to make your images and visuals truly engage the viewer. Color printing has always been expensive but now with the use of slide presentation software and website creation or inexpensive color copies, you have the ability to make things pop in useful and appealing ways. Just be sure that you are not detracting from the purpose of the visual. Color can also distract. Be sure to do the "is that ugly?" check before you finalize your visuals.

Does this pass the "is that ugly?" check?

Naaaah. Make some adjustments!

Sound

Whizzzzzzz! Bang! Pop! Click-click-click. It is possible to have visual aids be also auditory aids. Movies and audio files enable presenters to have images that not only move but also communicate for us. Ah—there's the rub. Noises send messages as much as visuals and your verbal presentation. When your presentation begins with a soft rendition of Cee

Lo Green's "Forget You"—be sure that you have downloaded the correct version and that no one is mistaking the lyrics. Too much sound, the wrong sound, distracting or confusing sound, and sound that gets the focus over your message are all problematic.

The question now is, "since I know what I want to display, what should I put it on?" This is when we consider mediums.

Visual Mediums

Before considering what type of software or visual medium to use, you really must consider what it is that you want to communicate and the visual content that will be needed to help you. Will you need full sentences, paragraphs, or even pages? Is it useful to show only key words? Is your message hinging on the ability to demonstrate exactly how something will look in a three-dimensional form? These are key questions! The type of visual aid medium that you choose will be guided by your answers.

Hopefully, the above section helped you to answer these questions. Once you have then you can now determine the **medium** (or presentation device) that will best show off your content. Your options include mediums with all the high-tech bells and whistles… and several that are both effective and basic.

Low vs. High Tech Mediums

There are essentially just two types of visual aid mediums – the low-tech and the high-tech. Most people, when imagining visual aid mediums, will immediately think of high tech mediums such as PowerPoint® or Prezi® or websites. Alas, you might be surprised to find that you have had more exposure to low-tech mediums and will likely use these more than any other type. The key is knowing which type is best suited for you, your audience, and your message.

Think of it this way: what is better than walking into a class or a meeting and seeing a huge projection screen that suddenly has images scrolling by in a Flash movie slideshow, bright and colorful fast-moving graphics as well as booming sound? A handout! OK, this may have confused you. Why on earth would anyone select a low-tech option when a high-tech visual option is available? That's easy. It is because low and high technology visual aids serve different purposes – and in many instances low-tech aids are more suited to your purpose.

Low technology, for our purposes, refers to any visual that does not use computer-generated elements and/or modern computer facilitated devices. Simply put, low-tech is referring:

1. **Handouts**
2. **Overheads/transparencies**
3. **Models**
4. **Whiteboards and chalkboards**
5. **Flip charts/posters**
6. **Picture slides**

These types of aids have numerous benefits individually, but also as a category. First, low-tech is cheaper! Low-tech products are typically far less expensive than high tech aids. Some conference set-ups will charge hundreds of dollars for a few hours of web connectivity, and even more to hook you up to their in-house speakers or projector system. Low-tech visuals are typically created off-site and brought in with little expense. In addition, low-tech aids are typically less attention-grabbing. Yes, this can be a good thing. If the aid does not become the focus of your presentation then your message have that focus, which is as it should be.

As you can see, low-tech visuals are actually easy to create and quite an effective means of connecting to your audience. If this is the case, why spend the time and money implementing high-tech visuals? It's simple. As mentioned above, all visuals have their own unique purpose with both benefits and detriments. If you have the skills, equipment, and the right rhetorical situation in which to use high-tech visuals then these are a fantastic means of engaging your listeners!

High technology, for our purposes, refers to any visual that is generated through or delivered to an audience using contemporary computer equipment or machinery. This include elements such as:

1. **PowerPoint® and Keynote®**
2. **Web or Internet Use**
3. **Video/Movie/Audio Visuals**
4. **Smartboards/ IWBs**

High-tech visuals have the pizzazz that low-tech visuals just don't. They offer color, movement, sound, and a capacity to change on the fly. You can't distribute a handout and then have it magically become something else when the audience asks you to discuss the third idea before the first one. A high-tech visual can do just that. It can change and adapt as you go.

Let us not forget that high-tech visuals have their own set of unique complications. The trick is not to use them just because you can and to remember to avoid the pitfalls.

Do and Do Not (Use Strategies)

Do not show a PowerPoint® presentation in a bright room. Do give a handout as you talk. Do not show a model to a middle to large size audience. Do spend more time on your presentation than your visuals. Selecting a visual medium is all about understanding the purpose of each type along with what to do and not to do with them!

Handouts (low-tech)

Handouts are detailed versions of visual information available to audiences at an individual level. Handouts can contain only images, only text, or a combination of both. Given this view of handouts, it would almost seem that they do not qualify as visual aids. In fact, they can be completely text and no images, which would fly in the face of our visual aids definition. Well, not quite.

Handouts are an offering of *visual support* for a presentation even in the form of text visuals. Let's say that you are speaking

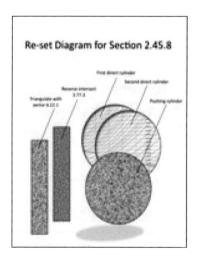

about the rules of visual aids to an audience and you want them to know the Four Golden Rules (mentioned above), you could show them on a presentation slide or give a handout that they could keep and reference later!

Like any other visual support—handouts must be offered at the time where their support is needed (Rotman, 2008). Some presenters (Heath, 2009) will tell you to never give handouts during your speech because it will interrupt your flow and draw audience attention away from your message. The choice for when to offer handouts is ultimately yours. If the handout outlines information being discussed in the middle of your talk and would help the audience to follow along, by all means, distribute away! If, however, your handouts summarize your talk to help audience members recall details at a later date… hold off the handing out until the end.

Handout Hints

Do	Do Not
- provide when audiences need to refer to information at their own pace - do include information referencing your specific talk (e.g., your name, topic, and contact info) - include significant white space - use for complex data	- use cluttered layouts - hand out when the information can distract from the verbal message - provide large visuals that can be shown at a single time and are not needed for *after* the presentation

Overheads/ Transparencies (low-tech)

Overhead transparencies have come a long way. If you remember you most ancient teacher rolling up a large cart with an odd looking contraption on it, flipping a switch to make a blinding square of light appear, and then using a pen to write on a clear roll of paper… well, then – you have been witness to the use of overheads!

Many folks in today's high tech world would argue that use of this medium is likely to show your audience that you have not mastered these new fancy gadgets called laptops—but you might remind them that overhead transparencies allow you to have an interactive visual aid that can be created *in the moment* with little or no preparation.

If you are writing on a blank transparent page (also a very inexpensive option) then you need no preparation for overhead use except the possession of a dry-erase marker. You can, however, use a computer to design basic overheads transparencies and subsequently draw or write on these during your presentation (Meilach, 1992). The key here is that overhead transparency visuals are highly interactive and require little to no technical savvy. If you keep your visuals relevant to your message and to reinforce your arguments then you have designed effective overheard transparencies (Heap, et al, 1994). (P.S…. have good handwriting!)

Overhead Transparency Hints

Do	Do Not
- use in very dark rooms	- use in bright rooms
- interact with audiences	- have bad handwriting
- number these to avoid sequencing issues	- use with small audiences
- leave lots of "white" space for writing	- utilize when under high-tech expectations

Models and Objects (low-tech)

In many instances (and in many industries), showing your audience the actual object about which you are talking is the best visual to offer. **Models** (or **objects**) "are simply three dimensional, scaled-down replicas of something you are talking about (like a building, a car, and so on) and are handled like objects

in a presentation." (Wyatt, n.d.). Many models are the actual item of discussion but when cannot get a full-size building into the room then a scaled down version is the next best thing (and far more cost effective).

Models, however, are not always replicas. A model or object can also be used to represent something else. For instance, if you are explaining how time will move quickly on the proposed project… a ticking stop watch set in the middle of the conference room table as your wrap up is a strong visual reminder of that sense of urgency.

Think about how models were used in your education. Annette Lester and Roger Lock (1998) discuss how something as simple as a sponge used in biology classrooms can help students to master the notion of red blood cells and heart function. These are the types of simple, low-tech, and low cost options that make big impacts.

Objects or models have the advantage of being very interesting but have their own unique drawbacks. First, it can be just plain difficult for a group of people to see the same object at the same time. Sure, you can hand something around and risk it getting broken or still being with the first person in the room while you moved on to discuss something else. Additionally, models can be *too* interesting. Like with all visual aids (and as developed below), you should be talking about the actual visual when it is shown and not allow it to be seen before. Models can be difficult to disguise before they are revealed and, thus, draw unnecessary attention.

Model and Object Hints

Do	Do Not
- use in very bright rooms	- use with large audiences
- give audiences plenty of time to see and absorb the model	- substitute for clear verbal information
- conceal models until they are relevant	- use models to conceal/ make up for a poor presentation

White and Chalkboards (low-tech)

Whiteboard and chalkboards serve essentially the same purpose. The former is far easier for audiences to read and is less messy—but both offer interactive visual support in a low-tech option.

You may be thinking that in a business setting that you will have little use of a chalkboard. This may be true—but, in the fields of education and construction, you will regularly use chalk. Most other industries will make significant use of whiteboards even in casual settings. Because of this, it is crucial for you to be an expert "whiteboard-er"!

Alas, these low tech options are difficult to prepare ahead and regularly difficult to see (close your eyes and imagine your college professor with the worst handwriting—rough, huh?).

Chalkboard and Whiteboard Hints

Do	Do Not
- use legible handwriting	- use cursive
- write in large, easy to see letters	- use fingers to erase
- keep information visually organized & laid out	- have audiences sit to the side of white or chalkboards
- regularly check in with audiences for clarity and comprehension	
- prepare key/ major notes ahead	

Flip Charts/ Posters (low-tech)

While technically two different breeds, flip charts and posters share enough of the same elements to have their merits and use discussed simultaneously. What's the difference? Well, a **flip chart** is, well,... flipped. It's that thing on the easel that you write on with markers and when you are ready for another page, you just flip to the next one. A **poster** is typically one stagnant display that is either shown or not shown and whose content is prepared.

Poster

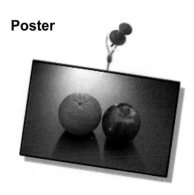

According to the training website, *Speaking Tips* (2004), "Unabashedly low tech, universally understood and easy to use, flip charts remain communication powerhouses. They continue to be popular because they are effective, portable, familiar, inexpensive and do not require electricity or telecommunications" (para. 1). With a sales pitch like that, you may think that flip charts are your new best friend. Allow them to be of good use to you but know how to use them.

Flip Chart and Poster Hints

Do	Do Not
- have legible handwriting on flip charts and/ or computer-generated or graphic posters - use along with other visual aids - pre-design elements - use 2-3 colors with vivid contrast - put blank pages between - bring tape or stands to hang	- use with large audiences (keep the group to approx. 20) - use 5 to 10 colors - set posters where they cannot be seen by all - leave or put up when not being referenced - use markers that smell too bad - keep your back to the audience

Picture Slides (low-tech)

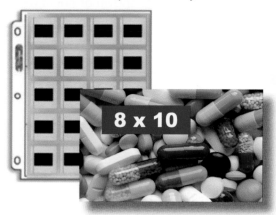

Going into art, advertising, graphic design? Then you will likely be using picture slides as visual aids. Some industries are adverse to high tech and (especially PowerPoint® or Keynote® presentations). No problem. In fact, the use of actual **pictures**, or high quality printed images, will give audiences a far more visually clear image than projected pictures (which is why these particular industries avoid the high-tech options).

Today, 35mm slides are used for more than your grandpa's slideshow of his trip to Orlando. Picture slides are a means of developing credibility with your audiences! After all, a picture is worth a thousand words and 35mm slides will give you the best picture quality.

Picture and 35mm slide Hints

Do	Do Not
- be in a very dark room - use projections with medium or large audiences - only show limited/ relevant pictures - coordinate pictures with other visuals - number images in clear notes	- use prints with large audiences - show numerous images at the same time - show small print sizes - print in low quality versions

PowerPoint® and Keynote® (high-tech)

We would be remiss if we did not begin our discussion of high-tech visual aids without a nod to the darling (and devil) of all business visuals – **PowerPoint® Keynote®** is Apple computer's answer to the pervasive use of PowerPoint® and **Prezi®** is a spatial presentation software newbie but all have basically the same function: create and show slides using text, tables, charts, graphics, images, and other multimedia elements.

PowerPoint® is the most debated visual aid of the modern day business and academic contexts. Why? Perhaps it is because PowerPoint® is the most *used* visual aid with the most amount of poor production (yes, even at the time of this publication, its use is still far beyond those of comparable softwares – no matter what else you are hearing!). This significant use has led to such poorly presented PowerPoint® slides that scholars have made their living trying to convince others not to use this medium (see Tufte, 2003, 2006). Critics of PowerPoint® would like us not to use this aid (or Keynote®) because:

- It diminishes a connection between audiences and speakers (Fried, 2004; Schwartz, 2003; Tufte, 2006)
- It limits textual content (Buss, 2006; Carroll, 2007; Thompson, 2003; Tufte, 2003)
- Offers poor visual quality (Tufte, 2003)

To leave our discussion at this might make you wonder why these aids are required in so many classes and expected at your office – especially since all of the above critiques are true!

PowerPoint® slides actually do have strong benefits when they are used appropriately, as best explained by Dale Cyphert (2004) in *Business CommunicationQuarterly*:

> It seems obvious that PowerPoint® is not a particularly good tool for creating visual aids (compared) to classical forms of verbal communication, but that does not address the ways in which presentation norms themselves have changed in the past century, moving from an age of verbal oratory to a visual era of film, television, and the Internet... I introduce PowerPoint as the business community's primary tool for incorporating the imagery, narrative, and serf-disclosure that are hallmarks of visual eloquence (80).

Cyphert's (2004) makes the excellent point that <u>presentational communication in an electronic age is better received by audiences in an electronic medium.</u>**The caution here is not to allow those mediums to detract from the message**.

Whether your choice be the more **linear** (one slide moving to the next) show producers such as PowerPoint® and Keynote® or the more **spatially oriented** (images and text that appears to all be floating and is sequenced to go back and forth between ideas) Prezi® software, you must use good communicator skills to utilize the benefits of these programs and not be hurt by them. Strategies for effective communication can include:

- designing visual elements that specifically connect to the presenter's audience (Beebe & Beebe, 2009; Foss & Kanengieter, 1992; Sawyer, 2011)
- limiting slide show effects and visual changes (Lowenthal, n.d.; Norman, 2004; Sawyer, 2011)
- creating links between visual and verbal arguments (Cyphert, 2004; Foss & Kanengieter, 1992)
- being as simple as possible (Beebe & Beebe, 2009; Sawyer, 2011)

PowerPoint Slide

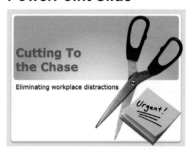

Prezi Slide Template

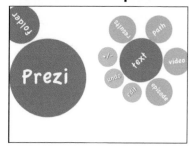

Keynote Slide Templates

Presentation Software Hints

Do	Do Not
- have the projection screen in a dim to dark area	- allow visual animation to predominate
- make clear visual connections to your audience	- use numerous types of animation
- have strong contrast between text and backgrounds	- rely on external connections (instead embed movie and sound files)
- create a line for the eye (clean layout with lots of white space)	

There are numerous books that will tell you how to create any of these slides (take a look at the "For Dummies" series or even the *PowerPoint 2010 Bible*). What's better… anything you don't know how to do, you can just look up online! There are hundreds of thousands of "how to" books. What is more limited are the texts that will teach you design elements – the books that explain WHY to use one design or why NOT to use another. As a first step, use the guidelines earlier in this chapter. As a second step consider such additional guides as:

- *Save Our Slides (second edition)* by William Earnest
- *Presentation Zen* by Garr Reynolds
- *PowerPoint Reality* by Kanan Sawyer

Internet Use (high-tech)

Web-based visual aids are more and more common in a day of ultimate connectivity. This may mean that videos are shown from an Internet site or inserted into presentation slides, that search engines are explored as part of a researching process, or even that images are shown right from server databases. Alone, the Internet is not an effective *visual aid* (in helping audiences to understand ideas, constructs, and arguments), however, paired up with a knowledgeable presenter – the Internet is a highly effective and engaging medium.

If your company has an existing website or if you can create one that will have all of the elements needed for your visual support, then access to this site can help you to present visual in three-dimensional views as audiences need them. The key to making this (and all moving elements) work in your presentation is to be sure that your website does not appear to be a generic website that you use for <u>all</u> presentations (connect it to *that* audience and *that* presentation) or that it does not smoothly provide access to details needed for specific areas of support at the time that they are needed.

As we know from previous chapters, some speakers seem to have major difficulties when relying on server-based visuals (e.g., Apple's Steve Jobs attempting to show off features of the new iPhone 4 but the server wouldn't connect). Most importantly, test your technology ahead of time and <u>be prepared</u> for technological failures.

Internet/ Website Hints

Do	Do Not
- link websites to specific presentations - embed hyperlinks in presentation slides as appropriate - check connectivity before the audience arrives - have a back up (e.g., handouts or screen captures)	- wade through generic sites - expect that audiences will all have technical or multi-media backgrounds to quickly follow along - become more engaged with maneuvering through the Internet than with your audience

Videos/ Movies/ Audio Visuals (high-tech)

It's no longer the day of VHS or Beta (ask someone over the age of 40 about that last one). Today, we have DVDs and Blue Ray and high quality image movies. Heck, commercial 3D players are starting to be just another typical video player option. Movies have a wonderful way of helping audiences to see not just what something looks like but how it *moves*. A movie can show a process as it goes along or even a person who is part of a process as it progresses from beginning to end. These may be what you are accessing in your connection to the Internet or even within PowerPoint® slides.

Movies have great benefits, but before you get too wowed with their appeals, you should consider how the actual playing of a movie can hurt your presentation effectiveness. First, movies can dominate both time and attention. If you show a movie then it may be all that is remembered about your presentation or, if it is too long, it may end up actually being the predominate piece of information in your presentation.

Movie support should be visible no longer than is necessary to clarify an argument or illuminate an issue for an audience. These 'clips' should be fluid with the rest of a presentation (e.g., embedded into a PowerPoint® slide or already up and ready to play when revealed by the projector).

Movies Hints

Do	Do Not
- use when movement and animation are needed for clarification	- generally let the time of this "aid" take up longer than a presentation's introduction
- stop movies when audiences stop finding them useful	- take presentation time to set up movies
- embed movies in presentation software for fluid shows	

Smartboards/ IWBs (high-tech)

Have you heard of IWBs? If you are not a teacher or studying pedagogy (a fancy word for the art of effective instruction), then you likely do not know this jargon. An **IWB** is a short-and way of saying 'interactive white boards' or Smartboards. And, while the terminology may not be important, the concept is vital for a business context.

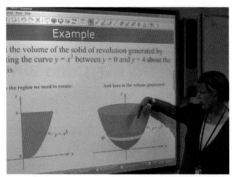

The IWB enables presenters and audiences to interact with all the functions of a desktop computer through the board's large touch sensitive surface.The IWB essentially acts as a port through which any computer run ICT function can be displayed and interacted with (Murcia & Sheffield, 2010, p. 418).

Smartboards or **IWBs** are visual aids that can integrate audiences into the creation of messages! Murcia and Sheffield (2010), in their compelling article *Talking About Science in Interactive Whiteboard Classrooms*, discovered that IWBs used in a science classroom actually resulted in *full* audience participation—and not in just some casually engaged way but in a substantial and meaningful discourse about science. Sure, you might not have science as your topic… but imagine if you are an accountant who is trying to explain financial windfalls to employees with no financial background. By involving the audience in the presentation through the use of a Smartboard, you can help them to <u>understand</u> and <u>engage</u> in all types of material (Glover, Miller, Averis & Door, 2007; Schuck & Kearney, 2007, 2008). (How cool is that? And how *useful* is that for business?!)

Smartboard Hints

Do	Do Not
- get training on the technology - use to explain technical data - ask that audiences help to manipulate and design visual elements of the presentation	- use with small audiences - expect that all companies or all industries will provide or desire this technology

DELIVERING MESSAGES WITH VISUALS

You are your best visual aid. Whether or not you are modeling an idea or product—or you are speaking with no other visual support – you must learn to move comfortably in your space and maintain the audience's attention. Presumably, you have read all about how to do this in the Presentation Chapter of this text. Now, you must learn to coordinate your fantastic presentation delivery with the 'delivery' of your visual aids.

Practice

Once you have prepared the visuals that you want to use in your presentation, you must practice using them. Do a full practice run, preferably with someone you know well and simultaneously (or subsequently) with someone you do not know well. These two types of practice audiences will give you different feedback and even have different understandings of your message.

No audience available? Alternatively, use a video or audio tape recorder, or a mirror. Then, go back and view your presentation with a critical and detached perspective. The more errors and issues that you can identify before the actual presentation, the more that you can adjust to make the actual talk run smoothly.

If at all possible, you should scope out the place of your presentation early. You will want to check technical equipment and/or physical set up of visual aids so that they can be seen from all points of the room. Practice using your visuals with the equipment provided! There will be differences between your machine and projector that can throw you off your game as you adjust in the moment. Do things like: know where the on/off switch is, be able to have the lights dimmed, and, if necessary, know how to have your slides or images ready to go but not revealed until their time has come!

Presenting on Others' Machines

If you have worked hard on presentation slides or websites and then went to show them at the venue only to find that they looked completely different—then you may have had an issue with **compatibility**. Perhaps the computer on which you were showing your slides had an older (or newer) version of the software. It may be the case that the projecting computer has only basic fonts, which do not link to the ones you have selected. Any of these issues will create a last minute panic and we never want that!

Achieving presentation effectiveness involves three things:
1. prior check of your space
2. prior check of your technology
3. prior check of your materials

Notice how both of these elements are about "prior" checks, which means that you cannot wait until the last minute. Even if you do wait to the last minute or you do not have access to these prior checks, be sure to "go with the flow" when something fails. If you show weakness then your audience will stop believing in your message. And… HAVE BACKUPS!

Staying In Sync

Isn't it distracting when a presenter pops out of a PowerPoint® presentation and hops over to the Internet? You get to see his or her desktop that displays an image from a recent beach vacation or snapshots of the dog all dressed up for Halloween? What about those times where the speaker is discussing her or his second area of content but the slides have moved themselves along to the fifth or even last discussion area? These are the delivery issues that make folks wish that speakers would just talk to us and not bring along any visuals at all.

Certainly, a no-visual-aid speech is always an option but if you need your visuals to portray a point, simply make sure that you have practiced enough to **stay in sync with your slides**.

Tips to staying in sync include:
* lots of practice while facing slides and then practice facing away
* video taping yourself speaking with slides
* avoid any type of auto-animation or auto-transitions
* pay attention to audience feedback and look for concerned focus on visuals
* LOOK AT YOUR VISUALS! ☺

A Final Word on Visual Stuff

Business presentations are the basic tool for sending messages in business contexts. Mastery of the verbal *and* the visual context allows you to be the most effective communicator possible. While you should spend the majority of your time crafting the verbal message, preparing visual support can be time well spent.

> Can you think of a way that a picture, chart, or real life object will help your listener better understand your point? Taking a few extra minutes up front to create this aid may save you time explaining and help you to be a more effective presenter. (Rotman, 2009, p. 32)

As you prepare any visual aids, remember that you are the expert on your subject matter. You should decide: 1) whether or not you need visuals 2) what content should be on them, and 3) through which medium your content should be displayed. If you become the master of these choices then you will be well on your way toward effective business communication!

Chapter Nine
Résumé and Cover Letter Communication

THE RÉSUMÉ & LETTER EXPERIENCE

So… you speak Finnish? Graduated top in your class? Were responsible for <u>100%</u> of your last company's profits? AND, you planned an initiative to create world peace?! Wow! Or, actually, whoa! Why do people think that lying on a résumé will somehow impress? Your résumé is an amazing tactic for creating a connection between you and a potential employer. It is also a fantastic hard copy of any lie that you offered that can be evidence to get you fired – or not interview you at all.

Let's start here: you don't need to lie. Ignoring the ethical ramifications of this (well, don't but let's leave those until later) and start to re-evaluate who you have to offer. First, it is unique. No one has the experience that you do—and no one has the characteristics that you have. Second, you *do* have something to offer. The reason that most people lie on a résumé is because they believe that they do not have enough of what a company wants to get a job. Well, you may not. If you are a sophomore in college and applying for a CEO position with only experience of babysitting on your résumé… you won't get the job! And, you won't want it. When people get jobs for which they are not qualified then they spend their time panicking, playing catch-up, and typically failing. That being said, if you have babysitting on your résumé then you have the experience of multi-tasking, crisis management, maintaining a safe working environment, and organizing group activities along with a calm, amiable personality. Wow! Now, that is impressive and it comes without a lie.

If you feel ill-prepared to write a résumé or you already have a great one but would like some expert thoughts on it, well, you are in the right chapter! This chapter lays out for you some very clear guidelines for preparing a professional résumé as well as an excellent cover letter. What you will read here is years of experience and a great collection of current research.

Before you begin to read, here is an important note: You might go online to Monster.com or "The Ladders" or another résumé source and find very different information. There is a reason for this and you should know it up front; résumé creation is very specific to industry, experience, style, and, yes, preference. This chapter will guide you through those varying opinions and give you a good sense of how to determine what works best for you! (But, if you find a different opinion—don't fret. With a good foundation, no matter what, you'll be on the right track!)

WHAT IS A RÉSUMÉ?

A résumé is more than a piece of paper that lists all the jobs that you have ever had. A résumé is a *mechanism for articulating your skills, experience, and accomplishments.* It is a vital tool in business communication because it is your first connection to potential employers or clients. If delivered well, your résumé can showcase your experience and land you that desired interview for that sought after job. Without a solid résumé, you will rarely have an opportunity to convince an employer that you are the ideal candidate for just about anything. Sound intimidating? Don't worry! You are about to find all the tools that you need in order to craft the ideal document!

First, good résumés are a *concise*, written summary of skills, knowledge, and experience that is relevant to the position to which you are applying. It is not an autobiography, so do not feel the need to cram in every experience and skill that you have. View it as a sales brochure where you will highlight your most relevant and impressive attributes.

Your résumé will *sell* you the best if it is:
- Clear, succinct, and easy for employers to quickly scan
- Inviting to look at—stands out from the others
- Persuasive—clearly showing that you are qualified, competent and can deliver results**

(** Important: *Persuasive does not mean inaccurate*. As we noted above, it is crucial to never create a document that will persuade the employer to hire someone that you are not. Any misrepresentation of your skills and experience is not only unethical, but can also cost you a job. If employers uncover inaccurate information on your résumé, you can kiss your chance of being hired, or even keeping a job for which you have already been hired, good-bye!).

Résumé Creation

If you are on the job market then you are likely considering more than one job – and should have more than one résumé. As you read the information in this chapter, you will see time and time again that the information on your résumé should be specific to a single job. It may seem daunting to draft dozens of documents. You actually won't. Begin your process by creating one document and then altering that document to fit specific positions. Here's the important part: save each one on your computer (actually in a few places to avoid technical failures) saved under the name of the job. Thus, when you get called for an interview with *Tri-State Public Relations*,then you will know to bring multiple copies of the "Tri-State Public Relations Res.docx" résumé to your interview.

So now that you know what a résumé is, it's important to know that they are not all the same. Sure, they have the same definition but within that definition you will find a vast array of formats and looks. Your job is to choose the one that works best for you!

Résumé Formats for YOU

Take a look at as many résumés as you can. Look online. Look at your friends' résumés. Look at every résumé that the company for which you want to work has posted. Notice anything? Résumés can look very different—and disappointingly… similar, too.

YOUR NAME HERE		
UNION AFFILIATIONS HERE		
Contact: 000-000-0000	Email Address Here		
Hair: Brown	Height: 0'0"	
Eyes: Brown	Weight: 000 lbs	
FILM		
Project Title	Type of Role	Studio or Director
Project Title	Type of Role	Studio or Director
Project Title	Type of Role	Studio or Director
TELEVISION		
Show Title	Type of Role	Production Co.
Show Title	Type of Role	Production Co.
Show Title	Type of Role	Production Co.
THEATRE		
Play Title	Type of Role/Character	Theatre Name
Play Title	Type of Role/Character	Theatre Name
Play Title	Type of Role/Character	Theatre Name

Templates and Trends

As you look at résumés, you will start to see trends. Résumé writers will use the same categories on their résumés. Time and time again, you will see the same layout and the same font. You will begin to notice that if you aren't looking closely, a lot of résumés look like the same document with a different name. They probably are. These résumés most likely have been created through the use of a template.

A **template** is a styling tool in a word processing program that provides a pattern, in which users can fill in details to produce a document. While using a standard format can help to get you started with the creation of a résumé (what goes on it and a sense of organization), you will soon realize the drawbacks with such a form. First, you will look like everyone else. Your résumé will not stand out. Second, you will not be able to include new categories that are not on the template and often you may not be able to add or delete the offered categories. Third, you will be forced to stick to a given layout that has been seen time and time again.

Avoid template downfalls by starting with a blank page and making your own decisions about what should go on that page. You should start by considering what layout to use, followed by considering what content to add to your masterpiece! The goal of every line of your résumé is to keep the employer reading. That person should want to know what comes next and be excited for the story that will unfold! By the time the employer reaches the end of your résumé story, you will have shown that you are worthy of an interview.

Organizational Formats

Putting together your résumé includes more than just designing a pretty page—it's about organizing your information to grab and inspire a potential employer. Organizational formats should suit your purpose and reveal your background in the most appealing way.

General Formatting

As you begin to produce your masterpiece, try to organize your résumé in a top down approach (meaning that the most important information should come first and the least important information last). This will likely be the order in which employers will read your résumé, so you do not want to save the most important information for the end as there is no guarantee the employer will get to the end of your résumé! At the initial stage of screening résumés, employers spend an average of less than 30 seconds scanning each résumé (Markey & Campell, 1996), so make sure that you do not hide the most relevant information!

The two most common formats for résumé writing are *chronological* and *functional*. These two formats are means of arranging the experience section of your résumé. Which one you select should be determined by how much experience you have and what you want to communicate in this section!

Chronological Format

The**chronological résumé format** organizes your experiences by, well, time. It directs you to arrange your experience from the most recent positions and works (no pun intended) down to least recent.

Example:

> ❖ **Manager**, *Cliffhanger Garage Band*, Austin, TX
>   May, 2006-Present
>
> ❖ **WaitStaff**, *Brunches R Us*, Grover Beach, CA
>   June 2004-April, 2006
>
> ❖ **Hostess**, *Johnny Brenda's*, Philadelphia, PA
>   January 2002-April 2004

(See how the most recent jobs come first and then go backwards to the least recent experience?)

This method helps an employer to see what you are currently *able* to do and how your experience *led* to those abilities. Thus, the reasons that you would use a chronological format include:
- to show a clear <u>history</u> of your experiences
- to highlight progressive career <u>growth</u> and advancement

When done well, the chronological format allows employers to quickly get a snapshot of your experience. For this reason, it is the most accepted format among hiring authorities. Many employers even expect it.

Now… just because something is expected, doesn't mean that you should automatically do it. There are actually problems associated with the use of this format. Avoid using a chronological format if:
1) you have gaps in your employment (a time sequenced order will make these gaps stand out),
2) have frequently changed jobs or careers (time order will make you look scattered rather than highlight groups of knowledge)
3) or have little to no work experience (time progression will highlight inexperience rather than allow you to draw attention to volunteer work, special projects, or coursework).

To make the problems with chronological formats more clear, consider the following example:

> Bob worked as an accountant for 20 years. Having never felt completely fulfilled by the work, he made the courageous decision to switch to a career in horticulture. In his accounting life, he became a skilled business manager, led his team, balanced books for clients in varied businesses, generally, became a rock star of business development plans! This experience will help Bob to become a key asset to help sustain and grow his garden center or nursery!

If Bob used a chronological résumé, his skill set would be buried while his seemingly sudden shift in careers would stand out like a sore thumb. Alas, there is hope for Bob. There is another résumé format that will show him off to his best advantage!

Functional Format

For those career-minded folks who see more problems than gains in presenting their experience with a chronological résumé format, consider instead the functional format. The **functional résumé format** organizes the experience section of your résumé *by specific skill sets*. If you have ever given a speech, this type of organization will make sense. A speech on fashion certainly could certainly be given based on time (e.g., moving from one decade to the next) but it could also be given by function/category (e.g., classic, couture, grunge, ready-to-wear). Functions are means of grouping your background by skills and accomplishments.

For example, let's go back to Bob. Here is how the content of his résumé might be organized (yes, it is missing the header, contact information, and details).

Functional Résumé Format Example:

Qualifications
(brief paragraph here about those)

Selected Accomplishments
 bulleted list
 details
 details

Professional Expertise
Management
details here
Horticultural Supervision
details here
Business Analysis
details here

Employment History
Job Title
Company
limited details here

Job Title
Company
limited details here

Highlighting Skills on the Functional Résumé

You'll note in Bob's example that (rather than organizing information on the résumé by time) the skills and accomplishments become the headers to organize this information. The skills are not inserted into descriptions of particular jobs (jobs are just listed), instead skills are grouped together to show a body of expertise grouped around a specific skill set.

Inclusion Of Job History On The Functional Résumé

Now, just because you show skill categories does not mean that you do not list job experience. You will de-emphasize your job timeline by placing it after your skill groups—perhaps even toward the bottom of your résumé (see above). The individual jobs will not need descriptions (those have been used for skills) but can simply be listed. Think of it this way, the functional résumé highlights *what* you have done rather than *where* you have done it!

Functional résumé formats work best for:
- applicants (or student applicants) with little to no experience
- career changers
- candidates who have gaps in employment (or those who have had frequent job changes)

While the functional résumé format may make flaunting your transferrable skills easier, it too should be used with caution. Since it is not the most widely used format and not as straight forward as a chronological format, employers may scoff at your functional style. If you are not careful, a functional format can lead to confusion, skepticism, or even annoyance if the amount of experience is unclear. Some employers may also think you are trying to hide something with this format (Olsen, 2006).

To counteract negative reactions to the functional résumé, remember to:
- be specific
- use numbers and quantify your experience wherever possible
- avoid vague phrases and lean toward concrete examples!

Now you know about the formats that are available to you for organizing your information and a bit about the pros and the cons but still might be unsure which organization will best serve your needs. To make this decision easier, you should next consider what you want on your résumé (the content) and then decide how to organize that information.

Content: What to Include and Not Include

The content of your résumé is the meat (or tofu)—the substance! This is where you will use careful language to craft a story of your experience. Never include unnecessary information or fluff on your résumé! Every word, phrase, and line on your résumé is valuable real estate; therefore, you must be thoughtful of what to include and what to *not* include.

It is important to look at your industry as well as the specific position for which you are applying to figure out what content is important to include and how to group it. All those résumés that you looked at when you first started this process—go back to those and see what important details are included in each! What organizational format do they use? What is the general look of the résumé? How long is it? What categories do they include? Now is the time to apply the answers to your résumé.

Length: How Long Should Your Résumé Be?

The first question that most folks ask when preparing a résumé is, *how long should it be?* What they are really asking is, *how much information should I include on my résumé?* Good question. Once again, there is no formula. Some people who have been in their industry a very long time or have made significant accomplishments will have résumés beyond 10 pages! Don't freak out. You likely will not have a lengthy résumé.

The industry (of most folks who hire) standard is one page. Even people with very long résumés are expected to have a one-page version of their longer documents. Although you may have limited experience, you'll want to fill an entire page (the rest of this chapter will help you know how to do that). Make good use of your page space and do your best to avoid excessive white space—this will give the impression that you lack experience. While most traditional college students and new graduates can typically summarize their education, skills, and experience in one page, you should not omit important information. If you have a good deal of experience to highlight, then going to a second page *may* be appropriate. Be sure that if you do so, you are not adding a single line or brief section. If you have spilled over to the next page—use it! Be sure to fill at least three quarters of your final page.

Crucial Contact

Once you start to fill your page, start with the crucial information— who and where you are! Having your name and contact information is necessary for all résumés. It doesn't matter what industry you hope to join—they want to know who you are and how to reach you. Your contact information should be clearly visible (typically at the top of your document). Unlike other sections of your résumé, this section does not have a special heading such as "Contact Information" (uh, we get that). Instead, simply place the information at the top of the page under or near your name.

> Your contact information should include:
> - your name—make this stand out by increasing text size (typically to about a 16 point font)
> - your permanent or campus address (choose <u>one</u>—employers won't hunt you down)
>   - put in full 9 digit zip code (research suggests that this will show you off as detail oriented)
>   - you generally should avoid abbreviating in a résumé but can do so for state but must do so accurately. (For example, the commonly accepted abbreviation is "PA" not "Pa.")
> - your phone number(use the number from which you are most accessible and have both a business-oriented message and/ or any "hold" music)
> - your e-mail address (yes, you should you have one) – make sure that the address you use is professional and be sure that you check it regularly
>   - unprofessional emails are one of the major no-no's of job searching (Southam, 2006).

Potential Categories

Categories are the groups of information that label (with headers) where you describe your applicable experience. Some folks might care if you were a lifeguard for five summers – others really won't. Some employers will look for a specified objective but for other jobs, this might actually hurt you. Select the categories that sell your skills best for this particular job! (DO NOT USE *ALL* OF THE CATEGORIES LISTED HERE. Remember to use what links to you and to the job!)

Objective Category

An objective is an optional element of the résumé. This is a hotly debated component of résumé writing, where some experts insist you need one (Hoheb, 2002; Smith, 2002) and others insist that it is highly problematic to have one (Ross & Young, 2005). Why? Well, the objective is of little value, as it does not offer any new information. If you are applying to a job posting, the employer knows your objective is to secure the job, so including one is a waste of valuable space. Your cover letter gives you the opportunity to expand on your goals, so again, this makes the objective redundant.

There are, however, some instances where an objective can be useful. One useful time may be if you are <u>not</u> applying to a position posted on a company's website or a job search site such as Monster.com, but instead sending your résumé to your dream company in hopes that they will have an opening. In other words, you are targeting a company you hope to work for, but they have not advertised any open position. If this is the case then it is important for the company to know what you are looking for and an objective can serve this purpose. Another situation where an objective may be useful is if you are looking for employment by networking. For example, you talked to your aunt, uncle, friend, professor—whomever—and they told you they would be happy to pass along your résumé. Of course, in this instance, there is not a posted position to which you are applying, so again, it becomes important to make clear what <u>you</u> are looking for in a position.

If you are indeed including an objective statement, here are some guidelines to follow:

- Be short and concise (one sentence, two at the most)
- Do not be so specific that you eliminate opportunities in which you *might* be interested (such as including specific job titles rather than focusing on a range of jobs you would be willing to consider)
- Try to incorporate your most marketable skills in the objective

Examples:

- *Not specific enough – BAD:* "To obtain an internship allowing me to utilize my knowledge and expertise in different areas."

- *More Specific – GOOD:* "To obtain a challenging internship in Human Resources, with a specific interest in training and development."

- *Wordy yet vague – BAD:* "Looking to obtain a successful career with a progressive company that will utilize my education, skills and experience in an executive capacity, where I can effectively contribute to the overall growth of the company in a way that best utilizes my diverse skill set."

- *Descriptive yet concise –* GOOD: "To secure an entry-level paralegal position at Smith Law Associates, exploring the field of tax law and collection."

Summary of Qualificationsor Skills Category
The summary section is another optional element that you can include in place of or in addition to an objective statement. Summary of qualifications are most likely found on résumés of those with significant experience or executives in the field – but can work for those who are attempting to highlight an element of one's vast experience.

Qualification summaries can work in tandem with an objective or instead of one. If you have decided to offer an objective then a subsequent summary can offer very specific details of how you have the experience to handle the desired work! Obviously, employers are more interested in what you can offer (summary of qualifications) than what you want from them (objective).

Consider your summary to be a teaser or preview for what is to come. Your goal is to convince the reader to read on! It should help the employer answer the question, *what can this person do for me?* To answer that question, include 3-6 high impact statements that showcase your strongest selling points for that particular position. Prioritize these statements so that the most important/ impressive/relevant come first (this is called the *law of primacy*).

Think about what makes you most marketable; that's what you want to highlight and, of course, tailor this section for each and every position to which you apply—what's important for one job is meaningless for another. How do you do this? Make sure you critically analyze the job posting and tailor the summary to the position. Does it ask for financial analysis skills? Are they specifically looking for someone who has led group meetings? Do your best to be concrete and make sure all of your claims are backed up in your résumé. For example, if your summary of qualifications states that you have three years of experience making presentations to diverse audiences then the descriptions of jobs where you have done that should list "spoke to a diverse audience of over 45 international sales directors at the National Sales Association conference" or the like!

Examples:

Editorial Assistant

Key Qualifications:
- Published author and conference speaker
- Three years experience as an English tutor
- Facilitated SAT prep training to diverse student population
- Skilled web page designer

Teacher

Professional Summary:
- Enthusiastic educator committed to student development and learning
- Five years experience teaching SAT prep courses
- Skilled in the design of challenging, enriching, and innovative activities
- Utilized a variety of teaching methods to accommodate diverse student needs

---

Sales Representative

Key Skills:
- Experience giving presentations to diverse groups
- Over two years of customer service experience
- Received Future Community Leader Award from the Montgomery County Chamber of Commerce
- Fluent in both French and Spanish

Education Category

The education section of your résumé is a chance for you to brag about your academic training! If you are in college or a recent graduate then BRAVO! You have specialized training that is not to be ignored. You may have taken fabulous classes (e.g., Business Communication!) or even achieved recognition on a Dean's list. You now must decide how to share this academic experience with potential employers.

Individuals who have a substantial amount of work experience might keep this section brief; however, if you lack work experience, you can expand upon this section to highlight some of your achievements and skills.

The following information must be included in this section:
- Universities attended/ attending (most experts say list all, but list at least the places from where you have earned or <u>will</u> earn any degree)
  - Name, city, and state of those universities
- Degree earned – write this out in its entirety rather than abbreviating (e.g., Bachelor of Arts)
  - if you are unsure if your degree is a Bachelor of Arts or Sciences, now is the time to check! (don't want to be selling B.S. when you have a B.A.)

- o If your major is not yet declared then just indicate "Major: Undeclared."
- Year and month of graduation, actual or anticipated

Example with Anticipated Graduation Listed

Education
West Chester University of PA
Expected Graduation May, 2011
Bachelor of Science; Department of Biology
GPA: 3.9

You may do more than just list this information. You may wish to add additional details that will help show what you have learned during your education. If so, keep the formatting clear and the information relevant.

These additional details may include:
- A double major
- A minor or concentration within your major
- "Relevant Course Work" or "Course Highlights" (a great addition for those with lots of schooling but limited professional experience)
  - o List only the courses that are most applicable to the position – not every course you have taken!
- Honors, awards, activities (this type of information can be included in a section of its own, but if you only have one or two items to list… this does not warrant an entire section – include them in the education section instead!)
- GPA (only include your Grade Point Average if it is impressive; i.e., above a 3.5 on a 4.0 scale for either overall or major GPA)
  - o Most readers will assume that your GPA is on a 4.0 scale but if it is not be sure to include the scale (e.g., 4.3/5.0 scale)

As you are compiling this section, you will start out with the most recent educational experiences and end with the least recent. For those who are pursuing a college degree, it is implied that you have earned a high school diploma; therefore, no need to include your high school information in the education section unless there is a compelling reason to do so (e.g., the school is very prestigious and will get the attention of the employer).There are many designs or layouts to use for this section but here are few good ideas to help you consider what works best for you!

Examples:

Education

West Chester University of PA
Bachelor of Arts: Department of Communication Studies
Anticipation Graduation: June 2011
Summa Cum Laude

Course Highlights:
* Principles of Public Relations   * Advanced Public Speaking
* Web Page Design   * Persuasion
* Principles of Marketing   * Computers & Applications

EDUCATION
❏ University of California San Diego
❏ **Bachelor of Science, Department of Finance/ Minor in Information Technology**
❏ AACSB Accredited University
❏ *3.8 GPA*
❏ Expected Graduation: December 2010

Education

West Chester University of PA
Anticipated Graduation: May 2010
Bachelor of Science in Science Education
Secondary Education Certification

Delaware County Community College,Media, PA
Graduation Date: May, 2007
Associate of Science in Biology

Consider Where to Put Education Information

When you are applying to internships or first entering the professional workforce, your education will typically be an important aspect of your résumé and, therefore, would likely be up at the top, just below your contact information (or after an objective or summary if you chose to use one of those optional elements).

On the other hand, if your experience sections are stronger (such as when you are an executive or much further into your career experience), then you'll likely want to move your education section to the end of your résumé. Be sure not to bury this section in the middle as it is either your primary and recent training (at the top) or your foundation (at the bottom).

Experience Category

Before beginning a discussion on experience, it is important to tell you – YOU HAVE EXPERIENCE! One of the most common concerns of those who are early in their career paths, including students, is that they have "no experience." That's not true. If you have lived past the age of ten, if you are in college, if you have helped just about anybody to do just about anything—then you have experience! Your concern should be how to best show off that experience and link it to the job for which you are applying.

An experience section emphasizes your past and present employment and/or your participation in relevant activities. It is likely the lengthiest portion of your résumé because this is the place where you show potential employers what you are capable of. Whether you have had one job or twenty jobs, the descriptions of what you have done should convey to a potential employer that you are a unique and worthwhile asset!

This means that your **descriptions** should:
- Not sound like job ads (don't just list responsibilities but let people know how you did the job!) (examples below)
- Give the most description for the most relevant jobs (no need to give more detail for the jobs you have had the longest if they aren't as applicable!)
- Be specific and give numbers where possible (e.g., size of budget, number of people supervised, percent increase in sales)

- Start each line with an action word
    - If you are having difficulty coming up with the best wording, there are countless online resources that have lists of action verbs for your résumé. These can be found with a simple Google search for "résumé and action verbs"
- Avoid repetition
    - Never repeating the same action word (this sounds like you have limited experience)
    - Do not use the same letter twice to start any descriptions (this can be a harder task but as employers give your résumé an initial glance, repeated letters give an impression of lack of breadth… even if you have tons!)
    - Be organized within themselves (chronological or even functionally—just like the résumé itself!)
    - Emphasize your strong stylistic language
    - Link to the job desired
    - Include the position title (if you did not have an actual title, create one that honestly fits your role)
        - Remember that job/ position titles are more important that the name of the company for which you worked – be sure to emphasize this element!
    - List the company or organization and its city and state
    - Provide dates of employment that include both the month and the year (e.g., June 2006 to August 2010)

Example/ Template for Experience Descriptions
(Remember that this is just an example of organization; you may be using a different look, which is great—as long as you include all the relevant parts!)

Position Title
Name of Company, City, State
Month/Year – Month/Year
- Job tasks, skills acquired, and accomplishments – starting with action word
- Do your best to keep each item to one line
- Be concise and avoid full sentences
- Use variety in language choice

Grouping Your Experience Details: Again, include the experiences that are most important and relevant first; however, within any given section, you need to organize in reverse chronological order – most recent first. So for example, suppose you are applying to a position as a web designer and you worked at a web design agency up until last year. However, your current job is an administrative assistant; and while these are certainly applicable skills, you know the web design experience is more likely to impress the employer. You can include a section called "Relevant Web Design Experience" (where you include your most relevant experiences in reverse chronological order) <u>above</u> a section called "Additional Experience" (where you include your remaining experiences in reverse chronological order).

You can customize your headings for this section, and it is a good idea to do so if you are tailoring your résumé for a specific position. For example, if the job ad calls for someone with editorial experience, you may want to create a section with the heading "Editorial Experience." This will obviously draw attention to your résumé. You decide the heading titles that work for your experiences and will make them most appealing to the employer. Some *possible* headings for your experience may be:

- Work History (for a brief list of jobs in a functional résumé)
- Field Work
- Volunteer Work
- Internships

- Research Experience
- Editorial Work
- Management Experience
- (Or any title linked to the position: Public Relations Experience; Teaching Experience; Broadcasting Experience; Nursing Experience; etc...)

You may discover you need *more than one section* to organize your experiences. This can help you to group your background in a very specific means to link to your desired job!

Link Experience to the Job: In many instances, you may not have experience that is in the actual field to which you are applying. This is normal for college students and recent college graduates. In fact, the whole idea of getting that first job is to get you some experience! That being said, you still do not want your background to seem completely irrelevant. Your task is to make a *connection* between your past experiences and the job you want. What skills, experience, and knowledge do you have from your past experiences (waitressing, babysitting, etc.) that will show the employer that you will be competent in this job (entry level PR associate, sales manager, etc.)?

You will connect by highlighting your commonalities. If you have in front of you the actual job description for the job that you want, find key words from the description and strategically place those words in your résumé when describing your experience. If they want "strong communication skills" then don't have your résumé simply list a public speaking class! No, instead be sure to have phrases such as "learned effective communication skills" or "applied communication strategies" to help describe your work at past jobs or in various clubs or volunteer work. As part of connecting you to the job, be sure to frame as much of your past experiences as you can in a way that makes their relevance to the job that you want really, really clear. For example, it certainly does not make sense to spend a great deal of time discussing your skill and aptitude for mopping a floor, as picked up in your janitorial job, when you are applying for an accounting job! While you do want to mention that your janitorial position helped you with being more thorough… no need to dwell on too many details! ☺

It's good to know, as you are attempting to link your (potentially imperfect) background to your (potentially ideal) job, that there are certain skills that will transfer from any job to any other job (e.g., communication, writing, computer skills, problem solving, team work, leadership, organization, decision making, and time management are all transferrable skills). Think about what the job you are applying to entails and requires, and then work on framing your previous experience so that it meets those requirements.

Examples:

Intern
Philadelphia Daily Times, Philadelphia, PA   Summer 2008
- Conducted interviews and wrote articles on a weekly basis
- Generated and researched ideas for feature stories
- Edited and revised stories created by other reporters
- Observed and interacted in all business aspects of a major publication
- Utilized Quark Express, Adobe Photoshop, and Microsoft Office Suite

Student Teacher: 10th Grade English
ABC High School, Philadelphia, PA   August 2008 – December 2008
- Prepared and implemented lessons, regularly assessing student progress
- Integrated technology into lessons, assignments, and classroom activities
- Served as mentor to writing club, increasing membership by 20 percent
- Established and maintained positive relationships with students and parents
- Collaborated with co-teachers to ensure student-centered instruction in inclusive classroom

Orientation Leader
West Chester University, West Chester, PA
August 2007 – Present
- Lead large (100+) and small (5+) groups of students through orientation
- Organize networking events to acquaint students to the university
- Collaborate with university faculty, staff, parents, and students to ensure smooth orientation experience
- Prepare and present professional presentations to students
- Attend leadership retreat to further develop leadership and communication skills

Activities and Honors Category

In some instances, what makes you the most marketable may be not be your work experience but something altogether unique, such as... out of the classroom activities and special awards. This section is optional but can be crucial if you lack work experience or training/background in the field. If you have a good deal of activities and/or relevant awards, you can make a fantastic impression! An awards and activities section might include the following:

- Academic awards and scholarships
- Membership in campus, national, or international organizations
- Leadership positions held in campus, national, or international organizations
- University and community service/volunteer positions
- Other distinctions...

Examples:

> **President, English Club**
> *West Chester University, West Chester, PA*
> August 2007 – Present
> - Organize and plan student networking events
> - Collaborate with university faculty to plan meaningful activities
> - Recruit students, resulting in 55% membership increase in one year
> - Plan and oversee essay writing contest
> - Tutor and mentor underprivileged youth in inner city
> - Coordinate fundraising efforts (raising over $5000 in two years)

> **ASU Campus Activities**
>
> | | | |
> |---|---|---|
> | Member | Student Government | August 2007 – Present |
> | President | Investment Club | January 2008 – Present |
> | Treasurer | Accounting Association | August 2009 – May 2009 |

Depending on the relevance of the activities and the amount of information you have to include on your résumé, you may choose to expand on a particular activity, as in the first example, or only list activities as in example above. Either way, be sure that the when (your were involved) and what (you did) are clear to a reader.

Computers and "Other" Skills Category

Ah… the infamous "other" category. What does it mean? If you have to ask—or worse, if a potential employer does—then these skills are not likely to sell you very well. Just like any other section, your skills section should absolutely link to the job that you want. First, the section is optional. Second, the skills that you list should also appear in the descriptions of past/current jobs (e.g., if you list that you are skilled in PowerPoint usage, make sure that you have this as part of your college training from your SPK 230 course—or if you state that you have mastered website design, be sure to describe how you put together the website for your summer job at *Claudia's Organic Farm*). Do not include unnecessary information!

Computer skills are perhaps the most useful and generally applicable skills. List only the computer languages and programs in which you have strong skills—and always be honest about your abilities!

Example of a Skill:

COMPUTER SKILLS
- Proficient with operating systems using all recent versions of Windows
- Skilled in using all Microsoft Office programs
- Visual Basic, SQL, and web page design expertise
- Certificate in computer security

If you only have a few computer skills to list then you can include these is a more general skills section that is titled to fit the job (e.g., Relevant Accounting Skills or Applicable Public Relations Skills). This more general section can include useful proficiencies such as from these areas:
- Foreign Languages
- Research Skills
- Specialized Training
- Budget Creation
- Writing Skills
- Certifications (although these may also go under education)
- Other (do not use this term but know that "other" skills besides these do exist).

Remember, the skills you include need to be relevant to the position. Walking on your hands is undoubtedly a pretty impressive skill, but there are few jobs to which it would be relevant!

High School Information—Non-Category

If you are a college freshman, it is fine to incorporate high school experiences. However, as your college career progresses, you should be acquiring new skills and experiences and should phase out the high school information (completely by your junior year!). Are there exceptions? Well, if you have truly exceptional experiences from your high school days (such as: you were the school valedictorian or you started and ran the school television station, etc.), then do include them on your college résumé. Be sure that even these are in some way relevant to the position for which you are applying. If you have nothing else to put on your résumé, then, of course, you will need to include high school experience; however, if you have reached junior year and have nothing new to add to your résumé, take notice of this issue and develop a plan for activities and experiences that will be beneficial when applying to post-graduation jobs!

Visual Language and Style

Regardless of the organizational format that you use, it is important to use styles and language that captivate but do not distract. The visual style of your résumé (i.e., design elements such as bold, italics, capitalization, bullets, text positioning, and fonts) should allow your résumé to look professional and be easy for the employer to quickly read.

Language

Your résumé is the best work of non-fiction that you could ever produce. It should be interesting, captivating, honest, and understandable. This is a chance to talk about you—but as all good communicators do – make it be what the audience wants. To do so, follow these basic guidelines for the best result:

1. **Treat your résumé document like a speech**
   - Have organized descriptions
   - Be specific with data
   - Make the language flow

- o Avoid jargon—or terms that the audience will not understand
- o Be clear
2. **Avoid empty claims**
   - o Prove aptitude with thorough discussion of accomplishments
3. **Avoid over used words and phrases** (or you'll sound cliché', see Zupek, 2010)
   - o No more of these tired and over-used terms:
     - ▪ People person, go-getter, team player, hard working, multi-tasker, self-starter, results, goal oriented
     - ▪ Avoid the use of "responsibilities" in any form—a term that holds lots of bad connotations (like that you did not want to do your work, but you had to!)
4. **Use numbers to quantify information wherever possible**
5. **Get the tense right**
   - o Currently held positions use present tense; positions you no longer hold use past tense
   - o "ing" (a present participle, if you were wondering) means that you are doing the action right there and then and is awkward to read (e.g., swap "writing" for "write" and "managing" for "manage," etc.)

Now that your language is on the mark—how does the whole thing look? We first talked about the layout and organization of your résumé in the beginning. You began by looking at a whole bunch of résumés online to get a feel for a layout that works for you. Once you begin to insert all of your information, however, you may find that you must tweak some elements of the design to make your information pop in all the right ways!

Style

There is no specific formula for what your particular résumé should look like – but there are several good indications of what it should *not* look like. The contradiction is this: you want your résumé to look different than others so it stands out (which is why you avoid using templates) but don't want the style to be so different that it becomes more of the focus than your information. The examples provided in this book are just that, examples. They are not the only way of formatting your overall résumé or individual sections.

You can arrange and format your résumé in a variety of ways; just make sure it is appealing to the eye and professional. Do not get crazy with use of color or font style. To keep your style useful and not distracting, be sure to give attention to these specific résumé elements:

- **Ink Color**
  - Color copies are harder to read and see than crisp black ink – if you use an element of color/color print, then use the highest quality professional print!
- **Font Size and Style**
  - Use no more than two kinds in the body of your résumé
  - 10-12 point (depending on font style) works best for content
  - Select a larger size for name (perhaps a 16 point size)
  - A smaller font size than content works best for contact info to not become an additional point of focus (but be legible)
- **Bullet Format**
  - Line up all bullets and tabbed content throughout the entire résumé
  - Do not use multiple kinds or levels bullets
  - Only use bullets if you have three or more items to list
    - For example, you do not need to bullet your education information unless you have at least three lines of information that you want to include under your degree
- **Formatting for Emphasis**
  - Be consistent with punctuation, tenses, and capitalization
  - Limit use of bold and formatting changes
  - Avoid making your e-mail as a hyper-link (this is where it turns blue and becomes underlined)
    - Hyperlinks are awkward visual style changes, difficult to read, and not useable when résumés are sent in most electronic forms
  - Create a line for the eye
    - Think of this: if you changed all of the words to fillers, would the look of the résumé still be easy to follow and the style clean?

Résumé Don'ts / Stuff Not to Include

As you begin to draft your message, there are few items that you should avoid including on your résumé or as part of your document. These elements will hurt the appeal of your information and perhaps communicate the wrong message about you. Some résumé potential pitfalls that will tell an employer to NOT bring you in for an interview include:

- Typos
- Grammatical errors
- Unprofessional email addresses (this is the time to scratch using -"hotmama@gmail.com" as your point of contact)
- An unprofessional message or song on your voicemail
- A personal picture (on domestic résumés)
- Unrelated hobbies
- Personal information (e.g., height, weight, eye color, etc.)
- Scenting your résumé
- Strangely colored or hard to read paper (avoid strong watermarks)

The Killer Typo

Typos are mentioned in the list above but deserve special attention. Avoiding typo issues will help you immensely. Of all of recommendations given in the chapter thus far, most importantly, make sure your résumé is consistent and error free. You must proof read over and over. Have friends, classmates, teachers, and co-workers review and critique your materials for you. The reality is that you may be able to earn an A on a paper with a typo or even two; however, this is not the case with a résumé. Your résumé is a representation of the work that you will do as an employee. It is the one and only piece of evidence that the employer has to determine if you are worthy of an interview. One teeny, tiny typo can be the difference between getting an interview or not!

Avoid "References Upon Request"

A blurb of "references available upon request" was the standard long ago. It said that you were able to provide contact information for people who could attest to your high qualities. Nowadays, however, no one will hire you if there are *not* folks to attest to your employment character. Thus, there is no need for this line on your page and it is, in fact, a waste of precious space.

Do Have a Reference Page Attached to Your Résumé

Removing this classic line does not mean that you shouldn't have references available! Before you send out your résumé, you should call the people that you would like to serve in this capacity (never list someone without their knowledge—and be sure to give them the respect and courtesy of a phone call rather than an email!).

Next, create a document separate from your résumé with your references listed. It should have the same header as your résumé (i.e., your name and contact info in the same font and space) with two categories:

- Professional References
- Personal References

Typically, you will offer about three of each type of reference unless your industry expects more or less. You can either send this along with your résumé document or wait until asked. Just imagine how impressive you will be when you get a call asking for references and instead of asking for time to get these out, you say, "No problem. Check your email… I just sent them to you!"

Now that you have the ideal résumé to describe your background. Your next step is to create a document that will introduce you to potential employers and give them a reason to read your fabulous résumé! That document is your cover letter.

COVER LETTER CREATION

"Dear Sir or Madam:
You have an opening for XY position. I am a great person to fill XY position. I have done great things. Please call me."

Does this sound all too familiar? Is it perhaps rather close to the ideas you have expressed in a letter to a potential employer? Or, have you looked at a template online and were told that your letter should look something like this? That makes sense. The basic elements are here but what is missing is the theoretical constructs of communication. Know and be about your audience!

What is the Purpose of Your Cover Letter?

 A **cover letter** is used to make an introduction to an employer, introduce your résumé, and get you an interview(Donlin, 2008). They can be sent to find out about jobs, to reply to an advertisement, to begin communication with an employer, or to take action on a job referral. Consider this your first interaction with the person who will eventually be your boss. As such, you want to both be yourself and be impressive.

Length of Your Cover Letter?

Just like your résumé, covers letters have no set number of pages but a single page cover letter is *typical*. The idea of the cover letter is to get a potential employer to read your résumé and a lengthy novel may hinder his or her enthusiasm for picking up the next document. Some industries will expect a lengthier introduction while others will not want much from you at all. To understand what is best for your industry, talk to your mentor, past graduates, those in the industry, and use the wonderful worldwide web to do a bit of reading.

The information you are required to include or hope to include to best connect to the employer will help to determine the length of your cover letter. You can include all of the elements described in this chapter with a single page cover letter. You can also use the skeleton or… template (not a design template, just an outline) to expand your work into a larger document!

Cover Letter Content

Unlike the basic elements above ("Dear Sir or Madam: Yada yada…"), communication theory directs us to make our messages about our audiences (see all of Aristotle's work on rhetoric as well as the presentation chapter of this text). What do *they* want? What will make *them* feel good? What will be respectful? Aristotle would say that the best means to persuade an audience is to use pathos (an emotional connection to the audience), logos (clear organization), and ethos (credibility of the speaker). Your cover letter can do all of this! The way that you connect to potential employers is through the strategic use of the content of your cover letter paragraphs.

Purpose of the Paragraphs

Most cover letters are produced to contain three components. These components may come across in three paragraphs on a single page to numerous paragraphs, bulleted lists, and data on several pages. For the purposes of clarity here, we will call them your three paragraphs.

Paragraph One

As noted in the résumé section above... you connect by highlighting links! This first paragraph is about those links. Most cover letters that simply use this first section to introduce the applicant and state the desired position. Can you imagine being an employer and reading hundreds of those? They would all blend together and not be very interesting to read. Now imagine that you pick up a page and the first thing you read is about YOU! It might be a compliment about a recent award. It may be recognition of the impressive goals that your company has set. You may even see that this letter is from the person that called you last week – and you know this because the first paragraph specifically mentions the call and something you two discussed. These are the memorable letters. To be memorable, make this paragraph about connecting you to the employer. Give examples of what you know about the person or company from your research. Do NOT include negative information about either or try to critique the company so you can be their problem solver (yikes!). Keep the information focused and have it lead to the reason why you are applying for this job with this company. Be sure to at some point tell them why you are writing—what position is desired!

Example

> Dear Mr. Cannizzaro,
> I so enjoyed our conversation in February. It was a good opportunity to catch up and I was excited to hear that All-tri is looking for new talent. As you know, I have had a long interest in and experience with Public Relations. My time as a Public Relations intern on the McDonald's Team this past summer at All-tri showed me that your reputation as one of the most prestigious organizations in the Austin area was well deserved. I hope to join your organization on a more permanent basis as an entry level PR associate.

Paragraph Two

Your second cover letter paragraph is about becoming a more real and substantial person in the eyes of your potential employer. Résumés are for listing your experience. Cover letters are for creating images through narratives. Once you have told the employer what job you want, you must get them to see you in the position. This means detailing a story (with a beginning, middle, and end) that applies a skill needed in the desired job. If the job needs you to work in groups, tell a story of how you led your team in a class-based project for your Introduction to Management course. If the position requires you to manage a budget, talk about the time that you worked on the university fall concert event and both allocated and managed thousands of dollars!

The best means of telling your story is to organize it just like you would in an interview—by first explaining the problem or situation, then your action, and finally the result. Give a specific instance/narrative rather than several vague examples. The story should relate to something on your résumé (i.e., if you tell a story about your summer job at *Home Depot*, make sure you have listed that job on your résumé). Even though this is a story, you'll need to make it short and to the point, using vivid and specific with great word economy. Finally, apply that skill to the current company or position.

Example

> Working in the Communication industry has allowed me to refine my skills working with the public. I wanted to relay to you an instance that occurred while I was working at Candy for all Occasions: A woman had placed an order two days before it was expected, and due to a miscommunication between her and another employee, her order was filled incorrectly. These circumstances put me in the difficult situation of mediating between the owner, who was on the phone, and the customer to rectify the situation by conforming to the language of each party, negotiating a resolution that would satisfy the customer's need while keeping the cost of reproduction at a minimum and saving face for the company. As a result, the situation left the customer satisfied and the order filled to her liking and me with an enlightened idea of what I would want for a career. With a background in customer service and a business background, I believe that my qualifications would be applicable in an agency setting—such as All-tri.

As you put together your story:
- Consider relating this information to something positive about their company
- A bulleted list of criteria is acceptable when appropriate for the job and employer
- Make it clear why you would like to work there
- Two paragraphs *could* be used instead of one but only if necessary

Paragraph Three

The last cover letter paragraph must leave a good impression with the potential employer. This is where you should be proactive. Think of how in the 1950s girls would like a boy and then sit at home on a Friday night waiting for that boy to call? Well, it ain't the 50s any more! Now is the time when women can ask out men, companies Google you before hiring you, the U.S. voted an African American man into the office of president, and the most powerful person in America is a female talk show host! (OK – that was a bit of a ramble, but you hopefully you get the point.) Now is the time to take charge!

As you finish your letter, let the reader know that you will be in touch. This will not mean that you are rude, pushy, or presumptive. Don't be obnoxious and state that this conversation will lead to an interview or other expectation. Do not say that you will be in touch *"to set up an interview"* or *"call at 9am on Monday the 21st to speak to you about the position."* If so, your letter will be handed around the office—not to showcase your skills, but as an example of how the next generation never learned manners. Instead, let the person know that you will follow up or check in and then, most important, do so!

Example

> I look forward to providing you with further details about my qualifications (in person, or via phone or e-mail). Please contact me at your earliest convenience. I will follow up with you to see what other information you may need from me during the week of June 28, 2010. Thank you for your time and consideration.

If appropriate, mention your enclosed résumé (if you have enclosed one) or any other materials. The great result of this paragraph is that you put the ball in your court. In this section, you can also thank the employer for reading your letter and considering you for the job.

Now be sure to sign off appropriately. Swap out statements such as "Holla Back" or "Kisses" for more professional formal endings such as "Yours truly/Sincerely/Sincerely yours" (or another formal ending).

Cover Letter Language

Like your résumé, a cover letter is a chance to prove your communication skills, and it is the first impression that you will relay. As such, you want to spend extra time on what and how you say it. Remember to avoid rambling – focus on what you can contribute to the employer (i.e., for that job – not just in general), including the experience, and the skills and knowledge that are needed by that particular position. Reduce your use of or any excessive repetition of the word "I" (although using this word IS acceptable). Yes, this document is about you but show the data rather than just going on and on about yourself. Too much "I" use can imply self-centeredness. Also, make sure your letter is neat. Avoid spelling errors, grammatical errors, typographical errors, smudged or unclear ink. Finally, have someone else proofread and critique your letter!!!!!!!!

The Look of Your Materials

As you can see from the examples given here, your cover letter can follow the "look" of your résumé. This means that using the header and style of your résumé for the cover letter will help you have a package to present when you send them. You will also want to put both on the same paper (avoiding a watermark), and clip together – but never staple these.

Signature

Your personal touch to your cover letter is your signature. While it is doubtful that any potential employer is using handwriting analysis to understand your personality from this turn of your pen, it is likely that your signature will leave an impression. Thus, always sign your letter. Use a good pen (no Sharpies, pencils, felt tip, or basic ballpoints, but you don't need a $300 Montblanc either). Gel pens and roller-ball fine point pens have clean dark lines with strong professional appeal. Because you are giving each document a personalized look (you don't want to look like this job is just another something at which you are throwing an application), never Xerox or copy your cover letter with a signature.

After writing your closing line (e.g., Sincerely, Kind Regards, etc.), hit theenter key three or four times to give room for your signature. Keep that signature the appropriate size, John Hancock scrawls are best left for the Declaration of Independence!

Example of Full Page Letter with Formatting

JENNIFER SMITH

12 South Drive
West Temple, PA 19460-9345
484.555.6987
js123smith@kanan.edu

All-tri Communications
c/o Mr. Tom Cannizzaro
200 South Broad Street
Austin, TX 19102-3899

June 5, 2011

Dear Mr. Cannizzaro,

I so enjoyed our conversation in February. It was a good opportunity to catch up and I was excited to hear that All-tri is looking for new talent. As you know, I have had a long interest in and experience with Public Relations. My time as a Public Relations intern on the McDonald's Team this past summer at All-tri showed me that your reputation as one of the most prestigious organizations in the Austin area was well deserved. I hope to join your organization on a more permanent basis as an entry level PR associate.

Working in the Communication industry has allowed me to refine my skills working with the public. I wanted to relay to you an instance that occurred while I was working at Candy for all Occasions: A woman had placed an order two days before it was expected, and due to a miscommunication between her and another employee, her order was filled incorrectly. These circumstances put me in the difficult situation of mediating between the owner, who was on the phone, and the customer to rectify the situation by conforming to the language of each party, negotiating a resolution that would satisfy the customer's need while keeping the cost of reproduction at a minimum and saving face for the company. As a result, the situation left the customer satisfied and the order filled to her liking and me with an enlightened idea of what I would want for a career. With a background in customer service and a business background, I believe that my qualifications would be applicable in an agency setting – such as All-tri.

From my experience, I refined organizational skills, participated in planning meetings, and enhanced networking skills. These learning experiences is why I am so interested in gaining further experience through your company; I consider myself a hard- working, goal oriented, personable, and resourceful worker who would like to work for a company with the same ethic. I look forward to providing you with further details about my qualifications (in person, or via phone or e-mail). Please contact me at your earliest convenience. I will follow up with you to see what other information you may need from me during the week of June 28, 2010. Thank you for your time and consideration.

Sincerely,

Jennifer Smith
Jennifer Smith

PDFs

After going through all of the effort with your résumé and cover letter, it would be a shame to have them arrive to an employer looking not at all like how you sent them. This will happen when you and the employer do not share the exact same operating systems, versions of word processing software, and/or if you use non-standard elements. Alas, you need not worry. Saving your documents in a PDF will save you from any conversion nightmares.

A Portable Document Format (PDF) is a picture of your document that is held stable when sent to other machines. You have likely viewed documents in this format for school, when doing research, or at work. If you have Word 2007 or above (or a MAC), you already have the ability to save your documents as PDFs. Just go to "Save As" and select PDF. Earlier versions of the software can create PDF files by going to the print window and "printing" the document as a PDF (it doesn't actually print—it just saves it as a PDF file—odd, we know!). Emailing or posting a PDF of your résumé, reference page, and cover letter will ensure that you formatting remains constant and that your look is just how you intended.

Note: If these directions are confusing, search the internet for 'create PDF free' to find a plethora of sites that are happy to do this for you!

Online Résumés and Portfolios

You might be posting your résumé all over the internet and uploading it to employers websites. We live in an electronic age and this is expected. What is becoming the new norm, however, is the online website. Many companies will offer you services for creating a professional/career-linked website, which will help you to post your résumé as well as various other materials about yourself. If you have a LinkedIn®account then you might have already taken advantage of such a service.

Here are some important ideas to keep when posting an online résumé. First, just like other online information, anything you post is 'out there.' Avoid putting contact information in a public place. Consider instead using the option for employers to contact you through the website email or service.

Second, you should know that many of the formatting elements discussed above will not pertain to an online medium. Having read the chapter on visual aids, you might remember the discussion about how PowerPointÒ slides serve a different purpose than a company website and so they will adopt different looks. The same idea applies here. A website may have different buttons (or pages) to show off each element of your information. Your contact information will likely not even be posted. You might need to choose a larger font because the one on your paper résumé is too difficult to read in this format. In addition, paper résumés allow you to tailor materials to a single job whereas what is online traditionally must be more generic unless you can provide different online versions to select employers.

While these issues sound like limitations, do not forget the huge benefits of online résumés. You may be able to link skills and experiences to examples. If you say that you are a certified nurse then you can hyperlink that statement to your transcripts and certificate. If you are looking for a job in broadcasting, you can only send along a CD with a paper résumé but on a website you can upload video examples in action!

As you turn your attention to posting, do not forget that your whole package of materials must work together. Allow employers to download a hard copy of your résumé from the online sites. Post your résumé in numerous places but only where you are willing to take a job. If you post your information on an international website but are not willing to move out of the country, it's just a waste of time for everyone. You should post only on sites that are advertising jobs in your specific area and where you have seen positions that you would certainly want. In the end, do not forget to think about costs. Most places will be free and it is important not to get dragged into paying for postings (heck, you don't have the job *yet!*).

A FINAL WORD

So, you now know what your résumé and cover letter should include, but how do you get started? It may seem overwhelming,but you can do it! It is important to take the time to brainstorm and figure out what information is relevant. Your first step is to have a clear sense of the type of positions you are qualified for and for which you would like to apply. Next, go online and look at other résumés and cover letters from folks in that industry. Get a sense of the type of impression that you would like to make—and begin the process!

Start out by making a list of what information is relevant to the position and jotting down all information you can think of that would convince an employer that you have the skills, experience, and knowledge they are looking for. It is better to start out with too much information and edit it down then trying to develop your résumé with too little information. Gather and summarize information about your education, employment, internships, volunteer work, activities, and any other experiences that would be applicable.

Since you are going to tailor your résumé for each position, it is useful to develop, save, and continually update a document that summarizes all of your experiences,skills, and accomplishments so that you can refer back to it when deciding what information to include for each position. Perhaps start with a document on your computer desktop that you can open and add to after any new experience (you can always go back and play with the look and language!).

Approach each of the steps listed here with confidence! Your first résumé may need quite a bit of work. Your first cover letter might not send the message that you hope it will. Heck, it is likely that your first job application won't get you the job. You may go through this process a few times. That's OK! You begin in school with mock job applications, résumé and cover letters turned in for a class, and applying to jobs on campus for a reason. If you are going to have a document that isn't perfect, then let it be in class or during school rather than when you finally find the job that you have always dreamed of. As you improve in this process, the look of your materials will reach a place where they can send just the right message – and get you just the right job!

Chapter Ten

Interview Me?
Interview You!

Two-Way Communication

If you have been watching the Real Housewives of New York, Tide Stain Stick or Pepsi Max commercials, or even if you've been trolling around YouTube, you have likely seen examples of some truly horrible interviews. These might be due to lack of preparation on either parties' part or simply bad behavior. Hopefully you will never need to experience fruitless interviews but we must admit that they happen and preparation is the key to turning things around.

Interviews are two-way, relational communication exchanges, which serve as a specialized form of oral task-related communication. The task? For those interviewing it is to evaluate the applicant's suitability for a job relative to all the other folks that have applied and for the person being interviewed it is to respond such that his or her feedback demonstrates the attributes on an ideal candidate! By understanding how employers are organizing and sending their messages to you, you will be better able to interpret and reply to those messages.

This chapter is broken up into two major sections. The first section helps you to become the best interviewer. The second section helps you to be the best interviewee. Both sections look at the organization of interviews and asking or answering questions. They prepare you for how not to ask illegal questions but how to answer them if they are asked of you. Most of all, they tell you how to send the message that you intend.

INTERVIEWING OTHERS

During your very first interview – look across the room; the person interviewing you was once sitting in your shoes. The reason that he or she can excel as an interviewer is because that person knows what it's like to be interviewed! Similarly, you are better prepared to be interviewed if you know the process of being an interviewer.

What Employers Want

Interviews are planned conversations. Er… well, they ought to be. These are times for, as said above, companies to evaluate your suitability for a job relative to others. Who are these others? They can be the other people that have also applied for the job or even an ideal person that the employer simply has in mind.

In either case, in order to do see how you compare, employers will have a set of criteria that serve as the basis for their evaluation. **Criteria** are standards for judgment. Employers will look to see if you particular foundational requirements and the levels that you have. These criteria may include:

- **Skills** – education, testable computer skills, languages, etc.
- **Experience** – past work in the field, types of work/training, management, etc.
- **Ability to learn** – accomplishments in past jobs, awards, honors, etc.
- **Personality** – demeanor, humor, approachability, respect, long-term goals that fit with company or position goals, etc.
- **Emotional intelligence** (see Leading and Meeting chapter) – adaptability, interpersonal ability, stress management, and mood (Chia, 2005).

To evaluate whether or not you have any of these criteria and how much of each, employers must *prepare* an interview such that it "tests" you.

How Do Employers Prepare

Oh gosh. Somebody has to say it… *not everyone who interviews you will be prepared*. Yes, this is true. However, that is no excuse for <u>you</u> not to prepare. The worst-case scenario is that they will have done their homework and you will not have! But, the level of an interviewer's preparation will vary significantly. The more that this person prepares then, quite obviously, the better he or she will be able to evaluate your fit for the position. While each step to do this is uniquely complex, the steps themselves are rather straightforward.

Steps to Interviewing
1) See a need.
2) Create an advertisement or job description
    a. for good info on how to do this, see: http://www.bnet. com/2410-13056_23-68811.html
3) Consider applicants (interns, out of house, job fairs, etc.).
4) Select candidates for interviews.
5) Organize and conduct interviews.
6) Make a selection.

Organizing the Interview of Others

Interviews are organized much like speeches. There is an opening, a middle, and a closing. The content of these parts differs from a speech, but just like a speech—they must be purposely structured!

The Opening

When you open a speech, you must **connect** to your audience (introduce yourself!) and then **preview** where the speech will go (let he or she know what you will be discussing). The same is true when you conduct an interview. Your job at this time will be to verbally guide the interview and make initial assessments.

Interview Opening Steps

1. **With a brief statement**: this is your time to develop rapport. Greet the applicant and help him or her to know your role as well as, if appropriate, the time that the interview will take (Rutgers, 2010).
2. **By defining the interaction:** given that there are many types of interviews, it is both useful and ethical (see ethics chapter) to let the interviewer know exactly what type of interview (e.g., informational, grievance, employment, etc.) will take place.
3. **By directing the time**: much like your speech preview, you will give the applicant an overview of the order of the interaction. You do not need to reveal information that will skew the process (such as letting the person know that he or she will be taking a computer skills test if this is supposed to gauge unstudied aptitude!).

After you have opened your interview, you can move on to the meat of the interaction!

The Middle

Interviews can be either structured or unstructured.**Structured** interviews have a clear plan of action and lend themselves to particular types of questions to gather specific information (Wiesnerf & Cronshaw, 1988). Whereas **unstructured** interviews, too often unplanned and left to the interviewer's whim and, thus, have less than half the success of gathering useful data (Wiesnerf & Cronshaw). Employers are moving away from purely unstructured interviews because structured interviews offer greater comparability among candidates and validity (Oliphant, Hansen, & Oliphant, 2008).

The middle of the interview is, of course, the most crucial information-gathering part of the process. It is where you probe the person (or people) in front of you. It is where you determine the viability of the candidates. The following sections (**Developing Probing Questions** and **TheQuestion Types and Purposes**) will guide you through this key section of conducting your interviews. Once you have developed those before your move to close the interview up.

The Closing

While the interviewing process may come to an end, that doesn't mean that the interview is actually over. After the last question, you still have some work to do. Wrap up the interview by taking out any ambiguity from the application process. The interviewee will likely have questions (Rennar, 2010) about the company and the process.

While you are making a determination (Rutgers, 2010):

- **Provide a timeline:** Thank the applicant for his/her time and explain what will happen next. Tell the applicant when the hiring decision will be made and how it will be communicated.
- **Answer questions and allow the applicant to add information:** The applicant's objectives are to gather information about the position and sell him/herself. Provide the opportunity for the applicant to accomplish these objectives.

An effective wrap-up will help to ease the candidates' mind (which results in less of those premature calls for updates!) whether you have decided to move forward with that candidate or not. Your last step for making your decision will likely relate to a combination of what you learned in the interview and what you will learn with a little modern day snooping. ☺

Developing Probing Questions

Interviews are organized much like speeches. There is an opening, a middle, and a closing. The content of these parts differs from a speech, but just like a speech – they must be purposely structured!

The Question Types

Interview questions will be developed in one of two ways: **closed-ended** or **open-ended questions.**

Closed-ended questions require short and pre-determined answers (some may call these dichotomous or saturated type questions). Closed-ended questions do not tend to probe (but can) and are restrictive enough to be answered in a few words (Richardson, 2002). Such as:

- To which job are you applying? *Public Relations Assistant.*
- Do you have experience using Quark? *Yes.*

- Have you completed the training program? *No.*
- What was your major? *Communication Studies.*
- Are you single? *Wha??* (OK—that one is closed-ended but also illegal. Read on for how to manage illegal questions!)

Open-ended questions solicit additional information from the applicant – and there is an infinite number of responses to these types of questions. Open-ended questions are broad and require more than one or two word responses (Richardson, 2002). Such as:

- What do you know about our company?
- Why do you want to work here?
- If you could have dinner with anyone alive or dead, who would it be and why?
- How have you trained to handle the requirements of this job?
- Can you give me an example of a time when you were a leader? (To be fair, this could be answered with either yes or no. In all likelihood, that response would be considered snotty and ruin your chances at landing the job. Use common sense to differentiate between question types and answer accordingly).

Expect most interviews to have both types of questions (Oliphant, Hansen, & Oliphant, 2008), but to, additionally, have the purpose of evaluating either your past behavior or how you might react in future situations.

Question Purposes

- *Have you worked on an Excel spreadsheet?*
- *What type of projects have you managed using Excel?*
- *Can you tell me about other database management systems that you have used?*

Do you catch a trend here? Clearly, someone asking these questions has a specific need to hire an employee with experience using the software program Excel or a similar database management program. This same interview may also ask about one's greatest strengths and weaknesses or other general questions, but this cluster shows a specific interest. Questions may be employed (no pun intended) to gather general information versus specific trait/skill information. These questions represent the difference between traditional and behavioral interview questions.

Traditional interview questions
Ask general questions. This type of interview is focused on the applicant as a general employee and perhaps a fit with the company or team. In this type of interview, how well a candidate manages the interview process will be highlighted. You will find interview questions such as:

- *What are your greatest strengths?*
- *Tell me about a weakness and how you manage it.*
- *If you were a tree, what kind of tree would you be?*
- *What do you admire in a boss?*

Behavioral-based interviewing is far more probing than traditional methods. **Behavioral interview questions** may not focus on how well a person interviews as much as what specific traits or actual experience the applicant offers (Oliphant, Hansen, & Oliphant, 2008). Questions may include:

- *What kind of leader are you?*
- *Would you rather work in a team or individually?*
- *How often did you consult team members during your training at GenEx corporation?*
- *Have you ever used your listening abilities to achieve goals?*

Behavioral interviews can be broken down into even more specific types based on question development – such as target selection questions or situational questions. Target selection works like a focus group system of asking questions with questions organized around specific key job criteria (Lazarus, 2008). See if these look familiar:

- *Have you worked on an Excel spreadsheet?*
- *What type of projects have you managed using Excel?*
- *Can you tell me about other database management systems that you have used?*

Situational interview questions pose specific job related situations. Situational questions are designed to elicit analytical or problem-solving responses but are on the spot and therefore give candidates limited preparation (note: case presentations, discussed below, are more elaborate versions of the situational question interview).

Interview Sequence

Again, the middle of an interview has many of the same characteristics as the body of a speech. Bodies of either of these amazing communication efforts will be structured in order to serve a particular purpose. As you learned when reading about speeches, particular information is best organized in a chronological format (e.g., talking about the history of the Urban Dictionary) whereas other information is best organized spatially (e.g., getting a tour of your college campus). Interview questions need organization as well—called interview sequencing.

Interview sequencing refers to the types of questions asked and in what order as a means of drawing out particular information (Hayes, 1994). The most common (but certainly not all of the) sequences are:
- Tunnel
- Funnel
- Inverted funnel

Tunnel sequences ask a series of closed-ended questions (i.e., those questions that have a set number or specific replies such as "yes" or "no" along with "male" or "female") (Hayes, 1994). It may be rare to offer this type of interview as you are hoping for more information from qualified applicants, but this will be useful as a pre-screening tactic before wasting time on long discussions with unqualified applicants. (Note… if you are interviewing and are only hearing closed-ended questions—or get cut off when you try to elaborate, remember that the interviewer is not angry at you! That person is likely pre-screening you so be happy to keep your answers short and to the point!).

Funnel sequences mix both closed and open-ended questions that begin with the general questions and then narrow the focus (like a funnel!) into more specific questions.

> For example, you might ask a respondent to describe his/her opinion about retail licensing policies in general before asking for opinions of specific policy options. This approach is useful if the specific questions will give the respondent information that could change his/her initial assessment. (UC Davis, n.d.)

Inverted funnel sequences also mix both closed and open-ended questions but flip the funnel upside down so that the most targeted questions come up front and the general ones conclude.

> For example, you might ask about the individual activities of a coalition before asking for the coalition's effectiveness overall. The respondent may give a more detailed response to the question about overall effectiveness because the earlier question will have made him/her think about the specific activities. (UC Davis, n.d.)

One of the best examples of a funnel interview includes our good ol' tax collectors at the IRS! If you were considering a job working for this all-powerful organization, according to John Brady (2007), author of *The Craft of Interviewing,* here is what you might experience:

> The inverted-funnel technique makes getting answers from a former IRS agent as easy as taking candy from a baby, as Max Gunther found one wintry day in New York.
>
> "When I walked into that interview, I wanted that ex-agent to tell me everything interesting that had ever happened to him in his tax-collecting job," recalls Gunther. "But how could I get him started? I could have asked a vague, general question: 'Has anything exciting ever happened to you in your IRS job?' But I didn't. It was too broad."
>
> Instead, Gunther asked the agent to itemize: "When you were auditing people's tax returns, did anybody ever try to bribe you?"
>
> "That question wound him up - in fact, very nearly overwound him," recalls Gunther. They talked for four hours. "I barely asked another question the whole time, and I came out of the interview with a wealth of fascinating material about the inner workings of the IRS. My broad question - Did anything exciting ever happen? - had been fully answered without my asking it." (para 6).

As you can see, there are many excellent means of putting together the body of your interview to best gather the right kind of information from your applicant. Once you have it, be sure to wrap it up well!

External Evaluations of the Candidate

Ah, the electronic age. Now is the day of Google, LinkedIn, Facebook, and Twitter. Now is a time with voyeurism and exhibitionism living hand-in-hand. More importantly, this is when an employer can find out just about anything about you! It is common practice for companies to conduct a thorough background check on you before they ever call you in for a job interview (and certainly before making an offer).

What They Look At

In this digital age, companies are resorting to checking your presence online. In a 2010 report commissioned by Microsoft, only 15% of respondents thought online information about themselves had an effect on job prospects. However, 75% of employers reported they conducted online research about applicants (Privacy Rights Clearinghouse, 2010). In other words, you should regularly check your online identity—i.e. be careful what you post! Now is the time to clean up your Facebook or other social networking pages. Delete of all those unnecessary photos *and* comments which you have posted; or your friends have posted about you. Another way to find website content related to you is to conduct a Google search on YOU. You may be surprised to see what will surface…

Certain jobs require specific types of checks. For example, if the job requires working with children, the employer will most likely do a criminal background check to make sure the applicant does not have a child abuse history. Clean driving records may be required for jobs where you will be doing a lot of driving. If a company decides to do a background check on you, it is their responsibility to let you know that it will be conducted. If you know you haven't done anything, don't be scared! This is not a personal reflection on their first impression of you—it's just the law!

At some point before an offer is presented, companies also conduct reference checks. You need to prepare a list of three to five names that your prospective employer can call. The purpose of these checks is usually to vouch for your character, and to ascertain how you have performed in a previous job (see résumé chapter for more about references). If you have not held a job before, you can include names of teachers or other respectable members of the community who can speak favorably about you.

It is your responsibility to brief your references about the position you are seeking, and what the employer is looking for (Navarro, 2006). Give them a copy of your résumé, and write them a thank you letter. Don't tell them what to say, but make sure they understand your qualifications for the job. (Definitely see résumé chapter!)

What They Can See

It is important to know that you have certain rights regarding what can and cannot be included in your background check. Federal and state regulations exist to protect rights with regard to information sought about individuals. For instance, medical records are often confidential and cannot be released without your consent. Contact your state's fair employment agency to familiarize yourself with your rights on this issue.

What To Manage

You may think that the most embarrassing thing in the world would be to have a potential employer hand you a picture off your Facebook page and ask you what you are doing. Worse… they look at the picture and decide not to bring you in for an interview at all. In order to be sure that you have the potential to get an interview invitation and that you aren't confronted with painful information when you get there, manage your online presence.

Dan Schawbel (2010) asks in *Manage Your Online Reputation—Before Someone Else Does*, "Did you know you're being Googled right now? You are." He tells us that almost 80% of recruiters are using search engines to look at you, and nearly 65% are using social networks to *check you out!* So, he recommends some unique ideas that go beyond simply changing your settings to private (not that those aren't easy to override) and taking down pictures (which will remain in cyberspace forever):

1. Purchase your own domain name.
2. Develop a blog and connect it with your name.

3. Claim your name on social networks before someone else does.
4. Contribute content to other sites so you can offer your own background/bio.

Finally, Schawbel (2010) gives all of us the following advice:

"Use reputation management tools. To protect, and monitor, your online reputation, use a variety of tools, along with Google Reader. Google Reader will capture alerts for your name as they appear across the Web. First, set a comprehensive Google alert for your full name, and common misspellings, so that when you're mentioned on a blog or in a news story, you'll be aware of it. Next, use Backtype.com to set an alert for your name within blog comments, and then BoardTracker.com so that you're notified when your name appears in a discussion forum thread. Use TweetBeep.com to get alerts for when your name is mentioned on Twitter. Finally, use Social Mention occasionally to search through all social sites for your name." (para. 11)

Now you have a good idea of what employers are up to during the interview process and it is your turn to offer them feedback that will land you the job! The means to doing that is learning how to best interact with potential employers when you are being interviewed....

BEING INTERVIEWED

Got good education – check!
Found ideal job – check!
Sent in résumé – check!
Called in for interview...
CONGRATULATIONS!

If you have gotten this far then you are well on your way to your first day at that fantastic job. There is, however, one important element standing between you and the offer. It is...(drum roll, please) the interview. While you may have an incredibly engaging personality coupled with superior experience, you are not a shoo-in! **Interviews are the employers' opportunity to assess/evaluate your suitability for the position relative to _others_.** So no matter how great you think you are, it also depends on how you will be with the people around you (isn't that called Communication?). In order to do well, you must take a lot of things into consideration... which means: you must be prepared!

Unfortunately, interview preparation is something that far too many applicants lack. According to Robert Half International and reported in the Wall Street Journal (Coombes, 2005), when 1,400 Chief Financial Officers were asked during what phase job applicants were likely to blow any chance of getting hired, they said:
- 9% do it in cover letters
- 21% in résumés
- 32% in the interview!

In fact, Clive Muir (2005), Professor in the Department of Management at Stetson University, argued that an applicant's performance in an interview has a greater influence on hiring than academic records or any other credentials. An A on your sophomore year psychology class doesn't necessarily mean that you are a good fit for the position! A professional, calm, and well-mannered presentation... well, that might get you somewhere.

OK, so you may be getting a little nervous (and wondering why you worked so hard to look good on paper). Do not worry—you are already on the right track. Your résumé and cover letter got you the interview and now you can learn how to ace this even more important step!

Interview Types

For our purposes and your interest from a Business Communication perspective, there seems to be just one type of interview – the one to get you the job. In truth, there are many types of interviews and knowing all of them can actually help you to do well with the others. Here are a few interviews with which in a business context you need to be familiar:
- **Informational** (applicant-initiated, typically pre-interview)
- **Performance** (employer-initiated, regular interval work assessment)

- **Counseling** (applicant or employer-initiated, therapeutic focus)
- **Interrogation** (employer-initiated, investigatory)
- **Grievance** (applicant-initiated, conflict resolution)
- **Exit** (employer-initiated, offer employer feedback)
- **Employment** (employer-initiated, evaluating applicant suitability)

As we move forward, this section will discuss only the **employment interview**, which will be your entrance into the business world! This is a time when an employer has reviewed your résumé and has decided to bring you in for a more personal evaluation. Whether or not you are one-on-one or with others will be up to that company's practices and needs.

Just Me? Or With Others?

Have you ever seen either of Donald Trump's reality shows, "The Apprentice" or "Celebrity Apprentice"? Trump provides an excellent example of the infamous group interview. Why infamous? Well, he turns the session into a dramatic finger-pointing session. In truth, group interviews are no different than individual interviews—you are being compared to the person that the company wants to hire (actual or imagined).

The **group vs. individual** ratio of people on each side of the table can vary. You are probably most familiar with the one-on-one setting—where you sit across from one company representative and have a discussion. Changes in our modern economy have created a surge in the number of applicants applying for individual positions (Chan, 2010). When this is the case, companies tend to bring in groups for initial screenings before having top candidates come back for secondary (or several) interviews. In some settings, it will be you speaking to a panel of people from the company. In other settings, you may be in front of one company representative surrounded by other interviewees. And, without making the math complicated, the situation can be a panel on both sides as well.

The number of the people in the room when you interview ought to simply be a matter of where to give your eye contact. When someone speaks, it is important that you look at that person. If it is someone interviewing you or someone sitting next to you being interviewed, look at him or her! Make sure that you give the speaker the attention that you would want. It shows an interviewer that you respect him or her and an interviewee that you are not intimidated.

Interview Modes

Not only will the number of people in the room vary – the room itself is a variable. Interviews are not always conducted in the traditional fashion of a company calling you in, sitting you in a room, and asking you questions. Today, interviews will happen in a variety of modes/ settings.

The Telephone Screening Interview

> It happens all the time: we get a résumé that everyone thinks is really exciting. Terrific grades. All kinds of powerful-sounding jobs… And then I call them up, and I can't stand talking to them… Before moving on to a full-fledged in-person interview, we usually use a phone screen to make sure that we're not wasting time and money on someone who is just seriously not smart. (Spolsky, 2006)

Phone interviews are time and money savers all the way around. Typically, phone interviews are conducted by secondary employees (i.e., not the big boss) or by a human resources representative. The time of the interview can vary from a few minutes to well over an hour. A strong benefit of phone interviews is that they cannot be visually focused (what you are wearing or look like) but instead must focus on qualifications (Spolsky, 2006). However, nonverbal communication does come through in phone interviews. Slouching over a desk, playing with pens or items around you, or a focus on something other than the discussion can all be heard right through the phone lines. Treat this interview as seriously as you would any other because even though interviews conducted using this medium are evaluated more positively than face-to-face encounters (Straus, Miles, & Levesque, 2001), they are still your first and only chance to make a first impression!

The Face-To-Face Interview

The employer's impressions about you based on an interview carries more weight than your résumé, so you should expect them to meet you face-to-face. In fact, Muir (2005) states that how you promote yourself is not as critical as how you appear to project behaviors that conform to the other party's desires. That's fancy talk for… *if you give the impression that something is true then others will believe that it is true*. Meeting face-to-face allows others to see how you project yourself.

Traditional face-to-face interviews

Traditional face-to-face interviews are exactly what you may expect in terms of coming in to chat with a person about a job. How they are organized can differ (as noted earlier in this chapter), but the purpose is the same. Company representatives want to see how you respond to specific questions when you are put in particular situations. The unspoken focus of these interviews will be nonverbal messages that you send in response to the setting. Practice behaviors that signal rapport like smiling and nodding your head, to signal that you belong in that environment. You can practice sitting up straight at your desk, shaking others' hands firmly when you meet someone new, and folding your hands (as to not fidget!) when you are listening to someone. All of these slight gestures will project confidence and comfort (Giles, 2010).

Technology Mediated

You may be asked to have a ***mediated* face-to-face interview** using videoconferencing technology. According to Barbara Kiviat's (2009) article in Time, *How Skype Is Changing the Job Interview*, such practices are becoming a trend to save travel time for applicants and company resources given to on-site interviews. As with any new business communication toy, this technology still has its bugs. Prepare and practice ahead whether you are the interviewer or interviewee. No matter how many miles separate you, this is still an interview. Dress as you would if you were meeting the interviewers in person, be sure to have good lighting, make sure your "backdrop" is professional, and above all – make the necessary preparations to ensure there are no interruptions (Bibey, 2010)!

Case Presentations

The case presentation interview is employed primarily by management-consulting firms, as well as investment-banking companies, and is increasingly being used by other types of corporations as at least part of the job-interviewing process. These interviews ask that applicants conduct research (even during a brief break in the larger interview) and come back to present findings or suggestions to the company. Wait a minute, this isn't school! That's *right* – this will be your career! Some employers are looking for up-to-date evidence of your capabilities.

Case presentation interviews are designed to scrutinize the skills that are especially important in management, consulting, communication, and related fields – such as: quantitative skills, analytical skills, problem-solving ability, communications skills, creativity, flexibility, the ability to think quickly under pressure, listening skills, business acumen, keen insight, interpersonal skills, the ability to synthesize findings, professional demeanor, and powers of persuasion.

Experts (see: Hansen, 2006)agree on many of the fine points for approaching case interviews:
- Practice extensively
- Listen carefully to the question.
- Remember that rarely is there one "right" answer.
- Don't be afraid to ask questions.
- Construct a logical framework with which to explore the critical issues of the case.
- Prioritize the issues and objectives.
- Don't be afraid to think outside the box. Creativity and brainstorming are likely just what the interviewer is looking for!

Skill Testing

If the position that you seek requires specific skills or knowledge, companies may require you to take a test to show that you have the skills required. These are often scheduled before the face-to-face interviews. Companies ask applicants to take these tests so that they can assess their reasoning skills and performance ability. Some examples of **reasoning tests** are verbal, numeric, abstract, spatial, and mechanical. Some examples of **performance tests** are typing skills, software skills, statistical knowledge, or computer programming languages. Tests may be multiple choice, timed, etc. (yep, just like school!) (Psychometric-success. com, 2009).

If your company asks that you take a test, consider going online to take several versions of a practice test before logging in to take the actual test. Previsor.com (formerly Brainbench.com) has an array of skill assessment tests and resources that are particularly helpful for this need. Be sure to ask what version of the software the test will be in and using what operating system – as differences in these elements may mask your actual aptitude.

Preparation Elements of Your Interview

Being called in for an interview is actually not the entire process by which you are evaluated. In fact, the **interview process** has several stages:

- Interview preparation
- Elements of the Actual interview
- Post-interview follow-up

Regardless of the size or nature of the company, these steps will (actually *should* but don't always) occur. If you interview with a small company, you may simply have a one-on-one with the store-owner or manager (e.g., your summer job between junior and senior year of high school). As you move forward in your career path, you will interview with larger companies or even moderate sized companies that want to make very sure that they hire the right person the first time. As your interviews become associated with higher level positions or larger companies, the actual interview phase itself can expand into a series of steps that may include all or any of the following:

- Initial interview with Human Resource representative
- First interview
- Technical test
- Second/Third/Final interview with hiring decision maker
- Background and reference checks

The key to doing well at any of these phases... is being prepared! (Surprise, surprise, right?)

General Interview Preparation

Have you ever gone into a test *knowing* that you were not prepared? How did that feel? Not good, huh? Going into an interview not prepared feels about the same. Oddly enough, according to Drs. Hansen and Hansen (2006), people go into interviews unprepared all the time.

> Most career experts agree that few interviewees prepare adequately for interviews (and) that, while college students spend in excess of 4,000 hours studying and attending class to prepare for their career, the average interviewee spends less than an hour preparing for a job interview(para. 4).

Perhaps this lack of preparation is because people are not sure *how* to prepare for an interview. It's actually easier than you may think.

Know the Company

The first means of doing well in your interview is **knowing who is interviewing you.** This knowledge is relatively easy to come by given the availability of information on the Internet. Sit down and look up some basics about the company, which will give you an edge in the interview, including the company's history, mission, goals, and performance (Pearce, 2010; Rennar, 2005). Armed with this information, you can build better rapport with the interviewer because you can tailor your responses to your audience and you will be able to answer crucial questions. Be prepared for questions such as: *"What do you know about this company?"* or *"How do you feel about our recent acquisitions?"* or *"Who do you think will be our biggest competitor?".*

Where can you find this information? Use a combination of sources for this research. First, go with the obvious: Google! Use Google™ to look up company details by trolling around on their website, finding out what others have written about the company as well as to looking up key personnel (yes, now you want to Google™ the execs and even those who are interviewing you).

Next, go a bit further to find out the stability of the company (you don't want to work for Enron just after the crash, right?) through sources such as Dun & Bradstreet (www.dnb.com). This website will allow you to check out company's credit information and, if the company is traded publicly, review its stock performance. After this, search news articles about the company and the field (e.g., what news is going on in the world of accounting?). Finally, conduct a few information-seeking interviews with experts in the field, or even with someone from the company itself. You can pick up some amazing tips and insights very quickly this way.

These search techniques are ultimately in your best interest. You might uncover dirt that makes you think carefully about whether you want to work with that company (Crawford, 2007). The last thing you want is to accept a position in a company that is about to close, has shady practices, or does not make good on promises to candidates. The interview is a two-way street. Sure, the employer evaluates you, but you should also be evaluating them.

Approach the interview with the mindset that you are entering into a negotiation (Mavunga and Kombe, 2008). As the job-seeker, you are coming from a weaker position than the employer. The more knowledge you have about the company, the better able you will be to ask questions that evaluate any opportunity and offer informed answers to questions.

Finding Practice Interview Questions

Finding Interview questions will help you to start the necessary rehearsal element of your interview. How so? Go into any search engine. Put "interview questions" in the search engine and you will find *thousands* of interview questions! Many of these questions are rather **expected** (e.g., tell me about yourself), some of them might be **dreaded** (i.e., something that you don't want to answer even if someone else might not dread it, such as, "if you were a color, what color would you be and why?"), and some of them could be **illegal** (e.g., "are you planning on putting on any weight in the near future?"). The point is that you can easily find any number of general questions. These become a useful tool to lay some groundwork. Next, ask people in the industry or those who have been at their careers long enough to have conducted several interviews for what questions they believe you might get.

The questions that you pull off the Internet (or gather from other sources) should pertain to you or the job. If you see questions on the Internet about your background in accounting and you are interviewing to be a hand model, well, likely these will not apply. Thus, go through the questions and pull out those that you could possibly be asked or even alter the questions so that they better pertain to you, the industry, or the position.

Alter Standard Questions to Be About You

The questions listed above offer examples simply pulled out of scholarly articles and Internet sites. Obviously, they are questions that are not specific to you, your industry, or your potential job. To allow these questions or others like them to help you to prepare for your interview, some alteration will be necessary.

Standard Question 1:
What were some responsibilities you had at your last job?
Alteration: What were your responsibilities at your summer internship with Dupont?

Standard Question 2:
What major challenges did you face in school?
Alteration: What major challenges and problems did you face in pursuing your Business Management degree? How did you handle them?

Standard Question 3: What didn't you like about a past job?
Alteration: What didn't you like about working at Rita's Water Ice?

Altering the questions will help you to consider specific examples. This way when an employer asks either a general question or one specifically from your résumé or experience, you will have something specific to offer.

Practice Answering Common Questions

You cannot guess as to what type of interview you will have (funnel, inverted funnel, no structure at all) or the specific questions that you will be asked (open-ended, closed-ended, dreaded, illegal) but this should not prevent you from being prepared. You can go through the process of preparation so that any situation you encounter will be a comfortable experience.

Select these common questions (altering them to fit your situation) and consider why the question would be asked and what the interviewer is hoping to gain from your answer. As noted above, the questions will likely fall into three categories: expected, dreaded, and illegal.

Expected questions are those that based on you, the industry, and the position you should just expect to get asked. If you are applying to a job that insists on PowerPoint skills then you should expect to get asked if you have these and about your particular skill level with the software. A **dreaded question** will be unique to you. You might get asked what type of tree you would be (a typical question to determine how you see yourself and if you can think metaphorically). This abstract question could be something that you absolutely dread while another person would actually look forward to the opportunity to answer this. Finally, you should be prepared to answer, and thus find several, illegal questions. There is a substantial discussion of illegal questions in the later sections of this chapter but. for now, know that an **illegal question** is one that hopes to evaluate you on criteria not associated with the job.

Here is a list of common questionsdrawn from a variety of sources and an indication of why they might be asked (Lazarus, 2008; Messmer, 2004; Navarro, 2006; Pearce, 2006; Thornbury & White, 2006; Williams, 2006; Woloshin, 2008). These have been broken down into categories of *expected* and *possibly dreaded*.

Expected Questions/ Behavioral Examples
Tell me about yourself.
- Employers do not want extensive history of your life. Pick the jobs that apply to the position and say one concrete achievement about each one.

What is your current salary/benefits expectation?
- Employers love to have you start this discussion (hopefully your offer is low and they can give it to you without you ever knowing your higher value). Avoid discussing salary and refocus on the job's responsibilities, and that you trust the employer will give a fair wage when he or she offers the job. If pushed, offer your mid-range dependent on benefits.

Why do you want to work for us?
- Employers want to know what you know about them and what qualifications make you a good fit to their existing needs.

Tell me about your biggest weakness.
- "None" is not an acceptable answer or even true (sorry!)— neither is "being too gosh darn perfect." Yuck. Employers want to evaluate your honesty and ethic to fix issues. For example, "Being so detail-oriented means I take a lot of time on projects. However, I make sure I allot enough time so I can meet deadlines." (Be sure to offer a specific—discussed below.)

Tell me about your biggest strength/most successful project.
- Employers are looking for specifics to gauge your idea of success. Frame this in terms of your past employers goals and be sure to link this strength with the prospective company's goals. (Don't take sole credit for any success that was not truly an individual effort.)

(Possible) Dreaded Question Examples

Can you explain this gap in employment?
- Employers want to be sure that you are not lazy and are attempting to see if you were fired. If you were laid off because of an economic downturn or quit because of a change in family situation, feel free to say so. Then talk about what you have to done to stay current in your field, such as volunteering in professional organizations.

Tell me about your worst employer.
- Never badmouth a past employer. Employers want to test your tactfulness. If your last boss was a schmuck then find something to say about how the environment was challenging but never slander!

Describe how you would successfully persuade a group to adopt your point of view. How did you achieve this?
- Employers hope to see what type of leader you will be (see leadership chapter). Frame your response to your then employer's goals, and focus on the importance of conflict resolution and interpersonal cooperation skills.

Organizing Your Answers

Specifics are the key to being memorable in your interview. Anyone can talk about their aptitude for leadership when asked about a good quality, but someone who can explain how he or she took on the head position for organizing the spring concert series at his or her university and detail exactly how that was done… well, now that is impressive!

Most job search sites have fun acronyms for how you should answer interview questions (STAR, PAR, SAR, S-PAR, etc.). Each of these means just about the same thing. First, each suggests that simply offering up a story or brief response is neither effective nor memorable. Second, they suggest that organization is a key way for you to craft interview responses so that they are easy to follow and easy to remember (if you have taken a Public Speaking class, these edicts of communication were likely impressed upon you often).

For our purposes, **PAR (Problem-Action-Results)** is the easiest response organization to use. This organizational method reminds you to begin your responses with a situation or problem, note what action that you took, and give detailed results of your action. Yes… then can happen in just a few sentences!

Here's a good example:
1. *What major challenges and problems did you face in your Business Managementdegree? How did you handle them?*

> **P**: "The workload was especially difficult because expectations in this major are so high—and realistic for post-graduation. The most challenging course that I took was Interviewing (COM 300) with Dr. Pfarrer."

> **A**: "While this course was demanding with Corporate Research Project, 3 speeches including an Elevator Speech about ourselves and 2 interviews, I found that working efficiently with a calendar and organizing small tasks helped me to feel proficient with my progress."

> **R**: "This tactic must have worked because I received a high grade in the course (a B+) along with a glowing letter of recommendation, which was included in my application packet given to you."

The above example is be a great means of being clearly articulate in your interview and offering memorable specifics but perhaps a bit difficult to use as part of your preparation. While the above may be what you actually say in the interview…. consider using an abbreviated form in your prep work so that you can easily draw to mind all of your prepared examples (see below).

---

1. What major challenges and problems did you face in your Business Management degree? How did you handle them?

P: Workload (Pfarrer class)
A: Work efficiently
R: High grade & letter of rec.

Be sure not to memorize your answers; the key to interviewing success is simply being prepared for the questions and having a mental outline to follow in responding to each question.

As you are preparing your PARs, keep in mind that this is an organized conversation and the natural you will be the best seller of you! Avoid clichés. "People-person" is overused. "I'm looking for a new challenge" gives the impression that you are about to be fired (Cejka & Taylor, 2007). Keep your responses succinct—don't rattle on and on. Being too chatty will backfire on you. Watch for signs that show the interviewer is getting bored, such as looking at the clock or watch, or if they stop taking notes (A word of caution for chatty job candidates, 2008). Be prepared to negotiate your expertise. Be familiar with the technical language of the job. Tailor your answers to include the company, showing that you have done your homework (Lipovsky, 2006).

As part of your homework, practice your <u>emotional</u> confidence. There is no crying in interviewing! Crying puts the interviewer in the position of being your psychologist (Hoffman, 2008). Avoid showing too much negative emotion. Even if you don't get this job—you might be offered the next one if you keep positive. And finally, remember to always be polite. Being defensive or argumentative with the interviewer will get you nowhere.

Tactics for When You Can't Answer a Question

As you prepare, be sure not to just get ready for the intelligent and seemingly appropriate questions. You will not believe what some people will ask you! Clive Muir (2008), noted above, put together a list of actual interview questions that were both asked and seem simply ludicrous.

- Would you like a cup of tea or coffee before we start? Don't worry,that isn't a trick question… or is it?
- Imagine you are a frog. Which beer do you prefer and why?
- If you won $20 million in the lottery, what would you do with the money?
- I know we're not allowed to ask this (ha ha), but what is your religion?
- Are you as personable a person in-person, as you are on the phone?
- Why the hell would you want to work here?

Depending on the question, you have several options. You could say, "I am not clear how that would relate to the job. Would you mind explaining this to me?" (Be sure to do this with a pleasant demeanor—snarky will get you nowhere!) Another potential response is "If I understand the question correctly, you would like to know (followed by a quick and relevant revision of the statement to something job pertinent)…" This demonstrates your ability to listen and communicate effectively (Thornbury & White, 2006). As you respond to your own revision of the question, make sure you spin your response in a solution-oriented way (Crawford, 2007).

Silence is not an option

Illegal questions need a response, even if this response is not a direct answer to the job (think of it as *strategic ambiguity;* see Paul &Strbiak, 1997). Neither is taking on a confrontational manner. Know how to respond, and your interviewer will remember you in a positive light.

The bottom line is that your answers should always draw the discussion back to the employer's needs. The employer has already reviewed your credentials (we hope!). What they are judging in the interview is your personal character to see if this is a good fit for them.

Managing Illegal Questions and Interactions

Illegal questions are going to get asked. You may not hear them in your experience (or you will) but they happen all the time. Some are intentional (e.g., "Wow, you look so young. How old are you?"), while others are just slips that happen as part of natural conversation (e.g., "I see you are wearing an engagement ring. Congratulations! When's the big day?"). Never feel obligated to answer an illegal question—but don't *not* answer it simply because it is illegal. If someone asks you what kind of accent you have (if you have one) and you feel comfortable letting people know, then do so. How do you know if it is illegal?

If you are wondering what actually constitutes an **illegal question**, the general rule of thumb is that any question that allows an employer to evaluate you based upon criteria that do not pertain to the job—is illegal. Neuson (2007), author of *Avoid discrimination claims when interviewing job candidates*, classifies illegal discriminatory categories into the following:

- **Age** - including questions that ask how many years you've been out of school; it is, however, acceptable to ask if you meet age requirements to work for the state or business
- **Marital status** – whether you have children, plan to have children, or your spouse's occupation
- **Gender** – including whether you are comfortable working with the opposite gender
- **Race/national origin** – where parents are from, where you were born, origin of last name, if English was a second language, language spoken at home, how long you lived here, if you are a citizen; it is, however, acceptable to ask for proof of eligibility to work if you are offered the job
- **Religion** – church you attend, if you attend church, religious holidays, if you can work on Sunday
- **Disability** – physical or mental limitations outside the purvue of the job; it is, however, acceptable to ask if you can do the essential functions of the job without accommodation and ask for physical checks on this if you are offered the job
- **Sexual orientation** – questions about relationships and partners or living arrangements

To be fair, some illegal questions may be asked because the employer hopes to understand your ability to do the job based on factors outside of work conditions. For example, "So, any kids?" may be a concern that children will hinder your ability to show up to work on time. Put the employers at ease by addressing what appears to be the true concern. Consider offering a statement like, "Some folks might be concerned that I will not be able to come to work every day because I have children. I can assure you that I am aware of the job's requirements and always prioritize my day to avoid any unnecessary conflicts with meeting those requirements."

Laws to Know

While you know the categories on which an employer may unfairly judge you, there are actually specific laws about what is legal in employment settings. Knowing these will help you be an informed and confident interviewee. The U.S. Equal Employment Opportunity Commission (2010), notes that these laws include:

- **Title VII of the Civil Rights Act of 1964 (Title VII):** prohibits employment discrimination based on race, color, religion, sex, or national origin

- **The Equal Pay Act of 1963 (EPA):** protects men and women who perform substantially equal work in the same establishment from sex-based wage discrimination

- **The Age Discrimination in Employment Act of 1967 (ADEA):** protects individuals who are 40 years of age or older

- **Title I and Title V of the Americans with Disabilities Act of 1990, as amended (ADA):** prohibit employment discrimination against qualified individuals with disabilities in the private sector, and in state and local governments

- **Sections 501 and 505 of the Rehabilitation Act of 1973:** prohibit discrimination against qualified individuals with disabilities who work in the federal government

- **Title II of the Genetic Information Non Discrimination Act of 2008 (GINA):** prohibits employment discrimination based on genetic information about an applicant, employee, or former employee

- **The Civil Rights Act of 1991:** among other things, provides monetary damages in cases of intentional employment discrimination

Is all this illegal stuff making you nervous? Well, don't be. You already have so many tools to a successful interview that you are miles ahead of the competition. In fact, you are so prepared that you will likely be asking some questions yourself!

Prepare Intelligent Questions to Ask

Effective interviews will give you, at some point, an opportunity to ask questions. Remember that this is a conversation, a two-way interaction, and that you should be prepared to ask questions. In fact, this is your chance to show your interest in the company and see how well you will fit in their organization! You don't have the job yet so questions about how well they will adapt to your desires and needs or the salary that you want may need to be held until you have an offer.

Rennar (2010) suggests questions*:
About the position
- Is position is newly created? If not, how long has the position been vacant?
- If hired, what resources would I have to accomplish the job's goals in first 6 months?

About the company
- How is job performance evaluated?
- What are the company's strategies to remain competitive and what is my role in that?

About environment
- Was the predecessor promoted or did s/he leave?
- What is the typical day or week like?

About expectations
- What qualities would the ideal candidate have, and what skills and abilities would go above and beyond expectations?

(*questions taken from: Conklin, 2007, Lazarus, 2008.)

Remember, it's not about *you*, but your <u>fit</u> with them. Understanding that fit is your job as much as theirs. So, ask questions… and do it with confidence!

Developing Confidence

What is the value of confidence? Motivational speakers make a whole bunch of money helping people *feel* confident. Athletes engage in visioning as part of their training– imagining they have won helps them perform better. If you feel you can do something, well then, your chances for success actually improve! Another term for this is **self-efficacy** (Tay, Ang, & Dyne, 2006). Bandura (1997) states that self-efficacy is a strong predictor of how an individual behaves in the future. Self-efficacy is related to greater effort and persistence—behaviors that lead to the achievement of goals.

There are several ways to develop your confidence in interviewing (Tay, et al., 2006). You could engage in vicarious learning (which means learn as other do) through strategies such as watching videos on good interviews and looking at examples of interviews that impressed employers. You could hire a coach to give you support (hey, wait a minute! You are in a class that does that!). You could role-play by doing a mock interview with a friend or classmate (Rennar, 2010)—again, likely an experience you will get in a Business Communication course!

A quick mini-visualization before you enter the interview scene gets you mentally prepared (Crawford, 2007). Envision yourself ending the interview with a firm handshake. Imagine that two days later you get a callback. Then go and make it happen!

"Day-Of" Interview Behavior

The big day comes. You may have butterflies doing the tango in your tummy or you may just be perfectly calm. After all of your preparation, it can seem difficult to imagine anything else that you must do before walking in the door—but here are a few tips to putting on the final touches.

Dress for Success

Have you ever gone to a party and realized you were over or under-dressed? Remember how awkwardly, painfully uncomfortable you felt? Imagine how you would feel if you walked into your interview and saw every employee in shorts and t-shirts while you were strutting around in a three-piece wool suit? Worse—what if the employer said, "We like you but don't you have anything more appropriate to wear?" This actual example of a question asked of an interviewee is a good indication of how the wrong look can throw off the whole interview experience even when you look 'professional'.

The person interviewing you is looking for *visual similarity and attractiveness* in interviewees. Yep, you better look like everyone else and be pretty—or handsome. Well, not quite… they judge whether you are a good fit, and, just like other places of social interaction (such as a bar), physical appearance plays a role in connection. Communication scholars, Neuliep and McCroskey (2001) say that people tend to view others of the same ethnicity as more attractive than those of other ethnicities. Nash and her colleagues—including some with L'Oreal cosmetics (2006) concluded that moderate cosmetics helped Caucasian women be perceived as healthierand more confident than those without.

Most studies ascribe to the less-is-more philosophy (e.g., some make-up or scent is viewed as positive but noticeable elements of either detract from the interview; see Cox and Glick's, 1986, *Résumé evaluations and cosmetics use: When more is not better*).

Once again, your research will serve you well in this area. For example, if you know that the company has a dress code of gray business suits for men but you are not sure what the women wear, you can dress similarly even if you are a woman because you have made an educated guess about appropriateness. What if the company is one like GoogleÒ, where the dress code may be informal or non-existent? Rejoice in that knowledge for when you get hired, but your best bet is still to dress a level above what you would be expected to wear on your dressiest day.

Still feeling a bit unsure of what to wear? Take a gander at these fun and useful resources: *Do not wear a tongue ring to your job interview* (Manley, American Libraries Journal, 2009); Revealing outfits aren't professional (Sewing, Houston Chronicle. 2010); *Work it Wednesday: Avoiding summer office wear mistakes* (Insley, NBC KARE 11).

Timeliness

If you show up early then you are on time. If you show up on time then you are five minutes late. This old adage works well for the interview setting. If you are late for an interview, your chance of getting the job is almost nil. Why? First of all, it implies a low value of the position. It reflects poorly on your future behavior if you do get hired. And finally, it is disrespectful to the people who have set aside their time to get to know you.Arrive ten minutes early (Thornbury and White, 2006). Any earlier than that and your nerves will start to fray.

To make it on time, incorporate your travel into your preparation. Travel to the location, when possible, a week or a few days before the interview—during the same time of day. Locate where to park, any funds you will need for parking or travel, and possible complications with your route or time. Allot yourself enough time on both ends—never have to run out of an interview that is going long because it is going well (Lazarus, 2004)!

Interaction Do's and Don'ts

By now, you should begin to feel confident in your ability to look professional and to answer common interview questions. Listed below are some tips about interaction on the day of the interview to help you be even more confident that you are well on your way to a new job!

How to Behave Once You Get There

You know how to behave—so, this isn't a critique of you. This is a guide for targeting your behavior to specialized circumstances and commonly forgotten elements of this unique interviewing situation. So:

1. **Be "on" during the last turn in the directions.** This means that as you turn into the parking lot, be aware that anyone could be seeing and evaluating you. Don't brush your teeth in the car,

change out of fuzzy slippers, or—god forbid—squeeze into your pantyhose.

2. **Silence anything that makes a sound.** This includes cell phones, beepers, and computers. Any gadget whose sound cannot be turned off should be left at home. This includes watches that beep at regular intervals.

3. **Bring copies of your résumé, a pad of paper, and a pen.** Take notes. It shows your interest in what the other person is saying. On the pad, write down your questions for them so you don't forget to ask.

4. **Don't panic.** If you do something embarrassing, like reaching over and spilling your interviewer's coffee, remember common courtesy. First, apologize. Second, you could try to lighten the mood by saying something like "I got so excited by what we were talking about… I spilled your coffee. I'm so sorry." Third, clean up the mess. Fourth, offer to pay for a replacement or to take care of any cleaning. And finally, apologize again in your thank you letter after the interview.

5. **Smile.** Watch your nonverbal behavior. Krunhuber et al (2009) studied different types of smiles and concluded that those with authentic smiles received higher personal, job, and expression ratings compared to those with fake smiles or neutral expressions.

6. **Practice your handshake.** Nothing conveys confidence better than a good solid handshake and a smile.

7. **Thank people.** Thank the interviewer/s, restate your interest in the position, and ask what the next step is and when you can expect to hear from them.

Post-Interview Follow-Up

You are still being interviewed even after you leave the interview. *Huh*? That must sound like a strange statement but it is true. Once you leave the meeting that you have had with the company or boss or even the initial screening with HR, you are still in the midst of needing to make an impression. Most folks forget this step but those who do not make the right impression and are more likely to land a job!

"Write" a Thank You Letter:

The most crucial element of your follow-up is a **thank you letter.**

> 'Thank you letters are important in this market, now more than ever,' said Lisa Verde, director of recruiting for Matrix Resources, Inc., an international IT recruiting firm. They are important, Verde explained, because hardly anyone sends them, yet companies expect them, and a thank you or follow-up letter can make the difference between getting a job and getting overlooked. (Joss, 2003)

Old-fashioned, hand-written letters are still preferable to e-mail (Powers, 2000) even if the latter is also becoming more acceptable. As a general rule of thumb, if the employer uses e-mail to contact you, it is acceptable to use the same medium to communicate back during the process, but a hard copy thank you should be used to conclude the process. Keep the letter short and spelled correctly. Mention something interesting that was discussed during your interview and then reiterate your interest in the position. Most importantly, mail this letter immediately, preferably on the same day.

When you are using e-mail during the interview progress, use proper etiquette with full text. This is a letter to a potential boss and not your Facebook postings. Don't capitalize all words or overuse exclamation points. Proofread your letter for grammar and spelling.

How to Inquire About Your Status

You felt good about that interview. Now you sit back and wait. How long should you wait before following up? If you ended your interview correctly, you should know the answer to this question.

Remember that at the end of the interview, one of the ways by which you show interest is by stating how interested you are or how great a fit you are for the position, followed by a question asking what the next step is or when you might expect to hear. Employers will usually give you a rough date, "a week" or "in the coming days".

You wait a week, and no one calls. What do you do now? Wait one or two more days before calling or e-mailing the main interviewer. Make sure you do not hassle the person before the specified date that he or she specified in the interview (Thornbury & White, 2006).

What to Do With an Offer

You will most likely receive a job offer through a phone call from the employer. Do not initiate any discussion of salary or benefits during initial interviews (Barclay, 2009). When you are offered the position, wait to accept until you know the terms of the offer—starting date, salary, and benefits. Feel free to say you are excited about the opportunity and get the details before rushing into the "YIPPEE! Of course, I will work for you!" exclamation.

Negotiating An Offer

If you are made an offer, you must be prepared to negotiate it from a position of knowledge. This is where research will be your best friend! List your needs and evaluate the offer to see if it meets most, if not all, of them. Do your research on the standard salary for that job, at that time, and in that location as well as benefits for similar positions in your area of residence. Use search engines such as Salary.com to find comparable wages.

In a survey of 150 senior executives by Account temps (*When is money worth mentioning*, 2009), respondents mentioned that the salary question was posed by 12% of employers in the initial phone call, followed by 30% in the first interview after that. Only 12% said that the issue was raised when an offer had been made. Why is this the case? If your salary expectations are too high, the employer does not want to waste time having you do lengthier interviews with hiring decision-makers. Williams (2006) smartly argues that you do your best to postpone this discussion until an offer has been made. And you should definitely NOT bring it up on your own accord early in your process.

If the employer brings up salary at an early stage, how should you answer this question? Resist the urge to give a potential employer any type of specific number because any offer will definitely be targeted to your initial suggestion—even if it is unreasonably low. Throw the ball into their court by saying something like, "Let's talk about job requirements and expectations, then determine a fair salary for the job." If you can get by with not giving a number first, you gain the upper hand; however, if you feel that the employer will not move on to the next level of interviewing unless you give an answer, be prepared to state the going industry rate in your area. This is where your research comes in useful.

Be flexible in negotiating. For example, the company may not be able to increase the compensation, but might be willing to throw in more vacation days, or allow you to telecommute once in a while. Begin negotiating by thanking the employer for the offer. And always, always ask graciously and respectfully.

Accepting an Offer

After verbally **accepting an offer,** confirm that your employer will send you a written version of the offer. If the employer states that the verbal agreement is sufficient, you need to make sure YOU write a letter that includes the details discussed. In this letter, thank the employer for the offer, reiterate your appreciation for the opportunity to work for them, and list the terms of employment.

Declining an Offer

If you decide not to accept an offer, do it graciously. Write a letter thanking them for the offer. You may state that you have accepted another offer that is a better fit for your goals and interests (if that is true!). You may also mention how tough it was to decide. Never say anything negative about the employer. Remember, you may want to apply for another position with that employer in the future. At the very least, keeping them as part of your contacts helps you grow your network of professional relations that can only be beneficial to your career.

LOOKING BACK ON INTERVIEWING

So… are you ready? Are you ready to hear messages and react? Are you ready to offer feedback that so impresses the person interviewing you that you are offered the job on the spot?! OK—you may need a bit of practice but the preceding chapter should get you well on your way.

Remember that your skills as an interviewer will build over time. If you have an interview that doesn't go so well, don't beat yourself up. The only way to get better is to practice. In college, your best be is to take many classes that offer interviewing opportunities. Don't take just one—take several. Ask your professors to help you with this skill and go online to find as many practice questions as you can!

Once you graduate from college, do not let your business interviewing skills get rusty. You will often interview even if you never leave the same company. You may interview for a new department or a higher level position. Keep your skills sharp. Keep gathering interview questions and writing your PAR answers. *Offer* to interview others and see how the process works from the flip side. You will be surprised at how much this can help you refine your own interviewing skills!

Some coaches will tell you to go out and interview for a job that you do not want. The logic with this is that you will be relaxed during the experience and, ultimately, acquire interviewing skills with nothing on the line if you mess up. That's great logic for you—but what about the person or company interviewing you. You are wasting their time and resources. Is this ethical? Is this nice? Well, certainly not the latter.

Questions of ethics do not have easy answers. We would never recommend in this text that you interview for jobs that you do not want but you have so many opportunities to participate in mock interviews (and mess up, fix it, try again) that you should certainly grab each of these as they come! It is also a great idea to ponder your ethical positions on business practices long before you encounter ethical dilemmas, so... read on!

Chapter Eleven

Ethical Business Choices – How are they Made?

COMMUNICATION ETHICS AT PLAY

Bernie Madoff took 50 billion dollars of other people's money and used it for his family and himself. Canada is attempting to overturn environmental guidelines in the U.S. in order to pump sand-oil over the border. California former Governor Arnold Schwarzenegger fathered a child with another woman while his wife was expecting their fourth child. You print out all of your school and personal documents at work because they have a great laser printer and it costs you nothing. Alright, you might be thinking that these do not all fit in the same category. The first three seem wholly unethical. They bring up the "how could they?!" response. The latter may bring up the "well, that's no sooo bad" reaction. The question of this chapter is *what makes something ethical versus unethical* and *how do we decide*? Nowhere is this a more relevant question than in modern business.

A discussion of ethics can happen at any time. Some texts begin with it while others leave it to the end or try to weave it throughout. We left it to the last chapter of this text so that you could base the answers to your questions about ethics on the foundational business communication information that you have gathered thus far. What if, however, you have decided to skip ahead (as often happens) and read this chapter before delving into the rest of this book? Not a problem. A consideration of ethics, as it is tied to business, is also a valid initial discussion as well. It may provide you with a lens through which to understand the concepts relayed to you throughout this text. Whichever decision of order you have made, you should begin your plunge into ethical philosophy by understanding the merit that such issues have in business communication settings.

An Ordered World

After the public fiascos displayed through Enron, Worldcom, Adelphia, and too many others, we could simply write off businesses as operating through unethical practices. That's just not so. Most business suffer when they act unethically. Certainly, the companies listed here are great examples of how poor choices can come back to bite you in the… bottom line.

So, what does it mean to be ethical. Well, let's start with this. Ethics are not doing what you feel is right. Ethics are not tied to a particular religion. Ethical behavior does not mean following laws. Furthermore, ethics is not what society tells you to do. **Ethics** are standards of behavior or the study of how we develop standards of behavior.

Standards of behavior are difficult to grasp because so many people do not always know why they do what they do. We have all done something based on a gut feeling only to realize that we messed up (yes, everything from buying that purse when the ole bank account was low to lying to a friend about where we were going so that he or she would not ask to come along). If we look at the examples above, then we know that doing what we think is right can hurt others, that devote religious people sometimes make huge ethical mistakes, and that not all laws are just.

With all of this ambiguity, deciding on standards of behavior – especially in a business setting—is a monumental task. The benefits to becoming adept at this task are also monumental. Even "Ethics for Dummies," (part of the *For Dummies* series) by Christopher Panza and Adam Potthast (2011), provides us with some really good reasons to 'be ethical':

- *Ethics allows you to live an authentic life with a sense of integrity.*
- *Ethics makes you more successful because unethical people tend to fail at interpersonal and relationship based practices.*
- *Ethics allows you to cultivate inner peace.*
- *Ethics provides for a stable society.*

(And they even content that…)

- *Ethics may help out in the afterlife.*

So, take this opportunity to consider your own standards and the ones that you would set for your co-workers and employees. Take this opportunity to reflect back on what you have learned so far with a critical eye and ask if you could have (or will) complete your practices in business communication with a higher ethical standard. Consider the rewards…

FOUNDATIONAL ETHICS PERSPECTIVES

Contrasting ethical philosophies may be best accomplished through a classic example. Imagine that you are at home late one night. There is a knock at your door and you open it in time to watch your friend run into your home hollering, "he's gonna kill me!" Your friend dodges inside and hides in a back room. Moments later there is a knock at the door and you answer it to find a strange man with a knife in his hand. He asks if your friend is in your there. Is it unethical to lie to the man? Could you ethically ask your friend not to involve you in these matters? Does it make you an unethical person if you do not protect your friend? The difference in both these questions and how you might answer them gives an indication as to the potential ethical positions that you may have already adopted.

For the sake of the context of this book (and because, let's face it, you aren't likely to have this scenario actually happen to you), let's put the dilemma into a business setting. You manufacture cars. You are happily conducting your business when someone comes to you and says, "this car has a flaw and if you don't fix it, people will die." Sadly, we have seen news lately that car manufacturers have been in this situation. We can pose to this scenario some similar questions: Is it ethical to let some people die if it will save your business and the jobs of thousands of people? How many people need to die and have their jobs saved before ignoring the issue is an ethical choice? Are you an ethical person if you decide to fix the cars in some instances and not in others? Ah… it just isn't that simple, is it?

Perhaps the best case is when you are prepared ahead of time with ethical standards to follow whenever you are confronted with an ethical dilemma. If you know beforehand what actions you view as moral, right, just, or dutiful then you can act swiftly and with confidence in your business (and personal) world. There have been thousands of books and millions of websites devoted to the philosophy of ethics. There are three that have stood the test of time as original, insightful, and, most importantly, have formed the basis of the three dominant traditions of ethical theory that we follow today: Immanuel Kant, John Stuart Mill, and Aristotle. The subsequent descriptions are not intended for you to understand every nuance of their positions (after all, you have graduate school to do that!) but to give you a foundation that can help to guide you in your business dealings.

Kant: Universalism and Deontology

Have you ever felt that it was your "duty" to do something? Maybe as part of being a good citizen or in your effort to help out your parents? Do you believe that everyone has a duty to be a good son or daughter? Is there any standard or rule that you think applies to everyone (such as "the Golden Rule")? The notion of duty is key to the philosophy of Immanuel Kant (1785).

Those adhering to Kant's philosophy are most appropriately labeled deontologists. A **deontologist** by definition is one who studies and follows the nature of duty and obligation. Kant (1797) rejected the notion that our ethics are situational (the "well, it depends" response). Instead, he asserted that there are particular duties to which all humans are bound. To be specific, "Ethical duties or obligations comprise a set of rules that are universal for all people and all times" (Neher & Sandin, 2007). For example, 'do not kill others' would be a duty.

While Kant (1797) does list some duties in his works, he does not produce for us an all-inclusive 'these are your duties' directory that we can use (wouldn't that be nice?). His work, instead, describes how to *recognize* our duties. To borrow from Carnegie Mellon professor Robert Cavalier's (1996) explanation, there is a distinction between the "I want" (behavior of self-interest) and the "I ought" (ethical behavior). Our attempts at ethical behavior are not spontaneous. For instance, if we see someone in need of help when we are busy then we might avoid that person but we will <u>recognize</u> that the person needs our help. In contrast, if we see a mother with a small child who is lying unconscious in the road, our busy lives suddenly seem less vital than providing assistance, which we will both recognize and act upon.

> Considering only those actions that are seemingly good (as opposed to actions that we ordinarily recognize as wrong), there is a DISTINCTION that can still be made within Duty itself: Actions IN mere ACCORDANCE (conformity) WITH duty and actions done FROM A SENSE OF duty. (Cavalier, 1996; emphasis in original)

Actions, in Kant's mind, are done from a sense of duty and not just because we attempt to conform. He believes that this duty is universal. It is that notion that sets up the Categorical Imperative.

The **Categorical Imperative** is a means by which we can evaluate our actions as moral or immoral. It is the rule that has us do unconditionally what should be used as a law for everyone (e.g., from Kant, "Act only on that maxim whereby thou canst at the same time will that it should become a universal law"). In other words, when you are thinking about whether or not to let people know that your cars could kill a few people— do what should be the act that *anyone* should follow *any time* this situation occurs. That would be universal. For Kant, an objective and rational mind is required for any consideration of morality. If you cannot rationally do this then you are not responsible (which is also the basis of the insanity defense in law!). If we are rational and recognize a duty—then "everyone must admit that if a law is morally valid…then it must carry with it absolute necessity"(p. 2). Yup, if it is moral then we *all* must do it. If we mess up, the important thing is that we intended to do something ethical.

Does this work for you? Do you like the universal applicability? Lying is bad—check! Don't kill people—check! These are moral and ethical duties. It may not be easy to be ethical but now we are in a position to evaluate when we are behaving ethically and when we are not. The beauty of Kant's position is that people can't wiggle out of moral obligations by rationalizing things in terms of consequences that *they* see as good. Of course, Kant would say, there are times when lying produces good consequences, but being a moral person sometimes means foregoing good consequences to do the right thing.

Before you reject the notion of absolutism (and the idea that you would need to be truthful with the killer who came looking for your friend), you must think about how our messy lives provide us with options even when we follow a strict deontological philosophy. For instance, WHY DID YOU OPEN THE DOOR?? If a killer comes to your house looking for your friend then you need to look at some other options besides opening up the door for a chat. You can be truthful in your call to *the cops*! You can be ethical by avoiding answering questions that would force you to choose between truth and safety. A deontological life means that we must look at bigger pictures and spend time evaluating rather than rushing into choices.

Critics of Kant

So, we can see that acting with a sense of duty may be a clear and useful path for us to follow in our quest for ethical business practices—or an ethical life. However, Kant is not without his critics. There are those who would argue (and perhaps rightly so, you decide) that while absolutes can allow us to be certain about issues,they make it difficult to see how we can apply the idea of 'morality' to real world situations and real people. C'mon, let's think about it. Real life is messy! We rarely can define real life in terms of absolutes. Take, for example, the notion of theft. Stealing is wrong, right? What about the whistle blower who steals information from his employer to help convict them of using toxic chemicals in children's toy manufacturing. Was that person wrong? Kant would say yes! Utilitarianism, a contrary ethical view, answers this question by recognizing that sometimes an action that is generally considered morally wrong (stealing) is sometimes morally acceptable; it all depends on the situation.

Mill: Utilitarianism

 John Stuart Mill (1972) came from the consequentialist school of ethics! Most people think of utilitarianism as the effort to do the most good for the most amount of people. That's true. But this notion is, first, only part of the larger philosophy and, second, based on a larger context. In the Mill school of ethics, a polar opposite position from the ethical school of Immanuel Kant, we do not judge an act based on a relationship to some external *duty* or even intention (e.g., 'I meant to do good but, whoops, it didn't go so well'). Instead, Mill believed that we use our rational ability to predict *consequences*. For example, if you are a manufacturing plant's safety supervisor and you come to work each day doing your best possible job but someone still gets hurt, you are not "ethically" responsible. If, however, you come to work drunk and do not watch for safety violations as your job dictates... then when someone gets hurt, you are ethically responsible. Why? Well, in the first scenario, you could not rationally predict that a safety issue would occur. In the second scenario, you knew that you were impaired and doing your job at a less than ideal level. In these second circumstances, it's fairly predictable that something could slip through the cracks and that you would miss it. It is our moral choice, says Mill, to do all that we can to avoid causing negative consequences!

On the surface, this sounds great. Avoid the negative stuff! So, if I'm in a bad mood and want to call out sick then Mill says, 'go for it', right? Maybe. Mill asks us to look at the larger context. If our calling out sick for our own personal happiness means that two other people have to be called in to cover our shift then 'Bad You!' What you have done is to negatively impact a larger group of people. When our actions have larger, rationally predicted, negative consequences than positive consequences then we have behaved unethically. (Does that whole "do the most good for the most amount of folks" thing make a bit more sense now?)
In this vein, as we are doing all of this good stuff for lots of people, how do we decide what is "good"? Mill has an answer for that as well. First, Utilitarians believe in the **Golden Rule**! Yes, we should do to others what we want done to us (Mill, 1972, p. 148). That is crucial to evaluating ethical behavior. If we go back to the example where a few of our cars might kill people, the Golden Rule would say that you should do what you would want done for you. But, which is it? Do you want to be told that your car might kill you or do you want someone to save your job? That's a hard decision. It seems like either decision means that we must give up something in some way.

Sometimes sacrifice is a necessary part of ethical behavior. It may be that in order to good by others, you must do some harm to yourself. Alright, et's not become martyrs… let's keep it realistic. Mill would not suggest that you dive in to save a drowning man if you cannot swim. That would simply sacrifice you both. He *would* say that you have an ethical obligation to help if you are a trained lifeguard and know what to do. Businesses these days can be a lot like a drowning man. If a business is going down and you have the financial ability or know-how to save the company, what would Mill say? You know the answer! He would say that you are ethically bound to dive in and help. You also know that if you will lose your business by helping another and that, ultimately, neither of you could survive then you are not ethically bound to sacrifice yourself. Utilitarians work towards to good of the whole, while still attempting to protect the interests of the individual.

When you compare Mill's Utilitarianism toKant's Deontology, you can see that they really do provide a counter balance to one another. The shortcomings of one theory are the virtuesof the other (and the other way around). For instance, one of the strengths of Utilitarianism is that it is flexible and practical. While most people agree that lying is wrong (Kant would say we have a duty not to lie), most people would also maintain that there are at least some cases where lying is acceptable (think of the killer at your doorexample). As critics of Utilitarianism point out, however, the flexibility of the theory might undermine its veracity… since people can to find ways to argue almost any action in terms of good *overall* consequences.

Aristotle: Virtue Ethics

Kant and Mill give us two very distinct ethical positions. It might seem easy to take one or the other. However, long before either of these philosophies was developed, Aristotle offered up what may be viewed as a middle ground. Much like it seemed surprising that Aristotle could help us in the development of visual aids (with ethos, pathos, and logos), his wisdom on ethics is useful in making business choices.

Aristotle (in his, *Nicomachean Ethics*) is not talking about consequences. He is not offering up universal rules or duties. Instead, Aristotle is talking about virtue. Virtue is something that, if we are being ethical, we aspire to be and to accomplish. It is not a single act or something that a single act can achieve for us. (So, for all you folks who spent a day with your co-workers cleaning up litter as part of a company project… that isn't enough). Aristotle saw **moral virtue** as the possession of particular qualities (e.g., self-control, courage, generosity, high-mindedness, gentleness, friendliness, truthfulness, etc.). He did not believe that people were born virtuous while others were not (yes, even Aristotle debunked the "Great Man Theory"). Instead, we grow and live in an effort to reach a virtuous way of being.

The basis of virtue theory is that morality or being a highly ethical person involves acquiring of good character traits as part of living your life. Those people who live in this way can, and sometimes do, perform spontaneous ethical acts (remember how Kant and Mill wanted lots of reflection and looking at the bigger picture or larger context – Aristotle doesn't go there).

The key to Aristotle's theory is that morality is intimately linked with our purpose and function as human beings!

Alright, you might be thinking that such a high standard cannot be reached. That living an ethical life in everyway so that you can be considered ethical is just too high a standard with too little pay off. *Wait*. Don't we apply these standards all of the time? **Phronemos** is Aristotle's idea of avirtuous role model. We all have role models that we look to as a guide for our actions. It could be your mom ("hhmmm… would *mom* submit Nestle's recipe as her own in a baking contest?") or your boss ("hhmmm… would *Mr. Simmons* fudge the numbers on this quarter's financial reports if he knew we would make it up next quarter?"). If you have seen a "WWJD" bumper sticker then you have seen Aristotle's view of virtue ethics in action!

Like with Kant and Mill's theories, Virtue Theory can be ambiguous without some clear guidelines. Mill may have the Golden Rule – but Aristotle has the **Golden Mean**. The Golden Mean is as close to prescriptive or advice-giving that Aristotle comes. He tells us that, by using some very practical reason, we can find the mean between a **vice by excess** and a **vice by default** (having way too much or giving up way too much). We do this by finding a middle ground (appropriate, since Aristotle is the middle ground between Kant and Mill). Aristotle was not proposing a Christian ethic but we can see how his ideas are in-line with the notion of avoiding the *Seven Deadly Sins*—which Dante also called the *Seven Deadly Vices*. A middle ground life would not advocate sloth or laziness but would also not suggest that one work to the point of physical and mental breakdown. A middle ground life would be one that had us avoid wrath without being passive to the point of being walked all over. In the same vein, our Golden Mean sees vice in gluttony but would not suggest a life of starvation either. The middle ground is different for different people (take the eating example… what would be excessive for a 110 pound college co-ed could be a snack for a Sumo wrestler). In making decisions, the ethical person has <u>a key sense of balance</u>.

Aristotle's virtue theory has direct implications for businesses. If we go back to the example where our cars have the likelihood of killing someone then we can see where balance can lead us to a virtuous path. Previously, we had suggested only two options: tell and go out of business or hide it and stay afloat. Car manufacturers like Toyota and Honda have managed to keep producing even amidst huge and embarrassing recalls. Virtue theory could guide us to the path toward fixing the problem in a way that does not destroy us financially. It is up to you to decide if this middle ground is what you see as the ethical choice.

What you should take from Aristotle is that virtue is in your character not in any act. Choices to not make us virtuous but our character makes gives our acts virtue. Today, we might make a particular decision about how to handle the car manufacturing issue and it would be virtuous. A few years down the road, we may in the same position and make a different decision. Just like a work, the best bosses are not those who make no mistakes but those who learn from their mistakes and work with others to improve. In deciding how to act, be it from the perspective of Kant or Mill or Aristotle, we cannot just go with our gut. The gut is not a standard. We must be able to explain how we made our choices and recognize that they are reflective of a particular ethical perspective that we find valid and have decided to follow.

An Over-Simplified Model

So – here we are. Three ways of approaching our business decisions and communication. Three ethical perspectives to help guide our choices. Now you simply must choose one… a task that no one would say is easy. You will be in the best position to decide on an ethical path if you feel that you can clearly differentiate each and apply them to real world scenarios.

Let's first be sure that you can differentiate. Each of the above philosophies is complicated and finely distinct. They revolve around the notions of duty, consequence, and virtue. While some might argue that these positions do not revolve around one another, we can also argue that each moral perspective has some relationship to the other. It might make things easier if we offer up a visual.

Below is a spatial model of the ethical philosophies discussed above. Now, we know from chapter one (the chapter on communication models) that merely offering a model to assist with understanding has some problems. Yes, they can help with clarity. However, they can also over-simplify information so that the nuances are ignored. Understand here that this is just a single visual of a complex connection!

An Ethics Diagram

• We go for absolutes based on higher duties (don't lie to the killer at the door).

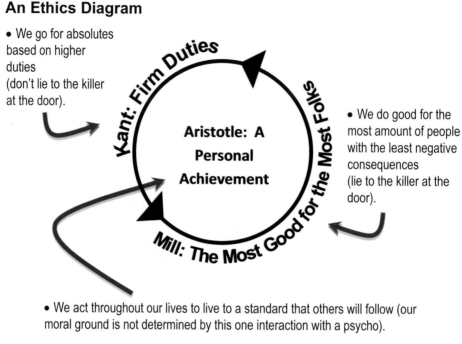

• We do good for the most amount of people with the least negative consequences (lie to the killer at the door).

• We act throughout our lives to live to a standard that others will follow (our moral ground is not determined by this one interaction with a psycho).

As you can see, Kant and Mill are opposite one another. If we were to put them on a flat line then you might assume that one leans to the left and the other to the right. You might assume that there is a particular distance between them. Not so. It is better to think of ethical philosophies as having a spatial relationship to one another rather than a linear relationship. Basically, you should remember that these two sit on opposite sides of that space. Aristotle, on the other hand, sits in-between Kant and Mill.

A FINAL RECAP AND REFLECTION

Ethics is not the study of what is *legal* or *socially accepted*; it is not even the study of what is right and wrong. Ethics is how we try to make sense of and discover reasonable general principles that can help us decide what we ought to do and what we ought not to do in <u>all</u> cases.

Many people think that obeying the law or following company policies or the Golden Rule is sufficient ethical behavior. But we know better. Laws and policies have loopholes. They begin and often remain incomplete. Turn to your own college policies or undergraduate catalog. Each year the text is edited, changed, and expanded upon because students have become more and more creative at figuring out what wrong things no one has thought to make a rule against in the past. Rules and policies grow in response to this creativity, but they will always be a bit out of date because we cannot create rules that will anticipate every possible bad act. In addition, you know that there are many legal activities or corporate actions that are not *morally* right to do.

The three long standing ethical traditions established by Immanuel Kant, John Stuart Mill, and Aristotle show us that there are options as to what standards we choose to adopt and follow. Once you realize that you are enacting a particular standard then you can:
- consciously see how you make your choices
- understand how others are making their choices
- take fuller responsibility for our choices

And this is an excellent place to leave you. You know the foundations of business communication and now can choose to adopt standards that will guide your choices of the options that inevitably come along with life in a business world. Be confident! Be strong! Be phronemos! Hopefully, you now are prepared to…

References

Chapter One References

Berlo, D. K. (1960). *The Process of Communication*. New York: Holt, Rinehart and Winston, Inc.

Daft, R. L. (2007). *The leadership experience*. Mason, OH: South-Western College Publishers.

Hall, S. (1980). Encoding/decoding. In Centre for Contemporary Cultural Studies (Ed.): *Culture, Media, Language: Working Papers in Cultural Studies, 1972-79* London: Hutchinson, pp. 128-38.

Jakobson, R. (1960): Closing statement: Linguistics and poetics. In Sebeok, T. (Ed.). *Style in Language*. Cambridge, MA: MIT Press. pp. 350-77.

Johnson, A. M., & Lederer, A. L. (Fall 2005). The effect of communication frequency and channel richness on the convergence between chief executive and chief information officers. *Journal of Management Information Systems, 22*(2), 227-252.

Mortenson, C. D. (1972). Communication models. In C. D. Mortenson (Ed.) *Communication: The study of human communication*. NY: McGraw-Hill. pp. 83-102.

Morreale, S. & Pearson, J. (2007). Why communication education is important: The centrality of the discipline in the 21st century. *Communication Education, 57, 2.*

Rubin, R. B. & Morreale, S. P. (2000). What college students should know and be able to do. *JACA: Journal of the Association for Communication Administration, 29,*1 53-65.

North, A. B. & Worth, W. E. (Sep96). Trends in advertised entry-level technology, interpersonal, and basic communication job skills, 1992-1994. *Journal of Employment Counseling, 33*, 3, 98-105.

Naval History & Heritage Command. (2009). Navajo Code Talkers: World War II Fact Sheet. *Navy & Marine Corps WWII Commemorative Committee*. Retrieved on July 12, 2010 from http://www.history.navy. mil/faqs/faq61-2.htm.

Russ, G. S., Daft, R. L., & Lengel, R. H. (1990). Media selection and managerial characteristics in organizational communications. *Management Communication Quarterly, 4*, 151-175.

Salzmann, Z. (1993). *Language, culture and society: An introduction to linguistic anthropology*. Boulder, Colorado: Westview Press.

Schramm, W. (1954). How communication works. In W. Schramm (Ed.), *The process and effects of communication* (pp. 3-26). Urbana, Illinois: University of Illinois Press.

Shannon, C. E. (1948). A mathematical theory of communication. *Bell System Technical Journal,27,* 379-423 and 623-656.

Shannon, C. E., & Weaver, W. (1949). *The mathematical theory of communication*. Urbana, Ill.: The University of Illinois Press.

Watzlawick, P., Beavin, J., & Jackson, D. D. (1967). *Pragmatics of human communication: A study of interactional patterns, pathologies, and paradoxes.* NY: Norton.

CHAPTER TWO REFERENCES

Bisel, R. B., Messersmith, A. S., & Keyton, J. (2010). Understanding organizational culture and communication through a gyroscope metaphor. Journal of Management Education, 34, 342-366. doi:10.1177/105256290934087.

Carzo Jr., R., & Yanouzas, J. (1969). Effects of Flat and Tall Organization Structure. *Administrative Science Quarterly, 14*(2), 178-191. Retrieved from Business Source Premier database.

Donaldson, L., & Hilmer, F. (1998). Management Redeemed: The Case Against Fads that Harm Management. *Organizational Dynamics, 26*(4), 7-20. Retrieved from Business Source Premier database.

Galbraith, J. (1973). *Designing complex organizations*. Reading, MA: Addison-Wesley Publishing Company.

Ghiselli, E., & Wyatt, T. (1972). Need satisfaction, managerial success, and attitudes toward leadership. *Personnel Psychology, 25*(3), 413-420. Retrieved from Business Source Premier database.

Johnpress, T. (Sunday, August 24, 2003). Transformational culture can percolate your firm. Austin Business Journal. Accessed December 28, 2010 from http://www. bizjournals.com/austin/stories/2003/08/25/smallb2.html.

Mayo, E. (1949) *Hawthorne and the Western Electric Company, The Social Problems of an Industrial Civilisation,* Routledge.

McGregor, D. (1960) *The Human Side of Enterprise.* New York: McGraw-Hill.

Pugh, D. S. (2003). The measurement of organization structures. In Handel, M. J. (Ed.). *the sociology of organizations: Classic, contemporary, and critical readings.* Thousand Oaks: Sage Publication. pp. 66-76.

Schramm, W. (1954). How communication works. In W. Schramm (Ed.), *The process and effects of communication* (pp. 3-26). Urbana, Illinois: University of Illinois Press.

Taylor, F. W. (1911). *The Principles of Scientific Management.* New York: Harper & Brothers.

Weber, M. (1947). *The Theory of Social and Economic Organizations.* Henderson, A. M., and Parsons, T. (trans.) New York: Oxford University Press.

Worthy, J. C. (1950). Organizational Structure and Employee Morale. *American Sociological Review, 15*, 169-179.

CHAPTER THREE REFERENCES

*Barker, L., Edwards, R., Gaines, C., Gladney, K., & Holley, F. (1980). An investigation of proportional time spent in various communication activities by college students. *Journal of Applied Communications Research, 8(2)*, 101. Retrieved from Communication & Mass Media Complete database.

Bierck, R. (2001). How to listen. *Harvard Management Communication Letter, 4(1),* 4. Retrieved from Communication & Mass Media Complete database.

Bordone, R. (2007). Listen up! Your talks may depend on it. *Negotiation*, 9-11. Retrieved from Communication & Mass Media Complete database.

Bugelski, B. R. & Alampay, D. A. (1961). The Role of Frequency in Developing Perceptual Sets. *Canadian Journal of Psychology, 15*, 205-211.

Dearborn, D. W. C. & Simon, H. A. (1958). Selective perception: A note on the departmental identifications of executives. *Sociometry, 21, 2*, 140-144.

DiSalvo, V. S. (1980). A summary of current research identifying communication skills in various organizational contexts. *Communication Education, 29,* 283-290.

Encyclopedia of Business and Finance. (2010). Listening skills in business. *Encyclopedia of Business and Finance.* Retrieved on July 30, 2010 from http://www.endnotes.com/business-finance-encyclopedia/listening-skills-busness.

Ferraro, V. & Palmer, K. (July 1999). Speaking and arguing: The rhetoric of peace and war. *Mount Holyoke College.* Retrieved on July 30, 2010 from http://www.mtholyoke.edu/acad/intrel/speech /listening. htm.

Festinger, L. (1957). A theory of cognitive dissonance, Evanston, IL: Row & Peterson.

Flynn, J., Valikoski, T., & Grau, J. (2008). Listening in the business context: Reviewing the state of research. *International Journal of Listening, 22(2),* 141-151. Retrieved from Communication & Mass Media Complete database.

Fredriksson, L. (1999). Modes of relating in a caring conversation: A research synthesis on presence, touch and listening. *Journal of Advanced Nursing, 30, 5,* 1167 – 1176.

Golen, S. (1990). A factor analysis of barriers to effective listening. *Journal of Business Communication, 27(1),* 25-36. Retrieved from Communication & Mass Media Complete database.

Hillyard, S. A., Hink, R. F., Schwent, V. L., & Picton, T. W. (1973). Electrical signs of selective attention in the human brain. *Science, 182,* 177-179.

Ifert Johnson, D. & Long, K. (2008). Evaluating the effectiveness of listening instruction in introductory communication courses. *International Communication Association, Conference Papers.* 1-19. Retrieved from Communication & Mass Media Complete database.

International Listening Association. (n.d.). Time Spent Listening and Communicating. *International Listening Association.* Retrieved on July 31, 2010 from http://www.listen.org/index.php?option=com_content&view=article&id=103:-time-spent-listening-and-communicating&catid=43:listening-facts&Itemid=74.

Janusik, L. (2002). Teaching listening: What do we do? What should we do? *International Journal of Listening, 165*. Retrieved from Communication & Mass Media Complete database.

Lee, D. & Hatesohl, D. (1993). Listening: Our most used communication skill. *University of Missouri Extension*. Retrieved from http://extension.missouri.edu/publications/DisplayPub.aspx?P=CM150.

Mayer, R. (2005). How to win any argument: without raising your voice, losing your cool, or coming to blows. Pompton Plains, NJ: Career Press.

McCroskey, J. C., Richmond, V. P., & McCroskey, L. L. (2006). An introduction to communication in the classroom: The role of communication in teaching and training. Boston, Pearson.

Posner, M, I. & Petersen, S. E. (March 1990). The attention system of the human brain. *Annual Review of Neuroscience,13*, 25-42.

Ramsey, R. & Sohi, R. (1997). Listening to your customers: The impact of perceived salesperson listening behavior on relationship outcomes. *Journal of the Academy of Marketing Science, 25(2),* 127. Retrieved from Communication & Mass Media Complete database.

RBH Employee Newsletter. (July, 2009). Talk more, listen less, learn more. Retrieved from https://www.myrbh.com/Portals/0/PDFs/Employee%20Newsletters/2009%20EENews/2009JulyEE.pdf.

Recording For the Blind & Dyslexic. (n.d.). Benefits of teaching listening. *Learning Through Listening.*Retrieved fromhttp://www.learning throughlistening.org/Listening-A-Powerful-Skill/Listening-and-Learning/Benefits-of-Teaching-Listening/93.

Schumacher, M. (March/April, 2008). How's your active listening? *Management File*. Retrieved from http://www.hazeninc. com/beta/images/activelistening.pdf.

Sypher, B. D., Bostrom, R., & Seibert, J. H. (1989). Listening, communication abilities and success at work. *Journal of Business Communication, 26,* 293-303.

Tufte, E. (September 2003). PowerPoint Is Evil. *Wired News* . Retrieved February 18, 2010 from http://www.wired.com/wired/archive /11.09/ppt2.html.

Wheeless, L. R. (1975). An investigation of receiver apprehension and social context dimensions of communication apprehension. The Speech Teacher, 24, 261-268.

Wolvin, A. & Coakley, C. (2000). Listening education in the 21st century. *International Journal of Listening*. Retrieved from Communication & Mass Media Complete database.

Zofi, Y. & Meltzer, S. (May, 2007). Listening takes practice (key component of effective communication). *Nursing Homes*. Retrieved from http://www.entrepreneur.com/tradejournals/article/165679069 .html.

CHAPTER FOUR REFERENCES

Benne, K. D., & Sheats, P. (1948). Functional roles of group members. *Journal of Social Issues, 4*, 41-49.

Bormann, E. G. (1990). *Small group communication: Theory and practice* (3rd ed.). New York: Harper & Row.

Borysowich, C. (May 24, 2005). Why your meetings suck! [blog entry]. Retrieved 12/26/2010 from http://it.toolbox.com/ blogs/enterprise-solutions/why-your-meetings-suck-4310

Chong, E. (2007). Role balance and team development: a study of team role characteristics, *Journal of Behavioral and Applied Management, 8*, 202-217.

Dewey, J. (1933). *How we think: a restatement of the relation of reflective thinking to the educative process* (revised ed.). Boston: D C Heath.

Fisher, B. A. (1970). Decision emergence: Phases in group decision making. *Speech Monographs, 37*, 53-66.

Goleman, D. (1998). *Working with emotional intelligence*. New York: Bantam Books

Gouran, D., & Hirokawa, R. Y. (1996). Functional theory and communication in decision-making and problem-solving groups. In Hirokawa, R. Y., & Poole, M. S. (Eds.), *Communication and group decision making* (2nd ed., pp. 55-80). Thousand Oaks, CA: Sage.

Hersey, P., & Blanchard, K. H. (1969). *Management of organizational behavior – utilizing human resources*. Englewood Cliffs, NJ: Prentice-Hall.

Hersey, P., Blanchard, K. H., & Johnson, D. E. (2007). *Management of organizational behavior* (9th ed.). Englewood Cliffs, NJ: Prentice-Hall.

Janis, I. L. (1972). *Victims of groupthink; a psychological study of foreign-policy decisions and fiascoes.* Boston: Houghton, Mifflin.

Janis, I. L. (1982). *Groupthink: psychological studies of policy decisions and fiascoes* (2nd ed.). New York: Houghton Mifflin.

Millard, D. (2007). Make the most of meetings by planning and following up. *Indianapolis Business Journal, 28*, 44, 19-19.

Mandell, B. & Pherwani, S. (2003). Relationship between emotional intelligence and TL style: A gender comparison. *Journal of Business & Psychology, 17(3),* 387-404.

Osborn, A. (1953). *Applied imagination.* NY: Charles Scribner's Sons.

Porteus, L. (7/11/2004). Group think led to Iraq WMD assessment. Retrieved December 23, 2010 from http://www.foxnews. com/ story/0,2933,125123,00.html

Rowan, J. M. (2003). Seating arrangements should support goal of meeting. San Antonio Business Journal. Retrieved June 12, 2010 from http://www.bizjournals.com/sanantonio/ stories/2003/11/ 10/ focus3.html.

Stogdill, R. M. (1948). Personal factors associated with leadership: A surey of the literature. *Journal of Psychology, 25*, 35-71.

Thomas, K. W., & Thomas, G. F. (2004). *Introduction to conflict and teams.* Mountain View, CA: CPP Inc.

Tuckman, B. (1965). Developmental sequence in small groups. *Psychological Bulletin, 63*, 384-399.

CHAPTER FIVE REFERENCES

Allen, M. & Preiss, R.(997). Comparing the Persuasiveness of narrative and statistical evidence using meta-analysis. *Communication Research Reports, 14*, 2, 125-131.

Baccus, J. (1935). Building a stock of illustrations. *Quarterly Journal of Speech*, 21(3), 373. Retrieved from Communication & Mass Media Complete database.

Bitzer. L. (1968). The rhetorical situation. *Philosophy and Rhetoric,1*, 1-14.

Bryman, A. (1998). Quantitative and qualitative research strategies in knowing the social world. In T. May and M. Williams (Eds.), Knowing the Social World. Buckingham and Philadelphia, Open University Press: 138 - 156.

Firestone, W. A. (October 1987). Meaning in method: The rhetoric of quantitative and qualitative research. *Educational Researcher, 16*, 7, 16-21.

Foss, S. K. & Foss, K. A. (1994). *Inviting transformation: Presentational speaking for a changing world.* Prospect Heights, Ill: Waveland Press.

Punch, K. F. (2005). *Introduction to social research: Quantitative and qualitative approaches, 2nd edition.* Sage Publications.

Vatz, R. E. (Summer, 1973). The Myth of the Rhetorical Situation. *Philosophy and Rhetoric, 6*, 3, 154-161.

CHAPTER SIX REFERENCES

Halford, G. S., Cowan, N., and Andrews, G. (June 2007). Separating cognitive capacity rom knowledge: a new hypothesis. *Trends in Cognitive Sciences,* 11(6), 236-42.

Monroe, Alan H. (1935). *Principles and Types of Speech.* Glenview, IL: Scott Foresman.

O'Keefe, D.J. (2002). *Persuasion: theory & research.* Sage Publications, Inc. (2) 220.

Perloff, R. M. (2003). The dynamics of persuasion, 2nd ed. Mahwah, NJ: Lawrence Erlbaum

Sprague, J. & Stuart, D. (2009). *The Speaker's Compact Handbook.* Wadsworth, Cengage Learning.

CHAPTER SEVEN REFERENCES

Ayres, J., & Hopf, T. (1999). Vividness and control: Factors in the effectiveness of performance visualization?. *Communication Education*, 48(4), 287.

Garber, R. I. (October 27, 2009). The 14 worst human fears in the 1977 Book of Lists: Where did this data really come from?. Joyful Public Speaking (from fear to joy). Retrieved on July 23, 2010 from http://joyfulpublicspeaking.blogspot.com/2009/10/14-worst-human-fears-according-to-1977.html.

Hayakawa, S. I. (1949). *Language in Thought and Action*. New York: Harcourt, Brace.

Hart, R. P. (1994). *Seducing America: How television charms the modern voter.* New York: Oxford University Press.

Maricchiolo, F., Gnisci, A., Bonaiuto, M., & Ficca, G. (2009). Effects of different types of hand gestures in persuasive speech on receivers' evaluations. *Language & Cognitive Processes*, 24(2), 239-266. doi:10.1080/01690960802159929.

McNeill, D., Cassell, J., & McCullough, K. (1994). Communicative effects of speech-mismatched gestures. *Research on Language & Social Interaction*, 27(3), 223. Retrieved from Academic Search Complete database.

Merten, R. K. (1948). The self-fulfilling prophecy. *Antioch Review, 8*, 193-210.

Pearce, W. B., & Conklin, F. (1971). Nonverbal vocalic communication and perceptions of a speaker. *Speech Monographs*, 38(3), 235-241. Retrieved from Communication & Mass Media Complete database.

Sato, W., & Yoshikawa, S. (2007). Enhanced experience of emotional arousal in response to dynamic facial expressions. *Journal of Nonverbal Behavior*, 31(2), 119-135. doi:10.1007/s10919-007-0025-7.

Smith, T., & Frymier, A. (2006). Get 'real': Does practicing speeches before an audience improve performance?. *Communication Quarterly*, 54(1), 111-125. doi:10.1080/01463370500270538.

Wachsmuth, I. (2006). Gestures offer insight. *Scientific American Mind*, 17(5), 20-25. Retrieved from Academic Search Complete database.

White, M. (1964). The Speaker's stand. *Today's Speech*, 12(2), 6. Retrieved from Communication & Mass Media Complete database.

CHAPTER EIGHT REFERENCES

Beaver, D. (April 2007). With visual aids, more is less. *ABA Banking Journal, 99, 4*, 61.

Beebe, S. A., & Beebe, S. J. (2009) *Public Speaking: An Audience-Centered Approach*. Boston, MA: Allyn & Bacon.

Buss, W. C. (March 2006). Stop death by PowerPoint. *Training & Development, 60 3*, 20-22.

Carroll, S. (March 2007). PowerPoint Abuse? Oversimplification Hinders Communication and Understanding. *FX One Seven Zero.* Retrieved February 15, 2010, from http://www.fx170.com/ ?q=article_ multimedia.

Cyphert, D. (March 2004).The problem of PowerPoint: Visual aid or visual rhetoric? *Business Communication Quarterly, 67,* 1, 80-84.

Foss, S. K. & Kanengieter, M. R.(July 1992). Visual communication in the basic course. *Communication Education, 41, 3,* 312 – 323.

Fried, J (August 2004). A little Tufte recap. *Signals vs. noise.* Accessed from http://37signals.com/svn/archives/000831.php.

Garcia-Retamero R. & Galesic M. (April 2010). Who profits from visual aids: overcoming challenges in people's understanding of risks. *Social Science & Medicine, 70 (7),* 1019-25.

Glover, D., Miller, D., Averis, D. & Door, V. (2007). The evolution of an effective pedagogy for teachers using the interactive whiteboard in mathematics and modern languages: An empirical analysis from the secondary sector. *Learning, Media and Technology, 32(1),* 5-20.

Heap, I. M., Burrill, L. C., Dewey, S. A., & MacDonald, G. E. (1994). Eradication of noxious visual aids: Slides and overheads that work. *Weed Technology, 8 (3),* 649-657.

Heath, M. (2009) Use of visual aids in public speaking. *Whitman College Rhetoric and Public Address Department.* Retrieve on June 18, 2009 from http://www.whitman.edu/rhetoric/84zvas2.htm.

Lester, A. & Lock, R. (Summer 1998). Sponges as visual aids--bath time fun for biologists?. *Journal of Biological Education, 32, 2,* 87-89.

Levie, W. H. & Lentz, R. (1982). Effects of text illustrations: A review of research. Educational Communication and Technology, 30(4), 195-233.

Lowenthal, P. (n.d.). Improving the Design of PowerPoint Presentations. *CU Online.* Retrieved February 17, 2010, from http://www. cudenver.edu/Academics/CUOnline/FacultyResources/Handbook/ Documents/2009/Chapter_12.pdf.

Mann, M., & Hill, T. (1984). Persuasive communications and the boomerang effect: Some limiting conditions to the effectiveness of positive influence attempts. *Advances in Consumer Research, 11(1),* 66-70. Retrieved from Business Source Premier database.

Meilach, D. Z.. (May 1992). Overhead transparencies designed to communicate. *Arts & Activities,111, (4),* 42-46.

Murcia, K., & Sheffield, R. (2010). Talking about science in interactive whiteboard classrooms. *Australasian Journal of Educational Technology, 26(4),* 417-431. Retrieved from Education Research Complete database.

Norman, D. (2004). In defense of PowerPoint. *Don Norman's jnd.org / user advocacy and human-centered design.* Retrieved February 15, 2010, from http://www.jnd.org/dn.mss/in_defense_of_p.html.

Phillips, A. & Donohue, P. (September 20, 2010) New Yorkers outraged as bureaucrats order city to change lettering on every single street sign, *New York Daily News.* Retrieved on May 29, 2011 from http://www.nydailynews.com/ny_local/2010/09/30/2010-09-30_ bureaucrats_order_city_to_change_every_street_sign_leading_ny_ to_say__it_is_just.html.

Rotman, E. (Jul/Aug 2009). Enhance Your Effectiveness with Visual Aids. Legacy. *National Association for Interpretation, 20,* 4, 32-32.

Sawyer, J. K. (2011). *PowerPoint reality: Slides in real time for real audiences with real easy steps.* Boston: Allyn & Bacon.

Schuck, S. & Kearney, M. (2007). Exploring pedagogy with interactive whiteboards: A case study of six schools. Australian Educational Computing, 23(1), 8- 13. [electronic version].

Schuck, S. & Kearney, M. (2008). Classroom-based use of two educational technologies: A sociocultural perspective. Contemporary Issues in Technology and Teacher Education, 8(4), 394- 406.

Schwartz, J. (September 2003). The level of discourse continues to slide. *The New York Times.* Retrieved February 22, 2010, from http://ied. unipr.it/~silve/tesi/the-level.pdf.

Speaking Tips. (January 26, 2004). Using flip charts. Speaking Tips. Retrieved on July 31, 2010 from http://www.speaking-tips. com/ Articles/Using-Flip-Charts.aspx.

Thompson, C. (December 2003) PowerPoint makes you dumb. *The New York Times Magazine*, p. 688.

Tufte, E. (September 2003). PowerPoint Is Evil. *Wired News .* Retrieved February 18, 2010 from http://www.wired.com/wired/archive/11.09/ ppt2.html

Tufte, E. (2006). *The Cognitive Style of PowerPoint* (2nd ed.). New York: Graphics Press.

Wyatt, A. (n.d.) Developing visual aids. Pathways to Tomorrow MMHS. Retrieved on July 31, 2010 from http://www.longview.k12.wa.us/ mmhs/wyatt/pathway/dvaid.html.

CHAPTER NINE REFERENCES

Brumberger, E. (2003). The rhetoric of typography: The persona of typeface and text. *Technical Communication, 50(2),* 206-223.

Crosby, O. (2009). Résumés, applications and cover letters. *Occupational Outlook Quarterly, 53*(2), 18-29. Retrieved June 9, 2010 from Business Source Premier.

Donlin, K. (June 12, 2008). Three Resume and Cover Letter Myths Exposed. Star Tribune. Retrieved on June 22, 2010 from http://www.startribune.com/jobs/career/11436521.html.

Hoheb, M. (2002). Résumé writing. *Scholastic Choices, 18*(3), 19-23. Retrieved June 7, 2010 from Primary Search.

Markey, B. T. & Campbell, R. L. (January 1996). A resume or curriculum vitae for success. *AORN Journal, 63*, 1, 192-202.

Needleman, S. E. (2009). Creating a résumé that sells. *Wall Street Journal - Eastern Edition, 254*(124), D1-D8. Retrieved June 7, 2010 from Business Source Premier.

Olsen, P. R. (2006, May 14). In a ghost-written résumé, your best incarnation. *The New York Times.* [electronic version].

Potvin, K. (2009). Landing the interview: How to get to the top of the résumé pile. *Public Relations Tactics, 16*(5), 20-20. Retrieved June 9, 2010 from Business Source Premier.

Ross, C. M., & Young, S. J. (2005). Résumé preferences: Is it really "business as usual"? *Journal of Career Development, 32,* 153-164. Retrieved June 7, 2010 from Sage Premier database.

Ryan, L. (2009). Six tips for following up on your résumé . *Business Week Online*, 10-10. Retrieved June 9, 2010 from Business Source Premier.

Schullery, N. M., Ickes, L., & Schullery, S. E. (2009). Employer preferences for résumés and cover letters. *Business Communication Quarterly, 72*(2), 163-176. Retrieved January 20, 2010, from Business Source Premier.

Schriver, K. A. (1997). *Dynamics in document design: Creating texts for readers.* New York: Wiley Computer Publishing.

Shaikh, A. D., Chaparro, B. S., & Fox, D. (2006). Perception of fonts: Perceived personality traits and uses. *Usability* News, 8(1). http://www.surl.org/usabilitynews/81/ PersonalityofFonts.asp.

Smith, P.G. (2002). Creating the perfect résumé. *Career World, 31*(3), 18-21. Retrieved June 7, 2010 from Education Research Complete.

Southam, K. (May 13, 2006). Email addresses that kill off job chances. The Advertiser (Adelaide) retrieved on July 22, 2010 from Newspaper Source.

Twardowski Career Development Center, West Chester University. (nd). Résumé and cover letter writing. Retrieved January 27, 2010 from http://www.wcupa.edu/_SERVICES/STU. CAR/students/RESUME2. asp.

Zupek, R. (2010). Top 10 tips for your 2010 résumé. Retrieved January 21, 2010 from http://msn.careerbuilder .com/Article/MSN-2143-Cover-Letters-Résumés-Top-10-Tips-for-Your-2010.

Chapter Ten References

Barclay, L. (2009). Acing the interview: How to ask the questions that will get you the job (review of the book by J. Beshara), *IEEE Transactions on Professional Communication, 52*(1), 113-114.

Brady, J. (October 2007). "The Craft of Interviewing" from Brady, J. (1977). The craft of interviewing. New York: Vintage Books. Retrieved on July 21, 2010 from http://www.concernedjournalists. org/know-your-funnels.

Cejka, S., & Taylor, M. W. (2007) People persons –and the job interview. *The Physician Executive (May/June),* 68-70.

Coombes, M. (2006). Interview Blunders Often Culprit For Missed Opportunities. *Wall Street Journal Executive Career Site.* Retrieved July 17, 2010 from http://208.144.115.170/ jobhunting/ interviewing/20051115-coombes.html.

Cox, C. L. &Glick, W. H, (1986). Resume evaluations and cosmetics use: When more is not better). Sex Roles, 14, 1-2, 51-58.

Bandura, A. (1997). *Self-efficacy: The exercise of control.* New York: Freeman.

Bibey, C. (2010). *How to Prepare for an Online Video.* MoneyCrashers. com. Retrieved July 22, 2010 from http://www.moneycrashers.com/ how-to-prepare-for-an-online-video-interview/.

Chan, C. (July 2010). Cabela's: Nearly 1,000 apply for 40 jobs at Glendale store, The Arizona Republic. Retrieved July 17, 2010 from http://www.azcentral.com/news/articles/2010/07/16/ 20100716glendale-cabelas-hiring-jobs.html.

Chia, Y. M. (2005). Job offers of multi-national accounting firms: The effects of emotional intelligence, extra-curricular activities, and academic performance. *Accounting Education, 14*(1), 75-93. Retrieved June 24, 2010 from Education Research Complete.

Conklin, J. (2007). Turning the tables: Six questions to ask your interviewer. *Quality Progress, 40*(11), 55.

Crawford, H. (2007). Job interviewing: Ten tips for success. *Contract Management, 47*(8), 4-6.

Giles, K. (2010). *Nonverbal Cues for Interview Success.* EmploymentGuide.com. Retrieved July 22, 2010 from http://www.employmentguide.com/careeradvice/Nonverbal_Cues_for_Interview_Success.html.

Hansen, K. (2006). Mastering the Case Interview. *Quintcareers.com.* Retrieved July 17, 2010 December 3, 2008 from http://www.quintcareers.com/case_interviews.html.

Hansen, K. & Hansen, R. (2006). Promising Interview-Prep Technique: Composing Written Responses to Interview Questions. *Quintcareers.com.* Retrieved July 19, 2010 from http://www.quintcareers.com/interview-prep_technique.html.

Hayes, J. (1994). Interpersonal skills: goal-directed behaviour at work. London, Routledge.

Hoffman, E. A. (2008). The emotionally challenging, open-ended interview. *Business Communication Quarterly (September),* 387-390. Retrieved June 24, 2010 from Business Source Premier.

Joss, M. (April, 2003). Tips and templates for creating an interview follow-up letter. Retrieved July 18, 2010 from http://articles.techrepublic.com.com/5100-10878_11-1057839.html.

Kiviat, B. (October 20, 2009) How Skype Is Changing the Job Interview. Time.com. Retreived on July 21, 2010 from http://www.time.com/time/business/article/0,8599,1930838,00.html.

Krumhuber, E., Manstead, A. S. R., Cosker, D., Marshall, D., & Rosin, P. L. (2009). Effects of dynamic attributes of smiles in human and synthetic faces: A simulated job interview setting. *Journal of Non-verbal behavior, 33*(1),1-15. Retrieved June 24, 2010 from Communication & Mass Media Complete.

Lazarus, A. (2004). Preparation is key to successful job interviews. *The Physician Executive (May/June),* 48-50.

Lipovsky, C. (2006). Candidates' negotiation of their job expertise in job interviews. *Journal of Pragmatics, 38,* 1147-1174.

Mavunga, G., and Kumber, F. (2008). Interviews as forms of negotiation. *Journal of Language and Communication (June),*66-77.

Messmer, M. (2004). Top 10 questions to ask during job interviews. *Strategic Finance (August),* 11-12. Retrieved June 24, 2010 from Business Source Premier.

Muir, C. (2005). Managing the initial job interview: Smile, schmooze, and get hired?, *Academy of Management Executive (February),* 156-158. Retrieved June 24, 2010 from JSTOR Arts and Sciences VI Collection.

Muir, C. (2008). Job interviewing. *Business Communication Quarterly, 71*(3), 374-390. Retrieved June 24, 2010 from Business Source Premier.

Nash, R., Feldman, G., Hussey, T., Lévêque, J., & Pineau, P. (2006). Cosmetics: They influence more than Caucasian female facial attractiveness. *Journal of Applied Social Psychology, 36*(2), 493-504. Retrieved June 24, 2010 from SocINDEX with Full Text.

Navarro, A. (2006). Employers want to know, "What can you do for me?", *The Physician Executive, (September/October),* 70-72.

Neuliep, J. W. &McCroskey, J. C. (2001). The influence of ethnocentrism on perceptions of interviewee attractiveness, credibility, and socio-communicative style. *Annual convention of the International Communication.*

Neuson, B. A. (2007). Avoid discrimination claims when interviewing job candidates. *Nursing Management (February),* 16-18. Retrieved June 24, 2010 from Business Source Premier.

Oliphant, G. C., Hansen, K., & Oliphant, B.J. (2008). A review of a telephone-administered behavior-based interview technique. *Business Communication Quarterly (September),* 383-386. Retrieved June 24, 2010 from Business Source Premier.

Paul, J., & Strbiak, C. A. (April 1997). Entrepreneur Magazine.

The ethics of strategic ambiguity. Special Issue: Ethics of Business Communication. The Journal of Business Communication, 34, [electronic version at: http://www.entrepreneur.com/ tradejournals/ article/19527181.html.

Pearce, S. (2010). A marathon, not a sprint. *Accountancy Magazine (March),* 48-49.

Powers, L. (October 2000). Anatomy of an Interview. AORN Magazine. 72, 4, 671.

Psychometric-succes.com. (2009). *Aptitude Tests – What You Need to Know.* Retrieved July 22, 2010 from http://www.psychometric-success.com/aptitude-tests/aptitude-tests-introduction.htm.

Rennar, H. S. (2005). Interviewing: Positioning yourself to get the offer. *Financial Executive (July/August),* 60-61. Retrieved June 24, 2010 from Business Source Premier.

Richardson, J. V. (2002). Open versus Closed Ended Questions In the Reference Environment. Richardson UCLA Faculty Pages. Retrieved on July 20, 2010 from http://polaris.gseis.ucla.edu / jrichardson/dis220/openclosed.htm.

Rutgers. (2010). Conducting an interview. *Rutgers Human Resources department.* Retrieved on July 19, 2010 from http://uhr.rutgers .edu/ stf/ConductinganInterview.htm

Schawbel, D. (June 25, 2010). Manage Your Online Reputation—Before Someone Else Does. Wall Street Journal Blog/ Hire Education. Retrieved on July 17, 2010 from http://blogs.wsj.com/hire-education/2010/06/25/manage-your-online-reputation—before-someone-else-does/.

Straus, S. G., Miles, J.A., & Levesque, L.L. (2001). The effects of videoconference, telephone, and face-to-face media on interviewer and applicant judgments in employment interviews. *Journal of Management, 27,* 363-381. Retrieved June 24, 2010 from Business Source Premier.

Tay, C., Ang, S., & Van Dyne, L. (2006). Personality, biographical characteristics, and job interview success: A longitudinal study of the mediating effects of interviewing self-efficacy and the moderating effects of internal locus of causality. *Journal of Applied Psychology, 91*(2), 446-454.

Thornbory, G., & White, C. (2006). HOW TO… be successful at job interviews. *Occupational Health, 58*(9), 22. Retrieved June 24, 2010 from Business Source Premier.

UC Davis (n.d.). Guidelines for Writing, Sequencing, and Asking Interview Questions. Tobacco Control Evaluation Center. Retrieved July 19, 2010 from ucce.ucdavis.edu/files/ filelibrary/5715/22448.doc.

U.S. Equal Employment Opportunity Commission. (2010). *Federal laws prohibiting job discrimination questions and answers.* Retrieved from http://www.eeoc.gov/facts/qanda.html.

Wiesnerf, W. H. & Cronshaw, D. F. (1988). A meta-analytic investigation of the impact of interview format and degree of structure on the validity of the employment interview. Journal of Occupational Psychology, 61, 275-290.

Williams, K. (2006). Can you ace 10 touch job interview questions?. *Strategic Finance, 87 (May)*, 23. Retrieved June 24, 2010 from Business Source Premier.

Woloshin, M. (2008). Starting over: On layoffs and new job searches. *Public Relations Tactics (July),*15. Retrieved June 24, 2010 from Business Source Premier.

CHAPTER ELEVEN REFERENCES

Aristotle [350 B.C.E.]. (1980). *Nicomachean Ethics.* Translated by W. D. Ross, 1908, revised by J. O. Urmson. Oxford, Clarendon Press.

Beamer, L (1992). Learning Intercultural Communication Competence. *Journal of Business Communication, 29*(3), 285-303.

Cavalier. R. (1996). Kant's ethics. Online guide to ethics and moral philosophy. *Carnegie Mellon University.* Retrieved on June 5, 2011 from http://caae.phil.cmu.edu/cavalier/80130/part1/ sect4/Kant.html

Kant, I. (1964). *The Moral Law.* Translated by H. J. Paton. London: Hutchinson & Co. Ltd.

Kant, I. [1785]. (1985). *Foundations of the Metaphysics of Morals.* Translated by Lewis White Beck. (2nd ed). New York: MacMillan.

Kant, I. (2003). "On A Supposed Right To Tell Lies From Benevolent Motives." Translated by T.K. Abbot. Retrieved on June 2, 2011 from http://core.ecu.edu/phil/mccartyr/kant/entry3.htm.

Mill, J. S. (1972). *Later Letters. Volume XVI.* Toronto: University of Toronto Press.

Mill, J. S. (1987). *"Utilitarianism" in Utilitarianism and Other Essays.* Edited by Alan Ryan. London: Penguin Books.

Panza, C. & Potthast, A. (2010). Why study ethics? Part of the ethics for dummies cheat sheet. *For Dummies.* Retrieved on June 1, 2011 from http://www.dummies.com/how-to/content/why-study-ethics.html